Applied
Management
Accounting

Tutorial

Aubrey Penning

Published by Osborne Books Limited
Tel 01905 748071
Email books@osbornebooks.co.uk
Website www.osbornebooks.co.uk

Design by Laura Ingham

Printed by CPI Group (UK) Limited, Croydon, CR0 4YY, on environmentally friendly, acid-free paper from managed forests.

British Library Cataloguing in Publication Data
A catalogue record for this book is available from the British Library

ISBN 978-1-911198-68-0

Contents

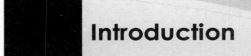

Introduction

Qualifications covered

This book has been written specifically to cover the Unit 'Applied Management Accounting' which is mandatory for the following qualifications:

AAT Level 4 Diploma in Professional Accounting

AAT Diploma in Professional Accounting – SCQF Level 8

The book contains a clear text with worked examples and case studies, chapter summaries and key terms to help with revision. Each chapter concludes with a wide range of activities, many in the style of AAT computer based assessments.

Osborne Study and Revision Materials

Additional materials, tailored to the needs of students studying this Unit and revising for the assessment, include:

- **Workbooks:** paperback books with practice activities and exams
- **Student Zone:** access to Osborne Books online resources
- **Osborne Books App:** Osborne Books ebooks for mobiles and tablets

Visit www.osbornebooks.co.uk for details of study and revision resources and access to online material.

1 Preparing budgets

this chapter covers...

In this chapter we begin our examination of the preparation of budgets.

We start by learning the purposes of budgets, and see how some organisations view particular purposes as more important than others. We examine how budget setting links with the organisation's objectives and strategy, and must be built around the key (or principal) budget factor – which is often sales.

Next we examine the various budgets that are usually prepared, and how they are sequenced. The key budget factor is normally forecast first, and the other budgets are based around this important data.

We then go on to examine the organisation of the budgeting process and the various roles of the budget committee and how individuals can participate. This leads us to an examination of responsibility accounting, and how it fits into budgeting. Next, we discuss some specific techniques that can be used to develop budgets.

We then move on to the numerical work involved in creating the budgets connected with a manufacturing organisation and how they fit together, including the master operating budget and the cash budget.

INTRODUCTION

In this book we are going to study the L4 unit 'Applied Management Accounting'. The book will generally follow the order of the learning outcomes in the specification. This is the order of study that is recommended by the AAT. The first topics that we will consider relate to budgeting, and these are covered in the first two chapters in the book.

THE PURPOSES OF BUDGETS

A budget is a financial plan for an organisation, prepared in advance.

In any organisation the budget provides the mechanism by which the objectives of the organisation can be achieved. In this way it forms a link between the current position and the position that the organisation's managers are aiming for. By using a budget firstly to plan and then to monitor, the managers can ensure that the organisation's progress is coordinated to achieve the objectives of the organisation. The specific purposes and benefits of using budgets are as follows.

1   the budget compels planning

By formalising the agreed objectives of the organisation through a budget preparation system, an organisation can ensure that its plans are achievable. It will be able to decide what resources are required to produce the desired outputs, and to make sure that they will be available at the right time.

2   the budget communicates and coordinates

Because a budget will be agreed by an organisation, all the relevant personnel will be working towards the same ends. During the budget setting process any anticipated problems should be resolved and any areas of potential confusion clarified. All the organisation's departments should be in a position to play their part in achieving the overall goals. This objective of all parts of the organisation working towards the same ends is sometimes referred to as **goal congruence**.

3   the budget can be used to authorise

For organisations where control of activities is deemed to be a high priority the budget can be used as the primary tool to ensure conformity to agreed plans. Once the budget is agreed it can effectively become the authority to follow a particular course of action or spend a certain amount of money. Public sector organisations, with their necessary emphasis on strict accountability, will tend to take this approach, as will some commercial organisations that choose not to delegate too much authority.

4 the budget can be used to monitor and control

An important reason for producing a budget is that management is able to monitor the actual results against the budget. This is so that action can be taken to modify the operation of the organisation as time passes, or possibly to change the budget if it becomes unachievable. This is similar to the way that standard costing is used to monitor and control costs, and can be used alongside that technique, as we will see later in this book.

5 the budget can be used to motivate

A budget can be part of the organisation's techniques for motivating managers and other staff to achieve the organisation's objectives. The extent to which this happens will depend on how the budget is agreed and set, and whether it is perceived as fair and achievable. The budget may also be linked to rewards (for example bonuses) where targets are met or exceeded.

THE BUDGET CYCLE

The budget cycle can be used to describe the various processes that need to be undertaken to implement a budget. They are carried out in the order shown, and generally apply to both large and small businesses, as well as public authorities. You may come across slightly different terminology used in relation to the budget cycle.

■ **budget preparation**

This involves bringing together the various data that is required. It also means making sure that all the relevant people are involved. There are many decisions that will have to be made by the participants, and these issues will be examined more fully as we progress through this section of the book.

■ **budget approval**

For a large organisation, this will be a formal procedure as we will see later. For a small business, it could be an agreement by the relevant managers.

■ **budget implementation**

This means that the budget is active from the start of the budget period. All relevant procedures must be adhered to, and the responsibility and authority as detailed in the budget will be followed.

■ **monitoring and evaluation of the budget**

This is a crucial step, and for many organisations is a main reason for budgeting. The budget should be compared with actual performance, and the results reported and acted upon. This can lead to changes to activities, or possibly revision of the current or future budgets.

THE MAIN TYPES OF BUDGET

Here we will briefly mention the main types of budget that you need to be familiar with. We will go into further detail regarding each type as we progress through our studies.

■ **operating budget**

An operating budget is a short to medium term budget (for example covering a year). It deals with the immediate requirements of the organisation, and it provides the initial steps towards the long-term strategic budget. We will examine the preparation and use of operating budgets thoroughly in our studies.

■ **capital budget**

This budget deals with the acquisition (and possibly disposal) of the non-current assets that are required to support the organisation. This budget differs from the operating budget (which is a revenue budget), since it is concerned with 'one-off' transactions.

■ **fixed budget**

A fixed budget is one that assumes a certain level of outputs – often sales. The budget is then built around this output level. This type of budget is appropriate if the output level can be forecast with a degree of accuracy – for example if there are sales contracts already in place. Even if there is uncertainty over the forecast output level, a fixed budget can be used for planning purposes, in combination with a flexed budget for monitoring and control.

■ **flexed budget**

A flexed (or flexible) budget is one where the **actual output** (for example sales) is used as a basis for the budget. This is carried out by using knowledge of cost behaviour to adjust the budgeted costs in the original fixed budget into line with the actual output. This would be carried out after actual output is known. An alternative would be to produce a series of budgets in advance to cope with a range of possible output levels. We will practise preparing flexed budgets later in this book.

THE INITIAL STEPS IN BUDGET PREPARATION

the aims of an organisation

Before an organisation's managers can begin to build a useful budget there are several initial steps that must be taken. These are based around the fundamental questions about the **aims** – the 'vision' – of the organisation:

'where do we want it to go?' and

'how do we get it there?'

These are essentially long-term issues, and once agreed upon would not tend to be changed very often.

objectives and strategy

For a budget to be of use to an organisation it must be a mechanism of helping the organisation achieve its **objectives**. The objectives are the targets that the managers of the organisation wish it to achieve. The way in which these objectives are expressed will depend upon the type of organisation and the way in which it operates. For example, a pet food manufacturer may have the specific objective of obtaining sales penetration of 25% of the UK dog food market, whereas an independent TV production company may have the objective of achieving a certain number of viewers on average.

The organisation must then develop a **strategy** for achieving those objectives. Several alternatives may need to be considered before the final strategy is decided upon. The pet food company mentioned in the above example may decide that it needs to develop and market a new food product for young dogs to help it to achieve its objective. The independent TV production company may have a strategy of producing pilots for ten new programmes each year from which it can then develop the most promising.

relevant data

Before any progress can be made in preparing a budget, relevant data must be identified and collected. We have already seen that information must be available about the aims, objectives and strategy of the organisation so that the budget that is prepared will be consistent with these. The following are examples of the types of data that can be used in developing the budget. The data is divided into data from internal and external sources.

data from internal sources

■ **accounting information**

This will include information about the accounting system (eg specific accounting polices) and how they will affect the budget, as well as data collected through the accounting system (for example historical costs).

- **wage and salary information**

  The resource of labour is clearly fundamental to many organisations, and sufficient information must be available to incorporate as appropriate.

data from external sources

- **information about suppliers and availability of inputs**

  Information must be available about suppliers' ability to supply the inputs required by the organisation, as well as data about relevant prices. This issue may be relevant to the consideration of limiting factors and can also force revisions to the budget.

- **information about customers and markets**

  It would not make sense to plan to make goods or provide services that were not required in the market place. Information of this type is fundamental to developing valid budgets.

- **general economic information**

  The impact of the economy on projections is discussed later in this chapter. No organisation can exist in a vacuum and those preparing budgets must recognise the importance of the health of the economy in which they operate.

Information from all these areas will be needed at various points in the budgeting process that is described in this chapter and the next.

limiting factors – the 'key' budget factor

When an organisation prepares a budget, it must first analyse its **limiting factors** – the issues that determine the level of its output. For a commercial organisation these could include:

- the size of its market
- the capacity of its premises
- the availability of raw material
- the amount of working capital
- the availability of skilled workers

One of the factors will be the main one that affects the activity level of the organisation – **the key budget factor**. This is the factor (sometimes known as the 'principal budget factor') that all the aspects of the operation depend upon. For most manufacturing or trading operations the key budget factor is **sales**; the assumptions that are made about the level of sales in the budget will affect all the other parts of the budget. This is because the organisation will plan to support the budgeted sales level and build the budgets and assumptions around this one factor.

Although sales level is the most common key factor, some commercial organisations may decide that a different factor is the most important in their particular circumstances. For example, if a manufacturer can sell all that it produces, but has production restricted by lack of skilled labour, then the assumed labour level would become the key budget factor. A similar situation would arise if there were production restrictions caused by shortages of raw materials, or limited machine capacity.

Non-commercial organisations will also need to identify their key budget factor, and build their budgets around their assumptions concerning it. Charities and government agencies may consider that there is a demand for their services that is virtually limitless; their principal (key) budget factor is the amount of money they receive to fund what they do. For example, the Government's healthcare provision is limited by the amount of funding it can get from the government spending allocation and from private enterprise. The demand for Oxfam's aid is very high, but its key budget factor is the amount of money it can expect to raise to fund that aid.

There may be times when a limiting factor changes during a budget period as a result of changing demand or availability of resources. The issues of dealing with limited materials, labour and production capacity are examined later in this book.

the initial budgeting process

If we combine the ideas just discussed then the initial budget process for an established organisation would follow the pattern in the following diagram:

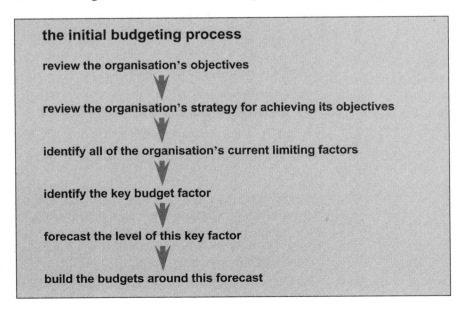

the initial budgeting process

review the organisation's objectives

review the organisation's strategy for achieving its objectives

identify all of the organisation's current limiting factors

identify the key budget factor

forecast the level of this key factor

build the budgets around this forecast

ORGANISATION OF THE BUDGETING PROCESS

the budget manual

For most organisations budget setting forms a vital part of the formal procedures: the organisation's method of budgeting will be set out in writing in its policy documents. These will include details of responsibilities and timetables. They may be combined into a **budget manual**.

The budget manual can be used to explain the 'why?' and the 'how?' of the organisation's approach to using budgets. It may include the following:

- the primary purposes of budgets for the organisation
- the types of budget that are to be produced
- what format is to be used for budgets
- how far in advance budgets are to be set
- who has responsibility for setting budgets
- who has responsibility for monitoring performance against budgets
- how often performance is to be monitored against budgets
- who has the authority to modify agreed budgets

the budget committee

The budget procedures may be the responsibility of a budget committee, chaired by the Managing Director or a person he/she has appointed. The composition of the committee may be set out in the budget manual, together with the committee's responsibilities. The budget committee may have the authority to modify the budget manual.

The committee will consist of senior representatives from all the departments, so that there is full communication and coordination throughout the organisation. This way, there should be full understanding about the overall objectives of the organisation, and the part that each department must play in the total picture. It would not make sense for the marketing department to plan a promotion of a product that the production department could not supply in sufficient quantities. This concept of everyone working towards the same result is referred to as 'goal congruence'.

It is important that all budget proposals are agreed with the budget holders, and because of the way it is comprised, the budget committee is an ideal mechanism for ensuring that this happens. Without agreement a budget is unlikely to form an effective tool. There must be opportunities at both the forecasting stage and the budgeting stage for relevant individuals to raise any queries and seek clarification of the data. Only by this process will all budget holders feel that they fully understand the budgets and the forecasts on which they are built.

The committee will not only set and agree the budget, but it will also be responsible for monitoring the budget once it is in place. For example, they may wish to monitor on a quarterly, monthly, or weekly basis, and will also want to decide on how quickly the information should be available and in what format.

It is important that the information produced in both the original budget and the subsequent monitoring reports is in a form that satisfies the needs of budget holders. The majority of the budget holders will not have accounting backgrounds, and the budget committee must carefully choose formats so that all users can understand and make full use of the documents.

In organisations where there is no formal budget committee, alternative ways must be used to ensure that budgets are fully agreed and coordinated, and that they are presented in a form that meets the needs of budget holders. In small organisations this responsibility may fall to the person who fulfils the role of management accountant, so they must be careful to carry out these duties effectively.

budget accountant

The budget accountant has a key role in the budgeting process within an organisation. Although the duties and responsibilities of a budget accountant will vary according to the organisation, typically the role involves preparing the budgets, monitoring the budgets against actual performance and reporting on the variances. The budget accountant's role should be outlined in the budget manual, and may have the following responsibilities:

- advise and assist functional managers in their budget submissions
- liaise with the budget committee and ensure that all budgeting activities are carried out in line with the budget manual
- ensure that all budgets are fully coordinated
- ensure that agreed budgets are communicated to functional managers and deal with any queries
- monitor budgets against actual performance and prepare reports on significant variances
- ensure that the budget timetable is followed by all participants

budget timetables

There are two main types of budgets used by organisations:

- **strategic** budgets
- **operational** budgets

They have different purposes, and are each based on different timescales. The budget committee will typically determine the way that these budgets are set and monitored, in line with the budget manual.

Strategic budgets will be produced well in advance of the period to which they relate. They are concerned with the long-term strategy of the organisation, and will therefore have the following features:

■ they relate to long periods of time (typically five years)

■ they are prepared a long time in advance of the budget periods

■ they are limited to outline information and are not set out in great detail

■ they are the responsibility of the senior management of the organisation

Some organisations may adopt a rolling programme of strategic budgets, perhaps five years ahead. Each year a further year would be incorporated into the far end of the budget.

Operational budgets will be produced for shorter periods of time – typically the next twelve months. They may be developed from the original strategic budgets for the budget period, but will take account of the fact that the business has information – facts and figures – about the immediate future. Operating budgets will therefore have the following features:

■ they relate to short periods of time (typically the forthcoming year, divided into manageable control periods)

■ they are agreed a relatively short time in advance of the budget period (typically several months before the year starts)

■ they are set up and agreed in considerable detail

■ they are the responsibility of the middle managers that control the operations of the organisation

capital expenditure budgets

The overall strategic and operational budgets must include **capital expenditure budgets** as well as revenue budgets. Capital expenditure can range from straightforward replacement of equipment, to moving to new premises or acquiring whole businesses. Capital expenditure can be defined as expenditure on assets that will benefit the organisation over more than one accounting period. In addition to following this general rule, many organisations will also set out a minimum cost of assets that are to be treated as capital. This is to avoid low value items that appear to satisfy the definition being treated as capital (for example a calculator or an electric kettle). The minimum cost of a capital item could be set at, say, £200, or for a larger organisation, perhaps £2,000. This amount would be set out in the organisation's policy documents. The coordination of the capital expenditure budget is particularly important to ensure that:

■ replacement equipment is acquired at the most cost-effective point for the organisation (before the old equipment becomes too costly to maintain, but not until the replacement is justified)

- planned production output that relies on capital expenditure is properly incorporated into both the appropriate revenue budgets and into the capital expenditure budget

- other resources are available to coordinate with the capital expenditure (for example installation, raw materials to cope with increased output)

- the labour requirements are available, and the workforce suitably trained

- suitable funding has been obtained to meet the capital expenditure

- appropriate planning has been carried out to phase in the use of the new non-current (fixed) assets

effective budgeting

The budgeting system must involve honesty, openness and transparency if it is to be effective. The system must be fair to all participants, and also be seen to be fair. Where decisions have to be made by senior managers about projects to be funded and the level of support to be provided to departments, the decision making process must be clearly laid out and then followed by all concerned. The opportunity for managers to feel that they have been badly treated by the process must be minimised by ensuring that the entire system is transparent.

For example, suppose the distribution manager has requested capital expenditure to replace the delivery vehicles, and the production manager has requested that some outdated manufacturing equipment also be replaced. If resources are limited, the procedure for deciding which capital expenditure should have priority should be objective and transparent and based on the best result for the whole organisation. In that way there can be no accusations of favouritism.

Where systems are not open and transparent, individual managers who feel that their projects or requests have not been treated fairly are likely to become disillusioned and demotivated. Similarly, if a manager is believed to have submitted over-optimistic forecasts in support of a project that he/she is advocating then grievances may be felt by other managers. There may be a role for the budget accountant in ensuring that data submitted is accurate and can withstand independent scrutiny.

accountabilities of senior managers

All senior managers have important roles in the budgeting process. They will probably sit on the budget committee as already mentioned, and they will therefore be jointly responsible for overseeing the development and implementation of the budget.

Individually, senior managers will participate in the development of the budget function that they have responsibility for. For example, the Sales Director would be responsible for participating in the development of the sales budget. To do this they would need to provide appropriate information. For example, the Sales Director would put forward historical data on pricing and sales levels, together with argued figures on what he or she believes the sales budget should contain. Depending on the level of participation in the budget setting process, the senior manager's staff may also be involved in putting forward their views, and these will be channelled through the senior manager.

Once the budget has been implemented, and the monitoring and control of actual performance against the budget started, the senior managers will be held accountable for the performance of their function. This is discussed in the section on 'Responsibility Accounting' a little later in this chapter. For example, the Sales Director would be responsible for the performance of the actual sales compared with the budget.

participation in budget preparation

A participative budget system means that those who will have to work to a particular budget are involved in its preparation. They are consulted throughout the process, so that they can input their specialised knowledge of the work involved and contribute to the planning process involved in budgeting. This is sometimes described as a 'bottom up' style of budgeting, as opposed to 'top down', which would refer to the situation where the budget is imposed on people by higher levels of management.

The main advantages of participative budgeting are:

- the budget takes account of information from those with specialised knowledge

- those involved will have improved awareness of organisational goals

- those involved will accept the budget and be motivated to work to it

- coordination and cooperation between those involved will improve

- participating in budget preparation broadens their experience and develops new skills

- participation in budget setting gives those involved a more positive attitude towards the organisation and this leads to better performance

It should be noted, however, that these advantages depend on the participation being genuine: if people are consulted, but their opinions later appear to be ignored, the effects will be the opposite of those listed above. (This is sometimes referred to as 'pseudo-participation'.)

Supporters of the idea of participation in budgeting may point to apparent improvements in performance as 'proof' of its motivating effect. However, coincidences can occur, and the improvement may have happened for some other reason: favourable cost variances can result from suppliers reducing their prices, for example, or sales volumes might increase because of purely external factors like changes in the weather.

Another reason for favourable results may be the introduction of **budgetary slack.** This means that managers have succeeded in obtaining a budget based on an over-estimation of costs or an under-estimation of income. They are then more likely to be able to achieve a good level of performance when measured against the budget. An argument against participation could be that it increases the risk of managers being able to introduce budgetary slack.

Research projects relating to participation in budgeting do not seem to have provided any firm conclusions about its motivational effects. It is not surprising that the effects seem to depend on the attitudes of the individuals involved, and different people react in different ways. Some employees may not want to spend time on budgeting, or may feel they do not have the necessary skills, so that participation would be seen as added pressure on them rather than an opportunity. They may feel that it is not part of their job, or that they have not been trained to carry out the task. Therefore, under some circumstances, an imposed ('top down') method of budgeting may be preferred.

Imposing a budget is also likely to be quicker than a consultation process, and sometimes the timescale will mean that a participative approach is impossible. Managers must be able to respond quickly to changing circumstances and maintain the progress of their organisation in the required direction. Part of this response may be to revise budgets at short notice.

RESPONSIBILITY ACCOUNTING

Organisations are managed as a group of different functions – for example 'Production' (for a manufacturing organisation), 'Sales and Distribution', 'Administration', and 'Finance'. This structure is illustrated in the sample organisation chart shown at the top of the next page. These functions can also be sub-divided into areas of control according to the needs of the organisation.

As well as each of these functions being controlled by individual managers, the accounting systems (both financial and management) will have been developed to operate with the same structure. As an important part of the management accounting system, budgeting will use the functional structure, and budgets will be developed within the functions and reporting carried out to the functional managers.

The term '**responsibility accounting**' is used to describe a way of looking at an organisation in terms of areas of responsibility, which could be functions or parts of functions. Such areas of responsibility are called **responsibility centres.**

An individual manager can then be held accountable for certain aspects of the performance of the particular function for which he or she is responsible.

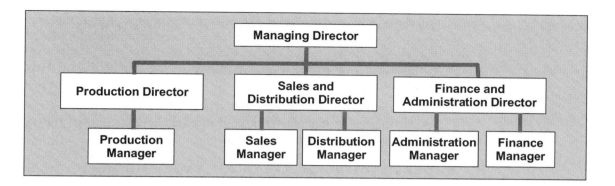

Which aspects of performance should a particular manager have to account for? Clearly, in a fair system, these would be those aspects which they can actually do something about, or over which they have some influence. This brings us to the concept of **controllability**, which is explained in more detail in the next section.

In order to be able to influence the outcomes of a responsibility centre, the manager must have the authority to take the necessary actions. Within a large organisation, there will be various levels of management from the senior executives to supervisors of small departments, each with an appropriate level of authority.

For example, the chief executive may have the authority to sign a contract for a major capital investment project, whereas a production manager has the authority to organise the week's production scheduling.

The extent of a person's authority is clearly linked to the area for which they can be held responsible. There are three categories of responsibility centre which are linked to different levels of authority:

■ A **cost centre** (or expense centre) is a responsibility centre where the manager has responsibility for costs. The manager has the authority to take certain actions in relation to the control of costs.

For example, an office manager can authorise the purchase of stationery and introduce controls to reduce wastage of paper.

■ A **profit centre** is a responsibility centre where the manager has responsibility for both costs and income, and hence profit. The manager has the authority to take action relating to income as well as costs.

For example, the manager of a branch office of an estate agent may have the authority to negotiate levels of commission with clients (perhaps within a specified range), as well as deciding on advertising expenditure.

■ An **investment centre** is a responsibility centre where the manager has responsibility for costs, income and some investments. The manager's authority is as for a profit centre, with the additional authority to buy and sell assets, up to certain limits. The manager therefore has some influence over the capital employed in this section of the organisation and Return on Capital Employed could be used as a measure of management performance. We will discuss Return on Capital Employed and other measures of performance later in this book.

For example, the manager of a division which makes some of the products of a large manufacturing company may have the authority to buy and sell machinery up to a given value.

budget centres as areas of responsibility

A **budget centre** is a department, activity or function for which a budget is prepared and the person who is responsible for implementing that budget is the **budget holder**.

In order to implement a budget, the budget holder must have sufficient authority to take the necessary actions, and can then be held responsible for the performance of the budget centre in comparison with the budget. Each budget centre is therefore a responsibility centre and may be any of three types of centre described above:

- a budget centre which is a cost (or expense) centre would have a budget for costs (or expenses) only

- a budget centre which is a profit centre would have a budget for both costs and incomes

- a budget centre which is an investment centre would have a budget for costs, incomes and capital expenditure

When the performance of a department, activity or function is measured against the budget, it is important to apply the principle of comparing like with like, and also to measure only those aspects of performance which the budget holder is able to do something about. These are the aspects which are described as controllable for that person, as explained below.

controllable costs and incomes

A particular cost or income is described as 'controllable' by a particular person if that person is in a position to influence it. It does not necessarily mean that the person has absolute control over it.

For example, the total cost of wages in a department can be said to be controllable by the manager of the department if he/she has the authority to decide how many staff of each grade to employ. However, the manager may not have absolute control over the total wage bill, because the rates of pay may be set at levels which he/she cannot change. The manager can influence the total wages and therefore it can be considered as being within his/her area of responsibility.

Whether something is controllable or not depends on the individual manager being considered, in terms of the post which they occupy and the level of responsibility that goes with it. Every cost or income can be influenced by someone in the organisation with a sufficiently high level of authority.

Factors such as bank interest rates, foreign exchange, inflation and so on are not controllable, but the costs affected by these factors can be influenced by management decisions.

For example, the cost of borrowing money is affected by interest rates, but decisions relating to amounts of borrowing and sources of finance can influence the total cost.

Controllability of costs or incomes is important for performance measurement, because clearly it would be unfair and demotivating to measure people's performance on something over which they have no influence.

Controllability of costs or incomes links to the idea of responsibility accounting: if managers have clearly defined areas of responsibility, where they can influence the costs or incomes or both, then they can be held responsible for those costs or incomes and their performance can be measured on the results.

The fairest ways of measuring performance would therefore be:

- On **controllable costs** in a cost centre – a possible method of measurement is variance analysis. The cost centre manager should not have to account for variances on costs which he cannot influence, for example apportionments of fixed overheads.

- On **controllable profit** in a profit centre – profit margin or contribution to sales ratio, as well as variance analysis, could be used for measurement, again applying the principle of excluding items which cannot be influenced by the manager, if possible. Difficulties arise because the exact boundaries between what can and cannot be influenced are not always completely clear cut: for example, by how much does a quality improvement affect sales volumes?

- On **return on capital employed** in an investment centre – here, the calculation of profit and of capital employed may be based where possible on controllable items. However, capital provided by the organisation as a whole and which is not controllable by the centre manager may be taken into account. This allows measurement of how well the total capital employed has been used by the manager to generate profits.

responsibility centres – allocation and recovery of costs

You will be familiar with the allocation of direct costs and the allocation and apportionment of indirect costs from your earlier studies. It is important that the allocation of costs is accurate, and that apportionment between responsibility centres is carried out in the fairest way.

For responsibility centres to work effectively it is also important that the recovery of indirect costs (e.g. cost absorption) is carried out in an appropriate way. The most appropriate method of recovery will depend on the type of organisation and responsibility centre, and it will also depend on the nature of the indirect costs involved. You will be familiar with this concept from your earlier studies. The following are broad examples of appropriate cost recovery mechanisms.

■ If a production cost centre is labour-intensive then using an absorption method such as direct labour hours is often an appropriate way to recover costs.

■ If a production cost centre is machine-intensive then using an absorption method such as machine hours is often an appropriate way to recover costs, especially if the majority of the indirect costs relate to operating machinery.

■ If a responsibility centre contains indirect costs that relate to activities that are consumed by products in differing amounts, then activity based costing (ABC) may provide a more appropriate recovery basis. This could apply, for example, to the indirect costs of running a stores section in a manufacturing organisation. We will study activity based costing in more detail later in this book.

APPROACHES TO BUDGETING

We have discussed how budgets are used based on responsibility accounting. Separate budgets will be prepared for each function of the organisation (divided up if appropriate) and individual managers will be held accountable for their department's performance against their budget.

The following alternative approaches can be taken to preparing these functional budgets.

incremental budgeting

Preparing budgets using incremental budgeting is the traditional approach. It involves basing the budget for a period on the previous period's budget (or actual costs), and then making adjustments for anticipated inflation and any other expected changes. In this way, incremental budgeting produces a series of budgets over time that change only gradually. This provides consistency and security within the departments, and can avoid conflict between departments as resources are allocated based on agreed principles.

There are, however, disadvantages to incremental budgeting:

■ there are no incentives for developing new ideas, or reducing costs. Managers may feel that they must spend all their budget to avoid it being reduced in future

■ over time the budgets may become out of line with the amount of work carried out in the department, or the usefulness of that work

■ if the departmental managers build in some 'budgetary slack' – by obtaining a larger budget than is really needed – then this may go unchallenged for many years

zero based budgeting (ZBB)

This method of budgeting takes the opposite approach to incremental budgeting. In each period the budget starts from a base of zero, with no account taken of the previous period's budget. Each cost that is agreed for the department has to be justified based on the benefit that will arise to the organisation from spending the amount allocated.

Often alternative 'decision packages' are prepared for the department showing the costs that would be incurred to deliver certain levels of benefits. For example, alternative decision packages for a credit control section could involve:

■ an option of a high level of interaction with debtors including active management of credit limits and a variety of appropriate actions on outstanding amounts to provide maximum receipts. This package would be labour intensive and expensive

■ an option involving a lower level of interaction with debtors, with fewer options to use to chase outstanding amounts. The receipts would flow into the organisation more slowly and bad debts may increase, but the cost of running the department would be much less than the first option

The costs and benefits of providing each level of service would need to be analysed and a decision made based on the outcome that was best for achieving the organisational objectives.

The following are some advantages of zero based budgeting:

■ it forces re-evaluation of the activities within each function, and how they contribute to achieving the organisation's objectives

■ it encourages innovation and links the uses of resources to the achievement of results

■ it avoids wastage and budgetary slack

However, there are some disadvantages:

■ the process is very time-consuming and expensive to operate

- it may focus on short-term benefits at the expense of the long term (for example when applied to training or marketing)

- the judging of decision packages may be difficult and subjective

One approach that could be taken is to rotate the use of zero based budgeting so that each budget centre does not go through the process each year. For example, a department may undertake a full zero based exercise once every five years, with incremental budgeting used in the other years. This would reduce the cost, but retain some of the benefits.

priority based budgeting

Priority based budgeting shares some of its ideas with zero based budgeting in that it can ignore previous budgets. It examines the outcomes that an organisation is attempting to achieve and prioritises them – allocating resources to the outcomes that are judged to be most important. It is a technique that is frequently used in the public sector where diverse services compete for limited resources, for example local authorities and police forces. It is especially useful for situations where resources are being reduced, and provides some rigour for making tough decisions.

Where appropriate, it can use input from the service users as well as the organisation managers. For example, views about the relative priority that should be given to public library services, rubbish collection, and street lighting could be sought from the public in a local area.

Some organisations use a scale (for example 10 points) to link to each element of a service provided ranging from 'critical' (must be funded) through 'desirable' (may be funded) to services that are unjustifiable. The resources are then applied to programmes or services working down the list from the most important until the budgeted resources are used up.

activity based budgeting (ABB)

Unlike the three approaches to budgeting that we have just discussed, activity based budgeting is often used to manage indirect costs **within** the production department and production support departments such as the purchasing department. Later on we will see how activity based costing could be used to allocate costs in the most appropriate way based on how activities use resources. Activity based budgeting links with ABC to provide a system that uses the same mechanism to budget as is used to develop costs.

Activity based budgeting uses the same cost drivers that were identified through ABC. The budgeting follows three stages:

- activities and their cost drivers are first identified

- the number of units of cost driver that are required to complete the required activity level is then forecast

- the budgeted 'cost driver rate' can then be used

For example, suppose the production department was planning to manufacture 5,000 units of a particular product using 10 batches of 500 units each. As each batch required one set-up (the cost driver) of the production machinery, the cost of 10 'set-ups' would be budgeted for. This would be a more precise way of budgeting than just considering set-up costs as part of general production overheads.

It would make sense to use activity based budgeting in conjunction with activity based costing.

rolling budgets

Rolling budgets are budgets that are continually extended into the future as time goes forward. For example, a yearly budget could be extended by one month every time a further month goes by, so that the budget is always for twelve months into the future. This can provide increased accuracy in the budget as it can enable changing conditions to be taken account of quickly. We will consider rolling budgets further when we look at how we can deal with future uncertainty.

contingency budgets

A contingency budget is a budget that is designed to allow for unexpected future events and their impact. Most budgets could include a contingency element (for example an amount to allow for future unknown price rises), but specific contingency budgets are primarily used in two circumstances. They are used as part of capital budgets (for example construction projects) where an amount above the expected cost is allowed to cover the cost of any unforeseen issues that may occur in the future. Another situation where they are sometimes used is by public authorities, where a contingency budget may be used to cover unexpected additional costs in a range of revenue expenditure budgets.

COORDINATING THE MAIN TYPES OF BUDGET

Once the key factor has been determined, and an appropriate forecast developed, the budgets for the whole organisation can be generated. For a manufacturing organisation these would typically include:

sales budget	usually generated directly from the key factor – the forecast data
production budget	based on the sales budget together with the anticipated finished goods inventory levels
materials usage budget	based on the production budget

materials purchases budget based on the materials usage budget, together with the anticipated materials inventory levels

labour utilisation budget also based on the production budget

plant utilisation budget this would show how the plant and machinery is used by the planned production level

Note that the above materials usage, materials purchases, labour utilisation and plant utilisation budgets could alternatively be presented as schedules to the production budget.

functional budgets to support the operation (often based on departments), for example administration budget, finance budget; these may not be so dependent upon the sales level as other budgets that are linked more closely

capital expenditure budget this would also have to be developed in conjunction with the revenue budgets to ensure that the agreed spending on new or replacement equipment was in place

cash flow budget this would take account of all the other budgets and their effect on the organisation's liquidity – note that this is not a functional budget, but is a part of the master budget

master budget the calculations from all the revenue and capital budgets contribute to the **master budget** which takes the form of a budgeted statement of profit or loss and a budgeted statement of financial position together with a cash budget

The choice and format of the main budgets will need to be appropriate to the organisation. Earlier we examined responsibility accounting, and how responsibility centres can be used. Appropriate cost centres, profit centres and investment centres will need to be defined, and the budgets will need to be structured accordingly. For example, if there are separate cost centres for 'administration' and 'marketing' then there needs to be administration and marketing budgets. In this way managers can be held to account for their department's performance. The term 'core costs' is sometimes used to describe non-operational overheads (for example, administration, marketing and finance costs).

the effect of changing inventory levels

You will have noticed several references in the list of budgets to **inventory levels**. Where inventory levels are to remain constant the situation is simple. For example, the production budget will be identical to the sales budget if the finished goods inventory level is to remain unchanged, i.e. the amount you will produce will be the amount you estimate you are going to sell. However, if the inventory level is to increase then the extra units of goods that will go into inventory will need to be produced in addition to the units that are to be sold in the budget period. This is a concept that we will return to frequently.

CREATING BUDGETS

Earlier in this chapter we examined the methods and implications of creating budgets and using budgetary control. We will now look at the numerical work that is needed to produce a budget. This will involve coordinating the various budgets so that they are all based on the same assumptions and fit together in a logical sequence. In any tasks involving the preparation of budgets, you may be requested to state the assumptions that they are based on.

The procedure that we will need to follow when creating budgets is based on the system described in the earlier section on coordinated budgets. Limiting factors need to be considered and the 'key' factor identified. For a manufacturing business sales volume is often the principal (key) budget factor. The system of budgets that will be created is shown in the diagram below and explained in the text that follows. The diagram also shows how the relevant budgets link with the cash budget.

sales budget

The forecast of sales units will need to be developed first, as this is fundamental to the whole series of budgets. The level of actual production that is required will depend on two issues:

- the amount of finished goods the business plans to hold in stock ready to be sold (inventory)

- whether any of the finished goods are likely to be rejected

sales revenue budget

The sales budget in units can be used to develop the sales revenue budget. This uses the sales units multiplied by the unit selling prices to arrive at the budgeted sales revenue. This budget will ultimately be used to develop the budgeted statement of profit or loss. The data from the sales revenue budget will also link with the cash budget, which will use information on the timing of the receipts.

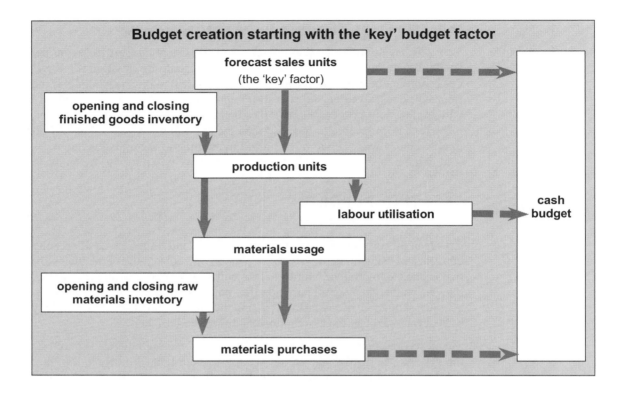

production budget

We will generally need to plan to produce the units that we intend to sell, but we can

■ plan to reduce our production by the intended fall in the level of finished goods inventory, or

■ plan to increase our production to increase the level of our finished goods inventory

The production budget in units for a period therefore equals:

Budgeted Sales Units

– Opening Inventory of Finished Goods

+ Closing Inventory of Finished Goods

This can be justified since:

■ the **opening inventory** of finished goods has already been produced, and can therefore be deducted from our calculation of what needs to be made, and

■ the **closing inventory** has yet to be made so needs to be added in to our total of goods to be produced

In summary, the common-sense rule is:

- if inventory of finished goods is to increase, then production must be greater than sales

- if finished goods inventory is to remain constant, production will be the same as sales

- if finished goods inventory is to fall, production will be less than sales

materials usage budget

Once the production budget has been developed in units, we can calculate the quantity of material we need to use. The **materials usage budget** is created to ascertain the amount of raw material that will be consumed in production. The use of materials can also be valued at this point if required. The data for these calculations may come from standard costing information, or some less formal estimates of the material content of production units.

materials purchases budget

The materials purchases budget can be created once the materials usage budget has been established. Here differences between the quantity of material to be consumed in production and the quantity to be purchased will be due to:

- the required movement in raw material goods inventory (adjusting for opening and closing inventory)

- any wastage or loss of raw materials

At this point we will consider the adjustments needed for raw material inventory movements.

The reasoning follows a similar pattern to the one described for sales, finished goods and production. If we already have raw materials in the opening inventory this amount does not have to be purchased, but the quantity that we plan to have remaining at the end of the period must be purchased in addition to the amount that will be used in production.

The **quantity of material purchased** (as recorded in the material purchases budget) will therefore equal:

Quantity of material to be used (per materials usage budget)

– opening inventory of raw materials,

+ closing inventory of raw materials.

The rule is therefore:

- if inventory of raw materials is to increase, then purchases must be greater than materials usage

- if raw materials inventory is to remain constant, then purchases will be the same as materials usage

- if raw materials inventory is to fall, then purchases will be less than materials usage

One vital reason for creating a material purchases budget is that the information on the timing of purchases will feed into the cash budget which shows when the payments will need to be made.

Case Study

FLUMEN LIMITED:
BUDGETS FOR MATERIALS USED AND PURCHASED

situation

A manufacturing company, Flumen Limited, makes a single product, the Wye. The sales forecast for February is 5,900 units. Each unit of Wye uses 5 kilos of Monnow and 3 kilos of Lugg.

The anticipated inventory levels at the beginning of February are:

Finished Wyes	1,400 units
Unused Monnow	350 kilos
Unused Lugg	200 kilos

The required inventory levels at the end of February are:

Finished Wyes	1,800 units
Unused Monnow	250 kilos
Unused Lugg	450 kilos

required

Produce the following budget figures for the month of February:

(a)   Production of Wye (in units)

(b)   Materials usage of Monnow and Lugg (in kilos)

(c)   Materials purchases of Monnow and Lugg (in kilos)

solution

(a)   Production units =

Budgeted Sales Units	5,900
– opening Inventory of finished goods	(1,400)
+ closing Inventory of finished goods	1,800
Production units =	6,300

Wyes

(b)   Materials usage
Monnow: 6,300 × 5 kilos = 31,500 kilos
Lugg: 6,300 × 3 kilos = 18,900 kilos

(c)   Materials purchases:
Monnow:

Quantity of material to be used	31,500 kilos
– opening inventory of raw materials	(350 kilos)
+ closing inventory of raw materials	250 kilos
Required purchases of Monnow	31,400 kilos

Lugg:

Quantity of material to be used	18,900 kilos
– opening inventory of raw materials	(200 kilos)
+ closing inventory of raw materials	450 kilos
Required purchases of Lugg	19,150 kilos

labour utilisation budget

This budget (also known as the direct labour budget) is developed based on the production requirements (in units) shown in the production budget. The labour utilisation budget is usually based on direct labour time in hours, but could be converted into full time equivalent employees.

At this point it will be determined whether there are sufficient basic labour hours available for the production requirements, or whether overtime will need to be worked. Sometimes the amount of labour time available is a limiting factor (as discussed earlier) and it may be that sub-contractors can be used to make up any shortfall. This is an example of the benefits of good budgeting – so that the labour resources can be planned to ensure that production can go ahead as required.

worked example – calculating overtime hours

During week 50, the production budget shows a requirement for manufacturing 12,083 units. Each unit takes 11 minutes of direct labour time. There are 52 direct labour employees, each working 38 hours per week. Overtime hours can be worked if necessary.

Calculate the overtime requirement, rounded up to the next whole hour.

Direct labour hours needed:

$\qquad$ 12,083 units × 11 minutes / 60 $\qquad$ = 2,216 hours (rounded up)

Basic rate hours available:

$\qquad$ 52 employees × 38 hours $\qquad$ = 1,976 hours

Overtime hours required:

$\qquad$ 2,216 hours – 1,976 hours $\qquad$ = 240 hours

worked example – calculating sub-contracting work

During week 51, the production budget shows a requirement for manufacturing 14,180 units. Each unit takes 11 minutes of direct labour time. There are 52 direct labour employees, each working 38 hours per week. Overtime hours can be worked if necessary, but only up to an average of 8 hours per employee. Production requirements in excess of those that can be carried out by employees must be sub-contracted to another company.

Calculate how many units can be made in-house (rounded down) and how many must be sub-contracted (rounded up to the next whole unit).

Total number of units to be produced: $\qquad$ = 14,180 units

Maximum number of units to be made in-house:

(52 employees × (38 + 8) hours) / (11 minutes / 60) $\quad$ = 13,047 units (rounded down)

Number of units to be sub-contracted:

14,180 – 13,047.27 $\qquad$ = 1,133 units (rounded up)

Note the way that the rounding is carried out in this example. It would not make sense to only make a part of a unit in-house. All units made must add up to the total requirement.

Once the direct labour requirement has been established, then costs can be calculated based on known basic labour and overtime rates. Where sub-contracting is also needed then these costs can be determined based on relevant quotations or estimates.

Indirect costs in the form of fixed and variable overheads can also be ascertained at this stage if required. If absorption costing is being used then the overheads may be absorbed using a direct labour hour rate. If marginal costing is adopted all fixed costs will be considered as relating to the time period rather than the production units.

plant utilisation budget

Another useful budget that can be prepared once the production budget has been finalised is the machine (or plant) utilisation budget. This shows the extent to which existing production machines are used for the planned production level, and also provides an opportunity to plan for short-term hire of additional machines.

worked example – calculating machine utilisation

During week 52, the production budget shows a requirement for manufacturing 10,120 units. The company owns twelve machines, each one is capable of producing up to 1,125 units per week.

Calculate the machine utilisation percentage (to the nearest whole percentage), and state whether all twelve machines are needed in week 52.

The maximum total machine capacity is 12 × 1,125 = 13,500 units

$$\text{Machine utilisation} = \frac{\text{production requirement}}{\text{maximum total machine capacity}} \times 100$$

$$= \frac{10,120}{13,500} \times 100 = 75\% \text{ (rounded)}$$

The unused capacity is (13,500 – 10,120) = 3,380 units. This is just over the capacity of three machines, so three machines are not needed at all during week 52.

If this production level was expected to continue for the foreseeable future, then consideration could be given to selling or scrapping up to three machines. However, care would have to be taken to avoid leaving the organisation with a problem should production levels rise.

Based on the current twelve machines, if the production budget had a requirement for more than 13,500 units, then additional machines may need to be hired. This is provided, of course, that there is sufficient direct labour for the expected production level.

wastage, inefficiency and rejects

You may come across situations where more inputs are required than are used in the products. For example, a manufacturing process could involve a percentage of the materials that is input to be wasted in production. You would then need to allow for this wastage, and budget to use an increased quantity of material.

worked example – dealing with wastage

A company makes a product that requires 3.6 kilos of material in each completed unit. There is expected wastage of 10% of the material that is input during production. During the period, the company plans to make 5,000 units.

The material that will be in the products is 3.6 kilos x 5,000 units = 18,000 kilos.

The material wasted will be 18,000 x 10/90 = 2,000 kilos.

The total material required will be 18,000 x 100/90 = 20,000 kilos.

The 20,000 kilos would then be incorporated into the material usage budget.

A similar calculation method could be applied to labour working at less than 100% efficiency. For example working at 95% efficiency during training. You would need to allow for non-productive time through the labour budget.

The calculation method would also apply to the expected rejection of finished goods. Here, more items would have to be planned through the production budget to allow for the anticipated rejects.

PRODUCING MASTER BUDGETS

It was explained earlier in the chapter that communication and coordination are key purposes of budgeting. The creation of a set of master budgets brings together the data from all the subsidiary budgets into a budgeted statement of profit or loss together with a budgeted statement of financial position and a cash budget. In this way all the budgets are coordinated and the results can be communicated to all parties. It enables all budgets to be checked for viability. For example, the sales budget must be achievable and link to production schedules that can be met and inventory levels that can be managed. The impact of all the budgets must be a budgeted level of financial performance (including profitability) that is appropriate. This must be achievable without putting undue pressure on the financial position (company assets and liabilities) or the organisation's liquidity (having sufficient cash and other resources to meet its financial obligations).

The following Case Study will reinforce the process, and demonstrate how the various budgets are coordinated. The term 'operating budget' can be used to describe a budgeted statement of profit or loss that ends with 'operating profit' (or loss).

Case Study

COORDINATION LIMITED: DEVELOPING AN OPERATING BUDGET

situation

Coordination Limited manufactures and sells a single product for £28.00 per unit. It has already developed a production budget (in units) for period 3, based on forecast sales of 13,000 units, together with anticipated finished goods inventory levels. The production budget for period 3 shows scheduled production of 12,800 units.

Materials:

Each unit takes 3.5 kilos of material to manufacture. The inventory of material at the start of period 3 is budgeted to be 22,400 kilos (valued at £39,200), and at the end of period 3 to be 25,600 kilos. The budgeted purchase price of material is

£1.80 per kilo in period 3, and this cost is also to be used to value the closing inventory.

Labour:

Each unit takes 45 minutes to produce. 50 staff each work 180 basic hours in the period at a cost of £12.00 per labour hour. Overtime is available at a rate of £15.00 per labour hour.

Overhead:

Variable overhead is absorbed at a rate of £2.80 per labour hour worked. Fixed overhead is budgeted at £9,560 for the period.

Operating Budget:

The budgeted opening inventory of finished goods has already been calculated as 2,500 units valued at £17.60 per unit. The closing inventory is to be valued at production cost per unit.

Administration costs are budgeted at £26,500 for the period and Marketing costs at £15,700.

required

- Complete a materials budget showing both kilos and value of inventories, purchases and amounts used in production.
- Complete a labour budget, showing time and costs of basic hours and overtime.
- Complete an overhead budget showing variable, fixed and total overhead for the period.
- Complete an operating budget for the period.

solution

Materials Budget:

	Kilos	£
Opening inventory	22,400	39,200
Purchases	48,000	86,400
Sub-total	70,400	125,600
Used in production	44,800	79,520
Closing inventory	25,600	46,080

Workings:

The order of calculation is important in this situation:

- The opening inventory (kilos and value) is given and can be inserted.
- The kilos used in production is calculated as 12,800 units × 3.5 kg = 44,800 kilos.
- The sub-total will equal the quantity used in production, plus the closing inventory 44,800 + 25,600 = 70,400 kilos.
- This sub-total will also equal the opening inventory plus purchases, so the purchases must be 70,400 – 22,400 = 48,000 kilos.

- The purchases can now be valued at 48,000 × £1.80 = £86,400.
- The value sub-total can be calculated as £39,200 + £86,400 = £125,600.
- The closing inventory is also valued at purchase price (from the Case Study instructions) 25,600 × £1.80 = £46,080.
- The value of material used in production must therefore be £125,600 – £46,080 = £79,520.

Labour Budget:

	Hours	£
Basic rate	9,000	108,000
Overtime	600	9,000
Total	9,600	117,000

Workings:

This is more straightforward than the materials budget.

- The total hours needed for production is calculated at 12,800 × 45/60 = 9,600 hours.
- The basic rate hours are 50 employees × 180 hours = 9,000 hours.
- The balance is made up of overtime hours 9,600 – 9,000 = 600 hours.
- The values are calculated for basic rate (9,000 × £12 = £108,000) and overtime (600 × £15 = £9,000).
- The total cost is £108,000 + £9,000 = £117,000.

Overhead Budget:

		£
Variable overhead:	9,600 hours × £2.80	26,880
Fixed overhead		9,560
Total overhead		36,440

Operating Budget

	£	£
Sales revenue		364,000
Cost of goods sold:		
Opening inventory of finished goods		44,000
Cost of production:		
Materials	79,520	
Labour	117,000	
Overhead	36,440	

		232,960
Closing inventory of finished goods		41,860
		———
Cost of goods sold		235,100
		———
Gross profit		128,900
Administration	26,500	
Marketing	15,700	
	———	
		42,200
		———
Operating profit		86,700
		———

Particular care needs to be taken with the valuation of closing inventory. Full workings for the operating budget are as follows:

- Sales revenue is 13,000 units × £28.00 = £364,000.

- Opening inventory of finished goods is 2,500 × £17.60 = £44,000.

- Materials, labour and overheads are taken from the budgets prepared earlier, and totalled to arrive at a cost of production of £232,960.

- The cost of production of £232,960 is divided by the 12,800 units made to give a production cost of £18.20 per unit to be used to value closing inventory.

- The closing inventory of finished goods in units is calculated as 2,500 + 12,800 – 13,000 = 2,300. This is valued at production cost of £18.20 to give a valuation of £41,860.

- The cost of goods sold is £44,000 + £232,960 – £41,860 = £235,100.

- The gross profit is £364,000 – £235,100 = £128,900.

- Administration and marketing amounts are inserted, totalled, and deducted from gross profit to arrive at the budgeted operating profit of £86,700.

Note that while all the budget formats used above are typical, there may be variations, and extra care must be taken if the format is unfamiliar.

CASH BUDGET

The cash budget is an important budget which illustrates the effect on cash flow of all the other budgets (including the capital expenditure budget). Cash budgets are usually prepared on a month by month basis so that fluctuations in cash balances can be anticipated and plans made for short-term borrowing or investment if necessary. A typical format is shown opposite, including sample figures. The actual descriptions of the receipts and payments will be tailored to the organisations' needs.

The key to preparing an accurate cash budget is to base it on the time that cash will be received or paid. This must take account of lagging – the difference in time between sales being invoiced and cash being received, and between purchases being made or expenses being incurred and when payments are made. You may be told, for example, that purchases are paid for after two months. It is also possible that receipts or payments may be split in terms of timing. For example, half of customers could take one month to pay and half take two months.

It is also vital to remember that 'non-cash' items are not recorded in a cash budget. Depreciation is the most important example of non-cash expenditure. However the initial purchase of non-current assets does need to be recorded in a cash budget, as do other non-operational payments like dividends and taxation.

Cash Budget	January £	February £	March £	April £
Receipts				
Receipts from Sales	10,000	12,000	10,500	15,000
Other Receipts		14,000		
Total Receipts	10,000	26,000	10,500	15,000
Payments				
Materials	5,000	4,800	5,200	4,300
Labour	4,100	3,800	4,000	4,250
Production Overheads	1,100	1,200	1,050	1,150
Administration Costs	500	450	480	500
Non-current Assets		12,500		
Dividends				7,000
Taxation	5,300			
Total Payments	**16,000**	**22,750**	**10,730**	**17,200**
Cash Flow for Month	(6,000)	3,250	(230)	(2,200)
Cash Balance b/f	10,000	4,000	7,250	7,020
Cash Balance c/f	4,000	7,250	7,020	4,820

Although preparation of a full cash budget, as above, may not be required in your exam, you must develop the skills involved and be prepared to calculate the receipts and payments as shown in the following examples.

worked example

The following budget has been prepared for Quarter 1 (January to March).

	January	February	March
	£	£	£
Sales	55,000	43,500	61,500
Materials	15,000	14,000	16,300
Labour	11,000	8,700	12,300
Overheads	10,000	10,000	10,000
Gross Profit	19,000	10,800	22,900

All sales are made on two months' credit.

Materials are purchased on one months' credit.

There is no inventory of materials.

Labour is paid for in the month that it is incurred.

Overheads include monthly depreciation of £4,000. Payments for overheads are made in the month incurred.

Required: Show the cash receipts and payments for March.

Solution:

		£
Receipts from sales	(January sales)	55,000
Payments for materials	(February purchases)	14,000
Payments for labour	(March labour)	12,300
Payments for overheads	(£10,000 – £4,000)	6,000

One way that receipts and payments can be calculated is to make use of our knowledge of how opening and closing balances interact with sales, purchases and expenses.

For example, if we know the forecast opening and closing trade receivables for a period as well as the expected sales, we can calculate what the receipts from sales should be. The receipts should equal (opening trade receivables + sales – closing trade receivables). You have probably used this idea in your other studies.

We can use similar calculations to work out payments for materials. If there are trade payables (or accruals) involved the calculation will be (purchases + opening trade payables – closing trade payables). Some overhead costs like insurance or phone calls may be paid before or after the cost is shown in the accounts. To calculate actual cash payments you may need to reverse accounting adjustments that have been made for accruals and prepayments.

**Case
Study**

CASHET LIMITED:
CASH BUDGET

The company has prepared the following operating budget for the next period:

	£	£
Sales Revenue		306,000
Less Expenditure:		
Materials usage	110,000	
Labour	123,500	
Depreciation	25,000	
Expenses	34,000	
	———	
		292,500
		———
Operating Profit		13,500
		———

The following amounts are forecast in the statements of financial position at the start and end of the period:

	Start	**End**
	£	£
Trade Receivables	45,400	50,100
Materials Inventory	21,450	22,500
Material Trade Payables	0	0
Labour Accruals	2,000	1,500
Expense Prepayments	12,400	13,100
Bank	43,500	

r e q u i r e d

Complete the summary cash flow budget for the period.

solution

	Cash Flow Budget £	Workings for information £
Receipts from sales	301,300	306,000 + 45,400 − 50,100
Payments for materials	111,050	110,000 − 21,450 + 22,500
Payments for labour	124,000	123,500 + 2,000 − 1,500
Payments for expenses	34,700	34,000 − 12,400 + 13,100
Total payments	269,750	
Net cash flow	31,550	
Balance b/f	43,500	
Balance c/f	75,050	

Chapter Summary

- Budgets can be used to compel planning, to communicate and coordinate ideas, and to monitor and control outcomes. They may also be used to help motivate managers and employees.

- Budgets must be in line with the objectives of the organisation, and the organisation's chosen strategy to achieve those objectives. Before starting to create a budget, the key budget factor must be recognised, and its numerical impact forecast. For most commercial organisations this factor is the sales level, but it could be based on specific resources or factors.

- The budgeting process is often overseen by the budget committee, assisted by the budget accountant. Participation in the budget setting process by a wide range of people has various advantages.

- Responsibility accounting is an important aspect of budgeting, so that managers are held accountable for the implementation and performance of their budget area.

- A range of techniques can be used to help create ongoing budgets for indirect costs and support activities. These include the traditional incremental budgeting as well as the more recent developments of zero based budgeting, priority based budgeting and activity based budgeting.

- Budgets that are prepared for manufacturing organisations typically include Sales, Production, Materials Usage, Materials Purchases, and Labour Utilisation, together with other budgets including various functional (including departmental) budgets, capital expenditure budgets and cash budgets. These are coordinated and amalgamated to form a set of Master Budgets.

Key Terms	**budget**	a financial plan for an organisation, prepared before the period starts
	key budget factor	the main factor (internal or external) that determines the planned activity level of the organisation
	budget cycle	the stages of preparation, approval, implementation and monitoring and evaluation
	operating budget	a budget that covers operations over the short to medium term
	capital budget	a budget used for capital expenditure
	fixed budget	a budget based on one assumed level of output
	flexed budget	a budget that is adjusted to correspond with the actual level of output
	incremental budgeting	preparing a budget by basing it on the budget for the previous period with adjustments for inflation and known changes
	zero based budgeting	preparing a budget without reference to the previous period, but by analysing the costs and benefits of a series of decision packages
	priority based budgeting	ranking outcomes into levels of priority as a means of budgeting only for those with the highest priorities
	activity based budgeting	using the techniques of activity based costing to prepare budgets based on activities and their cost drivers
	production budget	a budget that plans how much should be produced in a particular period, to allow for anticipated sales, inventory movements of finished goods, and rejections due to poor quality
	labour utilisation budget	a budget that details the labour input required to meet the needs of the production budget
	materials usage budget	a budget that plans the amount of materials that is required to satisfy the production budget, after allowing for wastage during production

materials purchases budget	a budget that plans for the level of purchases needed to meet the demands of the materials utilisation budget, as well as allowing for wastage before production and changing inventory levels
plant utilisation budget	a budget that shows the extent to which owned or rented machinery will be utilised by production
budget committee	a committee charged with the responsibility of setting and monitoring the budget. It will include senior representatives from all parts of the organisation
budget manual	a document containing information about how an organisation's policy on budgeting is implemented
strategic budget	a long-term budget produced in outline only
operational budget	a short-term budget produced in detail
capital expenditure budget	budget detailing approved expenditure on assets that will benefit the organisation for more than one accounting period
budgeted operating statement	budget based on the statement of profit or loss, showing the detail making up budgeted operating profit
cash budget	budget showing planned cash flows over the budget period
budget holder	the manager responsible for a specific budget and the actual performance that is measured against that budget
responsibility accounting	management accounting based on departments, activities or functions, each of which is the area of responsibility of an individual

Activities

1.1 Suggest the key (or principal) budget factors for the following organisations:

(a) A partnership of two craftsmen who make high quality violins for leading musicians. The work is labour intensive and highly skilled. They are able to easily sell all they produce.

(b) A transport company that has a contract to work only for a major supplier of turkeys. The turkey supplier is currently expanding, but there is an agreement in place for all their transport requirements to be met by this one company for the next 12 months.

(c) A company whose team of engineers has a contract to maintain the Metro in Manchester. They have no plans to seek other contracts.

(d) A company that has opened a new baked potato outlet on a busy business park. The firm has the sole rights to supply potatoes to the 3,000 staff on the site, and has the capacity to cook and sell 100 baked potatoes per day.

1.2 Who would you contact in each of the following situations?

(a) You want to identify the production capacity of the firm.

(b) You want to forecast the price of raw materials.

(c) The draft budget is ready for review.

Choose from:

- Trade union representative
- Managing director
- Buyer or purchasing manager
- Budget committee
- Production planning manager
- Marketing manager

1.3 An organisation has the following budgets:

- Personnel
- Cost of Production
- Maintenance
- Capital Expenditure
- Marketing

Select the most appropriate budget for each of the following costs:

(a)   Production wages

(b)   Printing recruitment application forms

(c)   Advertising

(d)   Customer demand survey

(e)   Raw materials

(f)   Spare parts for production machines

(g)   Warehouse extension

(h)   Sales commission paid to staff

1.4   Select an appropriate accounting treatment for each of the following costs:

- Holiday pay for production workers
- Material wastage in production
- Cost of the purchasing department
- Administrative wages
- Computing services
- Production equipment maintenance
- Depreciation of production equipment
- Redecoration of the sales showroom

Options available are:

- Allocate to marketing overheads
- Allocate to administrative overheads
- Direct cost
- Charge to production in a machine hour overhead rate
- Charge to production in a labour hour overhead rate
- Activity based charge to production cost centres

1.5 The following table shows the sales level in units planned for the next three months. The company policy is to hold inventory of finished goods at the end of each month equal to 20% of the next month's sales.

Period	October	November	December
Sales (units)	20,400	21,600	24,000
Opening inventory	4,080		
Closing inventory			
Production (units)			

Complete the table to show the opening and closing inventory and production in units for October and November.

1.6 A manufacturing company that makes kitchen chairs is planning its activities for month 5 in the current year. The following data is available:

Sales in month 5 are forecast at 1,800 units.

Each completed unit requires 4 kilos of raw material.

Planned inventory levels are:

	Raw Materials	Finished Goods
At end of month 4	1,200 kilos	500 units
At end of month 5	1,500 kilos	400 units

Required:

Calculate the following budgets for month 5:

- production budget (in units)
- raw materials usage (in kilos)
- raw materials purchases (in kilos)

1.7 During month 4, the production budget shows a requirement for manufacturing 25,430 units. Each unit takes 9 minutes of direct labour time. There are 22 direct labour employees, each working 160 basic hours per month. Overtime hours can be worked if necessary.

Calculate the overtime requirement for month 4, rounded up to the next whole hour.

1.8 Labour hours:

- 72,000 units of product M are to be manufactured in May.

- Each one takes 5 minutes to produce.

- 30 staff will each work 180 hours basic time.

How many overtime hours must be worked to complete the production?

Select from:

(a)	360
(b)	600
(c)	720
(d)	5,400
(e)	6,000

1.9 During month 5, the production budget shows a requirement for manufacturing 27,365 units. Each unit takes 9 minutes of direct labour time. There are 22 direct labour employees, each working 160 hours per month. Overtime hours can be worked if necessary, but only up to an average of 20 hours per employee. Production requirements in excess of those that can be carried out by employees must be sub-contracted to another company.

Calculate how many units can be made in-house (rounded down if necessary) and how many must be sub-contracted.

1.10 Department Y manufactures three products, A, B and C.

(a) Calculate the machine hours required to manufacture these in November, using the following table.

Product	Units	Hours per unit	Hours required
A	240	1.5	
B	210	2.0	
C	170	3.0	
Total hours for department Y			

(b) There are three machines in the department.

Each machine can be used for 300 hours in November. Additional machines can be hired if required.

Calculate how many additional machines should be hired.

1.11 A company that manufactures a single product (the Zapp) is planning for the next six months. Each unit of Zapp produced uses 2 litres of Woo and 3 litres of Koo.

Each unit of Zapp takes 0.5 hours of direct labour to produce.

The anticipated demand for Zapp is as follows:

January	5,000 units
February	4,000 units
March	6,500 units
April	5,000 units
May	6,500 units
June	5,000 units

after which the demand can be assumed to stabilise at 5,000 units per month.

It will be company policy to maintain raw material inventory at a level of 100% of the following month's usage, and to maintain finished goods inventory at a level to satisfy half of the following month's estimated sales. Inventory held on 31 December was 3,000 finished Zapps, 8,000 litres of Woo and 16,000 litres of Koo.

Required:

Calculate the following budgets for each month and in total:

- Production of Zapps (in units)

- Materials Usage (in litres of Woo and Koo)

- Materials Purchase (in litres of Woo and Koo)

- Direct Labour (in hours)

1.12 You are required to complete the workings schedules and Operating Budget (Budget Income Statement) below.

Workings schedules

Materials	kg	£
Opening inventory	2,100	2,000
Purchases	15,500	27,125
Sub-total	17,600	29,125
Used		
Closing inventory	1,000	

Closing inventory of materials is to be valued at budgeted purchase price

Labour

	Hours	£
Basic time @ £12 per hour		

It takes 4 minutes to make each item

Production overhead	Hours	£
Variable @ £2.00 per labour hour		
Fixed		4,625
Total Production Overheads		

Operating budget

	units	£
Sales revenue @ £2.60 each	29,000	
Opening inventory of finished goods	4,000	7,000
Cost of production	30,000	
Materials		
Labour		
Production Overhead		
Total		

	units	£
Closing inventory of finished goods*	5,000	

*Valued at budgeted production cost per unit

	£
Cost of goods sold	
Gross profit	

Non-Production Overheads	£
Administration	3,000
Marketing	4,000
Total	7,000
Operating profit	

1.13 Consolidation Limited manufactures and sells a single product for £15.00 per unit. It has already developed a production budget (in units) for period 6, based on forecast sales of 7,000 units, together with anticipated finished goods inventory levels. The production budget for period 6 shows scheduled production of 6,850 units.

Materials:

Each unit takes 1.5 kilos of material to manufacture. The inventory of material at the start of period 6 is budgeted to be 2,055 kilos (valued at £2,135), and at the end of period 6 to be 2,100 kilos. The budgeted purchase price of material is £1.05 per kilo in period 6, and this cost is also to be used to value the closing inventory.

Labour:

Each unit takes 15 minutes to produce. 10 staff each work 165 basic hours in the period at a cost of £12.00 per labour hour. Overtime is available at a rate of £16.00 per labour hour. Total hours required must be rounded up to the next whole hour.

Overhead:

Variable overhead is absorbed at a rate of £3.00 per labour hour. Fixed overhead is budgeted at £8,497 for the period.

Operating Budget:

The budgeted opening inventory of finished goods has already been calculated as 2,000 units valued at £6.50 per unit. The closing inventory is to be valued at budgeted production cost per unit.

Administration costs are budgeted at £16,500 for the period and Marketing costs at £23,450.

Required:

- Complete a materials budget showing both kilos and value of inventories, purchases and amounts used in production.

- Complete a labour budget, showing time and costs of basic hours and overtime.

- Complete an overhead budget showing variable, fixed and total overhead for the period.

- Complete an operating budget for the period.

1.14 Prepare a Cash Budget for May from the following budget data

Budget data	March	April	May	June	Cash Budget	May
	£	£	£	£		£
Invoiced sales	6,000	7,000	6,600	7,600	Opening cash balance	(430)
					Receipts:	
Purchases	2,000	2,200	2,400	2,200	Customer receipts	
Wages	1,000	1,020	1,040	960		
Other cash overheads	1,200	1,320	1,240	1,260	**Payments:**	
Capital expenditure	0	2,400	0	0	For purchases	
					For wages	
Average terms					For overheads	
Half of customers take 1 month to pay. Half take 2 months.					For capital exp.	
Purchases paid for after two months					Total payments	
Wages paid in the current month						
Other cash overheads paid after one month					Closing cash balance	
Capital expenditure paid in the current month						

1.15 Produce a cash budget for the month of March from the following information:

Operating Budget for Month of March	£	£
Revenue		56,500
Costs:		
Materials	15,500	
Labour	19,500	
Expenses	14,650	
		49,650
Operating Profit		6,850

Assumptions for March:

Trade receivables will decrease by £2,000

Inventory of materials will increase by £1,200

Materials are payable in month of purchase

Wages are paid in current month

Expenses payable will decrease by £650

2 **Using budgets**

this chapter covers...

We start this chapter by examining the constraints that may restrict the selling or manufacture of goods, which must be considered when budgeting. We discuss various ways that these limitations may be managed.

We then discuss factors that influence forecasts, including the product life cycle and competition and marketing. Next, we examine ways of dealing with uncertainty in budgeting, and the various approaches that can be taken.

The revision of a budget is then examined, and we see how to arithmetically manipulate budgets to take account of alternative scenarios.

The next section gives us an opportunity to practice producing flexible budgets by using our knowledge of cost behaviour.

The chapter is concluded with an explanation of management action that can be taken as a result of budgeting, including the ideas of feedback and feedforward.

SALES AND PRODUCTION CONSTRAINTS

In this section we will discuss a variety of constraints that may prevent an organisation from selling and/or producing more goods. You should understand the range of possible limitations on output and be able to work out the impact.

limited market share

It is almost impossible for an organisation to be in a monopoly situation and have access to 100% of the possible market for a product or service. There will always be a limit on the percentage of the market that an individual organisation can sell to.

For example, a restaurant will always be competing with other local restaurants for a share of the market for people who wish to dine out. The market share that is achieved will depend on the success of the organisation's marketing as well as the number and quality of the competitors and their pricing structure. It must also be remembered that there will be a limit on the total market for diners in an area – this will depend on the population, its habits, and its disposable income.

Effective marketing will increase market share to a certain extent, but this will always come at a cost. Care must be taken to ensure that any marketing undertaken generates more benefits than costs.

limited finance

When organisations have limited access to finance it can have wide ranging effects on the sales and production levels.

- sales on credit will be restricted if there is a lack of working capital to support a high level of receivables.

- inventory levels may need to be restricted. This can increase the risk of shortages of finished goods needed for sales and a lack of raw materials may interrupt production. Bulk discounts may also be unobtainable if the organisation only has the finance to buy in small quantities.

- capital expenditure may need to be reduced or stopped completely. This can lead to inefficient production and the inability to expand the business.

Access to finance will depend on the organisation's creditworthiness, and also on the economic outlook of the segment that it operates in as well as the country as a whole.

limited materials

Sometimes an organisation finds that it cannot obtain the amount of materials that it had planned to purchase. This could be due to a worldwide shortage, or to a more localised problem, perhaps just with the organisation's usual supplier. The problems with supplies could be simply temporary, or relate to a longer-term situation that is developing.

The range of tactics that can be used to overcome or lessen the effect of such problems includes the following, which can be used individually or in combination:

- **Utilising raw material inventory**. The planned production can sometimes be maintained by simply running down raw material inventory. This will only work in the short term, and will depend on the current raw material inventory level.

- **Utilising finished goods inventory**. If production needs to be reduced due to limited raw materials, sales may still be maintained if there are sufficient finished goods in inventory. This can also only be effective as a temporary measure.

- **Finding an alternative supplier**. This may be an obvious solution, although there may be cost implications, as well as quality considerations.

- **Substituting an alternative material**. Although some products can only be made from one material, for others there may be alternatives. Implications may include material cost and quality, as well as usage levels, including wastage. The labour force may also work less efficiently, and the suitability of current machinery and equipment would need to be considered.

- **Reformulating the product**. Changing the formula for manufacture can be carried out so that less of the raw material that is in short supply will be used. Clearly the quality of the finished item would have to be carefully considered, and the customers would need to accept the revised specification. This may involve using more of other raw materials to compensate.

- **Buying in finished goods**. This may be a possibility, although it begs the question of where the supplier of those goods obtained their raw materials. This solution would imply reducing in-house production, and losing profit. The organisation's manufacturing facilities would be under-utilised, and the labour force may need to be laid off unless an alternative product can be made on the premises.

- **Manufacturing an alternative product using different materials**. This may involve major changes in the whole production process. If it is to be a substitute for the previous product the new product must be designed and marketed to meet the same need, and customers will have to be persuaded of its merits.

limited labour

Where labour is in limited supply a range of alternative solutions are possible. Appropriate labour can usually be obtained eventually, even if it means paying a high rate and/or investing substantial amounts in training. Because of this, labour shortage problems are typically short-term ones. The range of ways to deal with a labour shortage includes:

- **Overtime working**. Although this probably involves paying a premium rate it is a logical way to tackle a temporary problem.

- **Utilising finished goods inventory**. If production needs to be reduced due to limited availability of labour, sales may still be maintained if there are sufficient finished goods in inventory. In the same way as dealing with an inventory shortage, this can also only be effective as a temporary measure.

- **Using sub-contractors**. This could include self-employed or agency staff within the factory, or possibly sub-contracting parts of the production process to another organisation and location. The latter may be a major decision with other implications. Any use of sub-contractors will have cost implications, although the responsibility for work quality may also lie with the sub-contractor, which may offset some of the disadvantages.

- **Buying-in finished goods**. This would be a major decision, and would have to be carefully costed. The loss of control over the production process would have to be considered, including quality issues and reliability of supply. It may also leave the organisation's own premises under-utilised.

- **Improving labour efficiency**. Although probably only a very limited change could be made in the short term, in the longer term training or better equipment may improve efficiency. Internal or external experts may be able to direct the organisation as to the best way to maximise the output of its labour force.

limited production capacity

When demand for an organisation's products is likely to outstrip its capacity to supply then the likely solutions will depend on whether the problem is believed to be permanent or temporary. The problems of production capacity are sometimes linked to shortage of factory space.

permanent inability to supply

Permanent inability to supply sufficient goods to customers can be solved by the organisation:

- increasing capacity by expanding premises or relocating

- increasing selling prices to reduce demand (and increase profit)

- sub-contracting or buying-in finished goods

temporary inability to supply

There may be temporary capacity problems caused either by:

■ unexpected demand, or

■ regular seasonal variations in demand

These factors can be dealt with by application of the following techniques:

■ **Manipulating finished goods inventory levels**. The most logical technique is to utilise spare capacity when it exists to build up inventory to deal with higher demand. This inventory can be used as a contingency against unexpected demand, or in anticipation of seasonal peaks. The cost of holding excess inventory should not be overlooked.

■ **Shift working**. This will have the effect of spreading the fixed overheads over a greater production level, and therefore reducing the indirect cost per unit. The direct labour cost may increase through shift premium payments, and the net effect on costs would have to be calculated carefully.

■ **Renting temporary premises or additional equipment**. There may be additional costs in these approaches that would need to be considered.

■ **Sub-contracting, or buying in finished goods, or improving efficiency**. The implications are as discussed previously when examining materials and labour shortages.

combination of limitations

There may be occasions when there is a limit on not just one resource, but a combination of two or more.

For example, if we originally planned to make 5,000 units, but find that we only have sufficient labour for 4,800 units, and enough materials for 4,000 units, then materials is the most pressing problem. It would not make sense to bring in temporary staff while there was still a materials shortage. If we can solve the materials shortage problem, only then should we turn our attention to the labour limitation. The issue that most constrains the output (as materials does in this example) is sometimes known as the **binding constraint**.

FACTORS INFLUENCING FORECASTS

Common sense tells us that there are events and developments going on locally, nationally and internationally which can affect our forecasts and should therefore be taken into account where possible.

the product life cycle

It is important when forecasting sales volumes to consider the effect of the product life cycle. Products typically go through a number of distinct stages between conception and finally being withdrawn from sale. The stages are:

- development
- launch
- growth
- maturity
- decline

These stages are shown on the following graph:

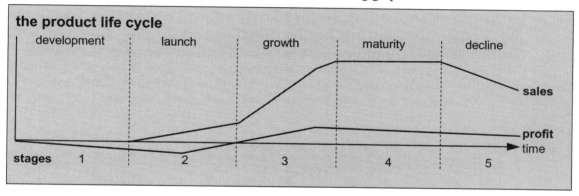

At the beginning of the cycle, development, production and marketing costs are high and so profit may even be negative. If the product is successful, a period of growth follows and sales accelerate up to the level of the maturity stage of the cycle. Here sales have reached a plateau, and demand may be sustained by making product improvements. After the market has become saturated, and virtually all potential buyers satisfied, sales of the product will go into decline. It may be wise to terminate production before all demand has been extinguished to avoid incurring losses, or alternatively repackage and revamp the product.

Marketing strategy during the launch phase of the product life cycle will have an important effect on revenue. One strategy that can work for products that initially have little competition (for example a high quality mobile phone that has unique technological features) is to apply **price skimming**. This involves setting a high initial price which will provide high profit per unit, and this should more than offset low unit sales. In this way it is hoped that development costs can be recovered quickly. The product may be bought by 'early adopters' who want to be seen with the latest products. As competitors launch their products, the price may then need to be reduced to sustain demand.

The opposite launch strategy is to adopt **penetration pricing**. This involves setting a low initial price to encourage a high level of unit sales, although there would be a low profit per unit. The purpose would be to tempt prospective customers who are currently buying from competitors, but who are only modestly satisfied with their purchases. This pricing policy is useful where the product has low development costs that need to be recovered, and it lessens the opportunity for competitors to reduce their prices below yours.

Throughout the product life cycle, the choices made about marketing (the 'marketing mix') will have an important impact on both the sales revenue and the profit.

While some products may move quickly from start-up to decline, others may have a longer life cycle and become what are known as 'cash cows', providing the business with a steady cash flow and source of profitability. Baked beans, for example, have been steady sellers for over 50 years!

It is clearly important to recognise the phases of the cycle, and to be able to identify what phase the products are in to improve forecasting. While a product during the mature phase may have a relatively steady sales level that should be easy to forecast, the approaching period of decline must not be ignored.

competition and marketing

There are major impacts on how forecasting is carried out, and how reliable the results are arising from what competitors are doing and what marketing is planned.

Competition from international organisations has increased dramatically in recent years as it has become easier to provide goods and services from remote locations. Not only is it important to know and understand the current strategy of competitors, but also to be able to appreciate the likely reaction of competitors to any action that your organisation make take. For example, it is unlikely that a price change or promotion campaign by one organisation would not provoke some reaction from its competitors.

Market research can be used to help with forecasting, particularly with the introduction of new products. If an advertising agency is used to assist with promotions, then they can also provide information and data on the promotion's likely impact on sales. The experience gained from previous promotional activity by both the organisation and its partners can be invaluable.

There are many external events that can impact on the reliability of cost forecasts. It is useful to consider the impact of external factors by using the PEST analysis technique. This looks at the influences by considering the categories of political, economic, social and technological factors. To give a few examples, political factors could include trade tariffs and taxation, and economic factors would include whether the country was undergoing a recession and what rate of inflation was anticipated. All these would have an impact on costs.

You may be asked to advise on the reliability of forecasts, and it should always be borne in mind that they can never be totally reliable. Perhaps a good guide to the confidence that can be placed on the reliability of forecasts is the amount of data from different sources that support the forecast. The more different sources and approaches that support the forecast, then the more reliable it is likely to be. A small market research survey on its own is unlikely to produce robust data.

Even products that are enjoying the maturity phase of the product life cycle will be subject to external influences from external events. One only has to look at the recent pandemic to see examples of products whose market has almost evaporated overnight, as well as products that have enjoyed an unexpected surge in sales.

DEALING WITH UNCERTAINTY

Because data produced from forecasts is inherently uncertain, organisations must use techniques to minimise the risks of basing budgets on inaccurate forecasts. There are several methods available, and managers may use one or more of them.

One method is to use 'sensitivity analysis' to model the impact of using different forecasts. This is closely allied to the 'scenario planning' or 'what-if analysis' technique that you may have studied. For example, if the employees' pay level for the budget period is not yet determined, then three alternative budgets based on, say, current pay levels, increases of 2%, or increases of 4%, could be drafted to evaluate the impact of the different amounts.

Another method could be to update forecasts regularly to ensure that recent events are taken into account. As the initial forecasts may be completed well in advance of the budget period, it would make sense to see if they are still valid as the budget period approaches. For example, a sales forecast based on trend analysis may initially be developed using historical data that ceases a year before the budget period. By re-forecasting using more recent sales data as it becomes available, the managers can reassure themselves that the forecast being used is still valid, or if not they can make appropriate changes to their plans.

Many organisations prepare one set of budgets for planning purposes, known as **fixed budgets**. An alternative is to prepare a range of budgets, each based on a different level of activity (typically sales). These are known as **flexible budgets**, and demonstrate the impact of different sales volumes on the budgets. Having prepared the range of budgets, an organisation may commit to one of the budgets as being its financial plan (and have all the managers working towards it), while still being aware of the impacts of achieving different sales levels.

Even when fixed budgets are used for planning purposes, flexible budgets are often used for monitoring and control purposes. This is so there is a fair comparison between the costs actually incurred and the budgeted costs for the same activity (or sales) level. We will examine this use of flexible budgets later in this chapter.

rolling budgets

Rolling budgets are used by some organisations. They consist of budgets that are continually extended into the future as time moves on. For example, a twelve-month budget could initially be prepared for 1 January to 31 December. As the organisation moves through January, the budget would be extended at the far end by a further month, so that a budget for 1 February to 31 January is created. This process would be continued each month (or other agreed period) so that there is always the same length of budget extending into the future.

This can provide improved accuracy and responsiveness compared to traditional static budgets, as information on actual performance can be fed into the budgets much more quickly. If necessary, the budget for the existing period (for example February to December using our earlier dates) can also be updated when the budget is extended. Rolling budgets are particularly useful for organisations that operate in fast-changing environments.

The disadvantages are that budgeting becomes time-consuming (and therefore expensive) and there may be confusion over trying to achieve ever moving targets if the existing budgets are constantly updated. This can lead to demotivation and the danger of participants putting the minimum effort into the budgeting process.

REVISING A BUDGET

It may sometimes be necessary to revise a budget either because the original budget is no longer appropriate, or to demonstrate the impact of an alternative strategy that needs to be considered.

Some of the techniques that you may need to use are cost behaviour, and the use of percentage calculations.

Revisions to a budget can include:

- changes to selling prices
- changes to sales and production volumes
- changes to costs

These changes may occur in combination (for example an increased selling price combined with a reduced volume) so care is needed to carry out the calculations accurately.

Often tasks will either be presented in marginal costing format or will assume that the sales volume is identical to the production volume. In either case, the complication of production output differing from sales will not apply. The following notes are prepared on that basis.

The following process should be followed when revising a budget.

sales revenue

The sales revenue is made up of sales units multiplied by selling price per unit. The unadjusted selling price may be given to you, or you may need to calculate it from the existing figures. You may then be provided with a percentage increase or decrease to apply to the original selling price. This price change would often be in combination with a sales volume change. Typically the higher the price is, the lower the volume falls. The revised sales revenue will be made up of the new volume multiplied by the new selling price per unit.

materials

Material costs are also made up of volume multiplied by material price. Be careful to ignore any selling price changes here – they are not relevant. A step-by-step method of calculation can be used as follows. An existing material cost per unit is first calculated, then revised, and then applied to the revised volume (since this is a variable cost).

Alternatively, an all-in-one calculation can be used. Both are illustrated in this example.

worked example

Material costs in the original budget are shown as £542,500, based on a volume of 155,000 units. The revised budget is to be for an increase in volume of 10%, together with a price increase imposed by the material supplier of 2%.

Method 1 Step-by-step

The current material cost per unit is £542,500 / 155,000 = £3.50

The revised material cost per unit will therefore be £3.50 × 102% = £3.57

The revised volume will be 155,000 × 110% = 170,500

The revised material cost will therefore be £3.57 × 170,500 = £608,685

Method 2 All-in-one

Revised material cost budget

= current material cost budget £542,500 × 102% × 110%   = £608,685

As you can see, both methods will arrive at the same answer – provided you are careful with the calculations!

labour

Provided the labour costs behave as variable costs, the calculations can be carried out in exactly the same alternative ways as explained above for material costs.

worked example

For example, direct labour costs are shown in the original budget as £750,000, based on a volume of 155,000 units. The revised volume is to be 10% greater, and the labour rate is to allow for an increase of 2.5%.

Using the all-in-one method gives a revised labour budget of:

£750,000 × 110% × 102.5% = £845,625.

In this example the step-by-step approach would result in a direct labour cost per unit that is not an exact number (even after seven decimal places). If you find yourself in this situation, it's best to use the all-in-one method above.

stepped costs

Some costs may behave as stepped costs. The key to carrying out revised budgets in these situations is to realise that each step is normally based on **up to** a particular volume of units. For example, if the original volume was 155,000, and each step of a certain cost was based on up to 15,000 units, then there would be 11 steps involved. Ten steps would take us up to 150,000 units maximum, but the extra 5,000 units requires another whole step.

worked example

Suppose the original volume of 155,000 is to be revised by an extra 10% (as in previous examples). The original budgeted cost is a total of £99,000, and increases regularly at every 15,000 units.

The original budget is based on 11 steps, so each step must have been for £99,000 / 11 = £9,000. The new volume is 155,000 × 110% = 170,500. This requires 12 steps (which takes us to a maximum 180,000).

The revised budget will therefore be 12 × £9,000 = £108,000.

fixed costs

Where costs are described as behaving as fixed costs, they will not alter for volume reasons provided the fixed volume range is not exceeded. If there is no mention of the range within which the costs are fixed, then you can assume that the costs are not influenced by volume. If a volume range is noted, be careful to apply any changes to the revised budget.

---

worked example

For example, suppose the fixed costs of £200,000 apply to volumes up to 160,000 units. If the volume exceeds 160,000 the fixed costs will increase by £5,000.

If the original volume of 155,000 units is increased by 10% to 170,500, the new fixed cost will be £200,000 + £5,000 = £205,000.

This is really another form of stepped cost – but with just one step, and of a given amount.

The following Case Study will illustrate the type of situation that you may be presented with.

Case Study

RE-VISION LIMITED: PREPARING A REVISED BUDGET

A draft operating budget has been submitted to the budget committee. The committee has requested that a revised budget is prepared based on an alternative scenario.

The assumptions made in developing the original budget were as follows:

- material and labour costs are variable

- an allowance has been made for a 2% increase in labour rates from the previous year

- production overheads is a stepped fixed cost, increasing regularly at every 20,000 units

The alternative scenario is based on the following assumptions:

- selling price will be reduced by 4%

- sales and production volume will increase by 10%

- material prices will increase by 3%

- labour rates will increase by 1% compared to the previous year

required

Complete the table on the next page to show the data and operating budget based on the alternative scenario.

Round figures (except selling price) to the nearest whole number if necessary.

Operating Budget	First Draft	Alternative Scenario
Selling price per unit	£8.00	
Sales and production volume	110,000	
	£	£
Sales revenue	880,000	
Production costs:		
Materials	220,000	
Labour	336,600	
Production overheads	120,000	
Total production costs	676,600	
Gross profit	203,400	

solution

Operating Budget	First Draft	Alternative Scenario
Selling price per unit	£8.00	£7.68
Sales and production volume	110,000	121,000
	£	£
Sales revenue	880,000	929,280
Production costs:		
Materials	220,000	249,260
Labour	336,600	366,630
Production overheads	120,000	140,000
Total production costs	676,600	755,890
Gross profit	203,400	173,390

Workings:

Selling price per unit:	£8.00 × 96%	= £7.68
Sales and production volume:	110,000 × 110%	= 121,000
Sales revenue:	121,000 × £7.68	= £929,280
Material costs: (affected by volume and price) (£220,000 / 110,000) × 121,000 × 103%		= £249,260

Labour costs:

(affected by volume and rate)
(£336,600 / 110,000) × 121,000 × (100 / 102) × 101%   = £366,630

Production overheads:

Original cost is based on up to 120,000 units
Revised cost is based on up to 140,000 units
(£120,000 / 120,000) × 140,000   = £140,000

FLEXIBLE BUDGETS AND VARIANCES

In order to monitor and control performance we need to compare actual results with budgeted results. Before we carry out the comparison we first need to ensure that the budget assumes the same level of activity as what actually occurred. In many situations the original 'fixed' budget will be for a different activity level, and so we will need to produce a 'flexible' budget.

A budget adjusted for a change in level of activity is called a 'flexed' or 'flexible' budget, which is more suitable if actual results are to be compared with budgets for the purposes of performance measurement, because it would mean that the comparison is of 'like with like'.

In order to prepare a flexible budget for revenue and costs, we need sufficient information to be able to calculate, for each element of cost:

- the variable cost per unit of activity
- the total fixed part of the cost

Some costs may be entirely variable or entirely fixed. For those which are semi-variable, the high-low method can be used if we have enough data. Some costs may behave as stepped fixed costs, and we must be able to adjust these costs. Once the costs have been analysed in this way, a budget can be prepared for any level of activity.

The cost behaviour identified may only apply within a relevant range, however, and therefore it may not be realistic to 'flex' the budget for very large changes in levels of activity.

A flexed budget is useful for preparing a performance report, where the actual costs and income are compared with the flexed budget applicable to the actual level of activity. Differences are shown in a 'variance' column, labelled as adverse or favourable. This form of report gives meaningful variances and is more acceptable to the person responsible for the budget.

preparing a flexible budget

To produce a flexible budget for the required level of activity, the total for each element of cost is calculated using:

- total variable cost = variable cost per unit × number of units

- total fixed cost remains unchanged

- total semi-variable cost =

  Fixed part of cost + variable cost per unit × number of units

- if, in a given case, there are any additional fixed costs which are incurred at certain levels of activity, or any step costs, these must be set at the correct level for the activity level of the flexed budget

Case Study

MAC LIMITED: BUDGETED COSTS

Mac Ltd manufactures a single product – a raincoat – using automated processes. The costs of production are budgeted, as shown in the table below, for outputs of 20,000 units per year and for 30,000 units per year.

Direct Labour consists of machine operatives' wages and the total wages behave as a step cost:

Output	Total Direct Labour
Up to 15,000 units	£20,000
Over 15,000 and up to 25,000 units	£35,000
Over 25,000 and up to 35,000 units	£50,000

Mac Limited: Budgeted Production Costs			
Output (units)	**20,000**	**27,000**	**30,000**
	£000s	£000s	£000s
Direct Material	140		210
Direct Labour	35		50
Machine running costs	90		110
Other production overheads	100		100
Total Production Cost	365		470

required

Complete the Budgeted Production Costs table by calculating the budgeted costs for Mac Ltd for output of 27,000 units. Note that Direct Labour is the only step cost.

solution

Mac Limited: Budgeted Production Costs			
Output (units)	20,000	27,000	30,000
	£000s	£000s	£000s
Direct Material [W1]	140	189	210
Direct Labour [W2]	35	50	50
Machine running costs [W3]	90	104	110
Other production overheads [W4]	100	100	100
Total Production Cost	365	443	470

Workings

(see working note references in the table above)

[W1] Direct Material is a variable cost:

£140,000 ÷ 20,000 = £210,000 ÷ 30,000 = £7

Therefore Direct Material = £7 per unit and £7 × 27,000 = £189,000.

[W2] Direct Labour is a step cost, as given, and for 27,000 units it would be at the level of £50,000.

[W3] Machine running costs are semi-variable, because they do not change in line with output. Using the high-low method:

	Cost		Units	
High	£110,000		30,000	
Low	£90,000		20,000	
Difference	£20,000	÷	10,000	= £2 per unit

Fixed cost = £90,000 – (£2 × 20,000) = £50,000

Total cost for 27,000 units = £50,000 + (£2 × 27,000) = £104,000.

[W4] Other production overheads are fixed at £100,000.

In the previous Case Study we illustrated how costs can be adjusted to create a flexible budget. We will now examine how both income and costs can be adjusted, and how the flexible budget can then be compared with the actual costs to produce meaningful variances.

Case Study

FLEXIE LIMITED:
FLEXIBLE BUDGET AND VARIANCES

The original March budget for Flexie Limited assumed sales of 30,000 units. The actual sales were 32,500 units. The following information is available about the budgeted costs:

- Materials, labour and distribution costs are variable.

- Energy costs are semi-variable. The variable element is £3 per unit.

- Equipment hire is a stepped cost. Each step is based on up to 3,000 units.

- Depreciation, marketing and administration costs behave as fixed costs.

The table below shows the original budget and the actual costs.

Original Budget		Flexed Budget	Actual	Variance Fav (Adv)
30,000	Sales volume (units)		32,500	
£		£	£	£
840,000	Sales revenue		861,250	
	Costs:			
114,000	Materials		123,950	
165,000	Labour		170,320	
126,000	Distribution		131,200	
105,000	Energy		113,300	
50,000	Equipment hire		61,500	
83,400	Depreciation		82,300	
51,300	Marketing		55,350	
44,950	Administration		45,100	
739,650	Total costs		783,020	
100,350	Operating profit (loss)		78,230	

required

Complete the table, showing the flexed budget and variances.

solution

Original Budget		Flexed Budget	Actual	Variance Fav (Adv)
30,000	Sales volume (units)		32,500	
£		£	£	£
840,000	Sales revenue	910,000	861,250	(48,750)
	Costs:			
114,000	Materials	123,500	123,950	(450)
165,000	Labour	178,750	170,320	8,430
126,000	Distribution	136,500	131,200	5,300
105,000	Energy	112,500	113,300	(800)
50,000	Equipment hire	55,000	61,500	(6,500)
83,400	Depreciation	83,400	82,300	1,100
51,300	Marketing	51,300	55,350	(4,050)
44,950	Administration	44,950	45,100	(150)
739,650	Total costs	785,900	783,020	2,880
100,350	Operating profit (loss)	124,100	78,230	(45,870)

Flexed Budget Workings:

Sales revenue	(£840,000 / 30,000) × 32,500	= £910,000
Materials	(£114,000 / 30,000) × 32,500	= £123,500
Labour	(£165,000 / 30,000) × 32,500	= £178,750
Distribution	(£126,000 / 30,000) × 32,500	= £136,500
Energy	Fixed element: £105,000 − (30,000 × £3) = £15,000	
	Total flexed cost: £15,000 + (32,500 × £3) = £112,500	
Equipment hire	Cost per step: £50,000 / 10 = £5,000	
	Number new of steps is 11 (up to 33,000 units) 11 × £5,000 = £55,000	

Depreciation, marketing and administration costs are unchanged.

flexible budgets in marginal costing format

As flexible budgets involve separating the fixed and variable parts of costs, they can easily be shown in marginal costing format if required. The variable costs are listed first (including variable overheads) and the fixed costs (which may include direct costs) are then grouped together. The Case Study that follows demonstrates this. The high-low method is not used because the information is given in a different way.

Case Study

TT LIMITED: MARGINAL COSTING

TT Ltd produces a single chemical product, TCH, which cannot be stored as work-in-progress or finished goods for technical reasons. For the year ended 31 August 20-3, the budget was for 10,000 litres of TCH to be produced and sold, but the actual production and sales for the period amounted to 11,000 litres. An operating results statement, with attached notes, is shown opposite.

Notes

1 There are no opening or closing work-in-progress or finished goods.

2 The cost of direct material is a variable cost.

3 The cost of direct production labour is a fixed cost, because the employees are paid a fixed wage. The employees available are sufficient to produce up to 12,000 litres of TCH.

4 The cost of power is semi-variable and the fixed part of the cost allowed for in the budget is £30,000. However, the fixed part of the actual cost is £27,660, due to renegotiation of the contract with the power company.

TT Ltd Operating results for the year ended 31 August 20-3

Volume (litres of TCH)		Budget 10,000		Actual 11,000
	£	£	£	£
Revenue		450,000		489,500
Direct costs:				
Material	80,000		90,200	
Production labour	95,000		98,000	
Power	46,500		45,700	
	221,500		233,900	
Fixed overheads	130,000		126,400	
Cost of sales		351,500		360,300
Operating profit		98,500		129,200

required

Calculate the following:

1   the budgeted unit selling price

2   the budgeted material cost per litre of TCH

3   the budgeted marginal cost (variable cost) of power

4   the actual marginal cost of power

5   prepare a marginal costing operating results statement, comparing the actual results with a flexible budget for 11,000 litres and showing the variances

6   explain briefly why the revised operating results statement is different from the original one, and state one advantage of flexible budgeting

solution

1   The budgeted unit selling price is £450,000 ÷ 10,000 = £45 per litre.

2   The budgeted material cost per litre is £80,000 ÷ 10,000 = £8.

3   The total budgeted cost of power is £46,500, of which £30,000 is fixed (note 4). Therefore the variable part of the cost is £16,500 for 10,000 litres.

    The budgeted marginal cost of power is therefore £16,500 ÷ 10,000 = £1.65 per litre of TCH.

4   The total actual cost of power is £45,700, of which £27,660 is fixed. Therefore the actual marginal cost of power is (£45,700 − 27,660) ÷ 11,000 = £1.64 per litre of TCH.

5   The answer is shown in the table on the next page, using the above answers to calculate the variable costs for 11,000 litres. Marginal costing format is used.

TT Ltd Flexible budgeting results statement for the year ended 31 August 20-3

Litres of TCH	Flexible budget 11,000		Actual results 11,000		Variance -	
	£	£	£	£	£	
Revenue W1		495,000		489,500	5,500	A
Marginal costs:						
Material W2	88,000		90,200		2,200	A
Power W3	18,150		18,040		110	F
Total marginal costs		106,150		108,240	2,090	A
Contribution		388,850		381,260	7,590	A
Fixed costs						
Direct Labour	95,000		98,000		3,000	A
Power W4	30,000		27,660		2,340	F
Overheads	130,000		126,400		3,600	F
Total fixed costs		255,000		252,060	2,940	F
Operating Profit		133,850		129,200	4,650	A

Workings:

Note these use answers 1 to 4:

W1 Budget = £45 × 11,000 and actual is as given. (Note that the sales variance is Adverse when actual revenue is less than budget.)

W2 Budget = £8 × 11,000 and actual is as given.

W3 Budget = £1.65 × 11,000 and actual is £45,700 − £27,660 or £1.64 × 11,000.

W4 Fixed part of the power costs are as given. Fixed overheads are also given.

solution (continued)

6 The revised operating results statement is different from the original one because the costs have been separated into their fixed and variable parts. A flexed budget for 11,000 litres can then be prepared, to show what the results should have been for this level of output and sales. This is not the same as the original budget because the budgeted revenue and some of the budgeted costs depend on the number of litres. This is emphasised by the marginal costing layout. The budgeted profit is higher than the original one, because there are more litres of TCH to contribute to the fixed costs and profit.

The revised statement has the advantage that the comparison is more meaningful when we compare like with like, ie both budget and actual figures are applicable to 11,000 litres of TCH.

This report presents relevant, useful information in a clear format.

MANAGEMENT ACTION

As part of the process for monitoring and control, there must be a stage involving some management action as a result of the monitoring. If there is no action, then the monitoring could be seen as a waste of time!

Actions are either to:

■ change the current situation to improve the 'actual' figures in future

■ acknowledge that the budget needs to be altered for the future

■ or a combination of these

feedback

Feedback is information obtained and reported after comparing the budgeted and actual results for a control period.

Feedback is used to determine the necessary control action if results are significantly different from the budget. What is meant by 'significantly different'? This would have to be decided in advance. It could be defined in terms of absolute amounts or percentages of the budget, that is, 'control limits' would be set.

Only when the feedback shows variances going beyond the control limits would they be reported for action to be taken by the appropriate person. This is called 'exception reporting', which has the advantage that only the 'significant' differences are brought to the attention of management, thus saving time and avoiding the risk of important figures being lost among a mass of data.

favourable variances

It is often thought that only adverse variances are significant, but **favourable** variances which are **beyond the control limits** are equally important and may require action to be taken.

The word 'favourable' is perhaps misleading because it suggests something good. Favourable variances may indeed indicate some advantageous situation which it would be useful to investigate to see if it can be continued, for example efficiency improvements. However, large favourable variances may not be desirable in some cases, for example favourable materials variances may result from using the wrong material or using insufficient material to maintain the quality of a product.

control action

The control action to be taken on receipt of feedback from the monitoring of budgets depends on the situation.

If the reason for the variance can be identified it may be possible to correct it, in order to bring the actual results for the next control period back in line with (or at least closer to) the budget. The **feedback loop** is shown in the diagram on the next page. The feedback loop is an important part of the Budgetary Control process.

Sometimes it is not possible to bring the actual results back in line with the budget, because there has been a permanent change in costs which is not controllable by the managers of the organisation. This could be due to external factors, such as national wage agreements or permanent price changes (increases or reductions). The action to be taken then involves adjusting the budget to plan for realistic costs, so that the feedback from the next control period is more meaningful. This brings us to the idea of feeding forward information.

feedforward

Feedforward is information about the current performance of an organisation and its environment which is used in budgeting for the future.

The budgeting process starts by identifying the organisation's objectives and translating these into desired results for the budget period. For example, if the long-term objective is to achieve a particular level of market share, the short-term aim can be expressed in terms of budgeted sales volume.

In a feedforward system, the initial budget is considered by looking at the results it is expected to achieve in comparison with the desired results. This process uses information about the current performance of the organisation (feedback) and information about the economic environment, together with the budget.

If the results, according to the budget, are significantly different from the desired results, then the budget may be amended to eliminate the differences. However, the organisation's aims and objectives may have to be reconsidered and brought closer to what is achievable. In either case, a revised budget and/or revised objectives should help to ensure that future results do meet the organisation's objectives.

The feedforward loop is shown on the diagram on the next page. Notice that the feedforward loop takes information to the Budgetary Planning process for the *next* period.

This whole process provides a cycle of continuous improvement. When rolling budgets are used the cycle may even be repeated on a monthly basis, as information on actual performance is used to revise budgets.

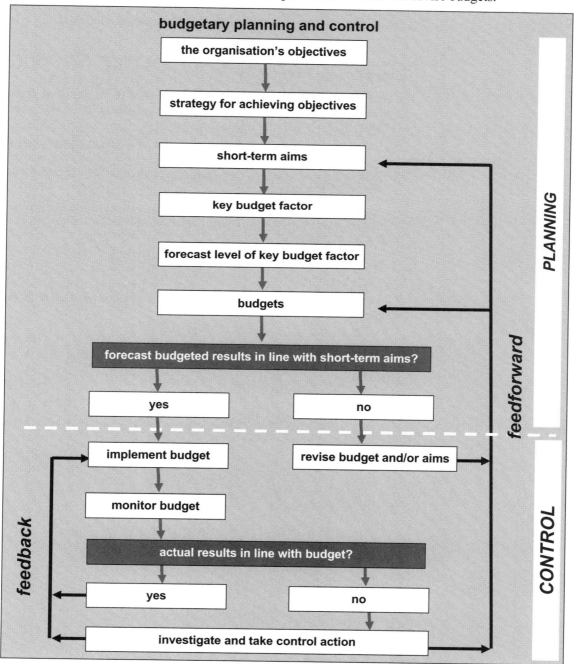

Chapter Summary

- Situations may develop where an organisation cannot obtain sufficient resources to carry out its intentions. Such constraints can range from limited market share, access to finance or shortages of materials, labour or production capacity. There are a variety of strategies that can be used to deal with these situations.

- Factors that can influence our forecasts include the product life cycle and competition and marketing.

- Sensitivity analysis, flexible budgeting and rolling budgets are some of the methods that can be used to help deal with uncertainty in the budgeting process.

- After the initial budget submission, budgets often have to be revised for a variety of reasons. Annual budgets may need to be divided into shorter periods, or revised altogether to take account of changing circumstances or alternative strategies.

- For budgeting, it is important to have information about how costs behave in relation to levels of activity. This is particularly relevant to the preparation of flexible budgets. A fixed budget is one which is prepared for a specific level of activity, whereas a flexed or flexible budget is one which allows for a change in the level of activity.

- After splitting all the costs into their fixed and variable parts, a flexible budget can be prepared by calculating the costs and income at the required level of activity.

Key Terms		
limiting factor	the factor that prevents the original planned production from being carried out. Examples of limiting factors are the available resources of direct materials or direct labour
product life cycle	The stages that a product goes through from development to ultimate decline
sensitivity analysis	the use of modelling to assess the impact on budgets of various different volumes, prices and costs
fixed budgets	a set of budgets based on a single set of assumptions about sales levels; these budgets are often used for planning purposes
flexible budgets	a series of sets of budgets based on different sales levels; these may be used for anticipating different outcomes at the planning stage, or for monitoring actual costs against an appropriate budget
rolling budget	Budgets that are continually extended into the future as time goes on
feedback	information obtained and reported after comparing the budgeted and actual results for a control period – feedback is used to determine necessary control action if results show significant differences from the budget
feedforward	information about the current performance of an organisation and its environment which is used in budgeting for the future – a feedforward system attempts to ensure that future results will meet the organisation's objectives
exception reporting	the practice of reporting only the information which is significant. In terms of variances it could involve only reporting variances outside the agreed tolerance level (control limits)
management by exception	the use of exception reporting to help concentrate management efforts on significant issues

Activities

2.1   A manufacturer has a temporary shortage of direct labour. Consideration is being given to either using overtime working of the remaining staff, or sub-contracting part of the manufacturing process to another organisation.

Suggest possible advantages and disadvantages of each approach.

2.2   A company has budgeted to make and sell 200,000 units in the coming year.

Each unit takes 0.5 labour hours to make and requires 2kg of raw material.

The quality control department can test 16,000 units each month.

A contract has been placed to purchase 300,000kg of raw material at an agreed price.

Further supplies can be obtained on the open market but the price is likely to be much higher.

The company employs 50 production workers. Each worker works 1,750 hours a year in normal time.

Complete the following analysis.

There is labour available to make . . . . units in normal time. Therefore, ... hours of overtime will be needed.

The raw material contract will provide enough material to make . . . . units. Therefore, . . . kg will have to be purchased on the open market.

Quality control can test . . . . units in the year. It will be necessary to make alternative arrangements for . . . . units.

2.3   Supervision is a stepped fixed cost for a particular organisation. Each supervisor can manage the production of up to 20,000 units in a year. The cost of supervision is budgeted at £360,000 when annual output is 170,000 units.

Calculate the budgeted cost of supervision for annual unit production of:

(a)   160,000 units

(b)   175,000 units

(c)   185,000 units

2.4 A company has already produced budgets based on its first scenario.

Assumptions in the first scenario:

Materials and labour are variable costs

Depreciation is a stepped fixed cost increasing every 12,000 units

Occupancy costs and energy costs behave as fixed costs

There is an allowance for an energy price rise of 3%

The alternative scenario is based on:

An increase in selling price of 2%

A decrease in sales volume of 4%

An energy price decrease of 1%

An increase in occupancy costs of 4%

Apart from the selling price per unit, do not enter any decimals. Round to the nearest whole number if necessary.

Complete the alternative scenario column in the operating budget table and calculate the increase or decrease in expected profit.

Operating Budget	First Scenario	Alternative Scenario
Selling price per unit	£17.00	
Sales volume	150,000	
	£	£
Sales revenue	2,550,000	
Costs:		
Materials	600,000	
Labour	637,500	
Depreciation	312,000	
Energy	123,600	
Occupancy costs	235,000	
Total costs	1,908,100	
Operating profit	641,900	
Increase / (decrease) in profit		

2.5 A monthly operating statement is shown below with some explanatory notes. You are required to flex the budget, calculate variances and show whether each variance is favourable or adverse.

Monthly Operating Statement

	Budget	Actual
Volume	31,500	34,000
	£	£
Revenue	2,520,000	2,856,000
Costs		
Material	441,000	510,000
Labour	567,000	616,250
Distribution	6,300	7,000
Energy	151,000	164,000
Equipment hire	32,000	35,000
Depreciation	182,000	180,000
Marketing	231,000	235,000
Administration	186,000	189,000
Total	1,796,300	1,936,250
Operating Profit	723,700	919,750

Monthly Operating Statement

Volume 34,000

	Flexed Budget	Actual	Variance Fav/(Adv)
	£	£	£
Revenue		2,856,000	
Costs			
Material		510,000	
Labour		616,250	
Distribution		7,000	
Energy		164,000	
Equipment hire		35,000	
Depreciation		180,000	
Marketing		235,000	
Administration		189,000	
Total		1,936,250	
Operating Profit		919,750	

Notes:

Material, labour and distribution costs are variable.

The budget for energy is semi-variable. The variable element is £4.00 per unit.

The budget for equipment hire is stepped, increasing at every 4,000 units of monthly production.

Depreciation, marketing and administration costs are fixed.

2.6 The following table shows the original budget and the actual costs for a period.

Original Budget		Flexed Budget	Actual	Variance Fav (Adv)
60,000	Sales volume (units)	57,300	57,300	
£		£	£	£
960,000	Sales revenue	916,800	945,250	28,450
	Costs:			
138,000	Materials	131,790	134,950	(3,160)
234,000	Labour	223,470	222,390	1,080
72,000	Distribution	68,760	70,400	(1,640)
85,000	Energy	83,650	82,350	1,300
88,000	Equipment hire	88,000	86,950	1,050
91,400	Depreciation	91,400	92,300	(900)
59,600	Marketing	59,600	65,300	(5,700)
66,500	Administration	66,500	65,250	1,250
834,500	Total costs	813,170	819,890	(6,720)
125,500	Operating profit (loss)	103,630	125,360	21,730

Notes:

Materials, labour and distribution costs are variable.

Energy costs are semi-variable. The variable element is £0.50 per unit.

Equipment hire is a stepped cost. Each step is based on up to 8,000 units.

Depreciation, marketing and administration costs behave as fixed costs.

Required:

Complete the table, showing the flexed budget and variances.

3 Standard costing – direct costs

this chapter covers...

In this chapter we will start to examine one of the major topics of this Unit – standard costing. This chapter concentrates on using standard costing in conjunction with direct costs – we will examine overheads in Chapter 4.

The chapter commences with an overview of the background to standard costing and how it can be useful. It then goes on to see how standard costs are built up and how standards can be set.

A large part of the chapter is devoted to the calculation of variances relating to direct costs. These are the differences between standard and actual costs that are related to specific components of the cost. It is vital that you understand fully how the variances are derived so that you can carry out a variety of calculations if required.

The main variances covered in this chapter are:

■ *total direct material variance*

■ *direct material price variance*

■ *direct material usage variance*

■ *total direct labour variance*

■ *direct labour rate variance*

■ *direct labour efficiency variance*

■ *direct labour idle time variance*

The chapter is rounded off with a summary of the main underlying causes of direct cost variances.

STANDARD COSTING SYSTEMS

Different organisations will have developed individual systems to control their revenue and costs which depend on their managers' needs. These control systems often simply use existing accounting information to monitor performance. Where this performance is measured against budgets that have been prepared in advance this is known as a budgetary control system. Many manufacturing organisations which produce standardised ranges of products may choose to go beyond just using budgetary control systems, and develop their own standard costing system. A standard costing system is a formal method for calculating the expected costs of products. The system can then be used for monitoring and controlling performance by comparing actual costs with standard costs.

It differs from general budget setting (which is normally concerned with the costs of sections of the organisation), because it focuses on the cost of what the organisation produces (the 'cost units'). It is often used in conjunction with budgets, so that they work together consistently.

Standard costing establishes in detail the standard cost of each component of a product, so that a total cost can be calculated for that product.

Standard costing is ideal for situations where components are identical and manufacturing operations are repetitive.

advantages of standard costing

The main advantages of operating with a standard costing system in place are that the standard costs can be used:

- to help with decision making, for example as a basis for pricing decisions

- to assist in **planning**, for example to plan the quantity and cost of the resources needed for future production

- as a mechanism for **monitoring and controlling** costs: the standard costs for the actual production can be compared with the actual costs incurred, and more detailed variances can be calculated than with standalone budgets, allowing more targeted control activities.

Advantages of using standard costing to assist with monitoring and control of costs include:

- Standard costs include details of both price and quantity of inputs. This will provide much better information than simple cost variances. The use of responsibility accounting in which managers are held accountable for performance of specific parts of the organisation fits in with this approach and enables the managers to control the costs armed with good information.

- Because the data will be input on an ongoing basis as part of the clerical process, an effective standard costing system will be able to provide cheap and accurate information in almost real time. This enables action to be taken quickly if necessary. Contrast this with the calculation of budgeting variances that are normally produced after the period end.

- Information can be provided in the form of operating statements that reconcile the actual costs with the standard costs of the output through the various standard cost variances that we will examine shortly. This will provide a very clear analysis of the differences between actual and expected costs – all the way to profit differences if required.

In addition there may be other benefits to setting up and using a standard costing system:

- The preliminary examination of current production techniques and resources may reveal hidden inefficiencies and unnecessary expenditure.

- The fact that costs are to be monitored may increase the cost consciousness of the workforce (and the management).

- The system lends itself to exception reporting. For example, a company may decide that only when costs are more than 2% away from the standard should the variances be reported.

There are therefore a variety of arguments for developing and using a standard costing system. The main uses that a particular organisation intends to make of the system will determine how it goes about setting standards.

SETTING STANDARDS

We will now examine in more detail how standards may be set, and how this can have an impact on our interpretation of variances.

types of standard

There are four main types of standard that may be set:

1 **Ideal Standard** makes no allowances for inefficiency or wastage of labour or materials, and therefore assumes perfect conditions.

2 **Target Standard** is set at the level that the organisation wishes to achieve under current operating conditions. It is designed to be a challenging but attainable standard.

3 **Normal Standard** is set at the level that is expected to be achieved under current operating conditions. It may be considered more realistic for planning purposes than a target standard, but it does not provide as much challenge. Both target standards and normal standards may be considered as attainable.

4 **Basic Standard** is an historical (and therefore effectively out-of-date) standard that allows comparisons to be carried out over long periods of time.

IDEAL STANDARDS AND THEIR IMPLICATIONS

the tendency for dual standards

When an organisation implements a standard costing system, the way that the standard is set will affect the interpretation of the variances. If an ideal standard is used, with no allowances for wastage or inefficiency, then the variances for material usage and labour efficiency will tend to be adverse. This in turn will mean that managers will come to expect adverse variances, and that action will only be taken when the variances are outside what they consider to be a reasonable tolerance level. If the use of an ideal is extended to setting material cost and labour rate standards by using the cheapest prices and the lowest labour rates, then the managers will become used to finding that all the variances recorded are adverse. They will tend to ignore the adverse variances that are reasonably small, and concentrate their attention on the larger variances. In this way they will have started to operate a system of informal **dual standards**, whereby the standard that is set is not the one that it is expected will be achieved.

This has important implications when standard costing is used to help a business with its planning. Where standards set at an ideal level are used for planning purposes then the result will always be inaccurate. For example, when using ideal standards to specify the amount of materials or labour time that will be required, the resources will tend to be underestimated. This could result in lower production being achieved than was planned, or additional resources being needed to complete the required production. This is because the ideal standards do not incorporate any allowance for the wastage or inefficient working that will always occur to some extent. Managers may get around this problem informally by adding an additional amount into their resource requirements. They are then effectively using their own version of a standard. The same situation will occur with material prices and labour costs, so that unless an amount is added to the standard when the anticipated production is costed, the result will almost invariably be under costing.

the dangers of informal standards

It could be argued that making such adjustments as described above is just a logical extension of the setting and use of standards. But problems could arise if different managers had different ideas of what tolerance levels were acceptable. Management by exception, where management time is concentrated on situations where actual results vary significantly from plans and exception reporting, can only work effectively if there is genuine agreement about the level at which results should be reported and acted upon instead of ignored. A situation could develop where not just informal dual standards were in operation, but a range of standards was in use by different managers for different purposes.

---

practical example

Consider the following situation:

The Production Scheduler may add an allowance of 10% to the standard usage of materials when planning the amount to be bought for a production run and requisitioning the goods. The Production Supervisor may consider that a usage variance of up to 8% from standard is reasonable. The Production Manager views a tolerance level of 5% as being within an acceptable range.

If the variance is reported at 6% then the Production Supervisor may feel that he/she has performed well, whereas the Production Manager is expecting answers from him/her as to why the usage is so high. Meanwhile the excess purchases of raw material are sitting in the stores!

This situation would not be a good demonstration of how to use standard costing and variance analysis as a form of responsibility accounting. In order to make different managers responsible for different variances they must be clear as to exactly what standards they are expected to achieve. This can be difficult enough with the impact of the interdependence (interrelationship) of variances, without the additional confusion created by having different informal versions of the standards in existence.

ideal standards and motivation

A further area that is influenced by the way that standards are set is that of **motivation**. As discussed earlier, variances resulting from a system where standards are set at an ideal level will generally be adverse. Whether linked to a reward system or not, targets will only tend to work well if they are considered fair and achievable. It cannot be easy to motivate staff at any level to perform well if all you can measure is by how far they have fallen short of the standard on each occasion. The natural human reaction may be to feel that since the standards cannot be achieved there is no point in even attempting to work efficiently. The standards may be felt to be irrelevant by the staff – hardly the atmosphere of cost-consciousness that most businesses would like to develop!

The use of ideal standards will also effectively prevent businesses from setting up a traditional labour bonus system based on paying a percentage of time saved compared with the standard time. It will be clear that if the standards are set at an ideal level, then there will never be any time saved, and therefore no bonus is likely to be payable.

ATTAINABLE STANDARDS AND THEIR IMPLICATIONS

Setting standards at an attainable level (ie target or normal standards) should avoid most of the problems identified with setting ideal standards, and most businesses using standard costing opt for some version of attainable standards. Where the standards are carefully set, the resultant variances should typically be a mixture of adverse and favourable, as the organisation will tend to sometimes exceed the standard and sometimes not quite achieve it.

Not everybody considers what is 'attainable' as being the same thing, and there will be no standard that will be considered fair by everyone. It could be thought of as a range rather than a single point. If standards are set following consultation within the organisation there will always need to be some compromise as different managers and employee groups argue from their own perspectives. There are common problems arising from encouraging participation in the setting of both standards and budgets. While standards which are set by making use of the expertise of a range of participants will tend to be more easily accepted and 'owned', the conflicting needs and desires of the personnel involved can make the standard setting process long and difficult.

BASIC STANDARDS AND THEIR IMPLICATIONS

Maintaining standards at a 'basic' level will tend to have several disadvantages. Since the standard was set some time ago its relevance may be questionable, and large variances will tend to become normal. This will mean that comparison is most useful if it is based on the **trend** in variances and this procedure will enable managers to identify with ease the way in which costs have changed over a long period.

A clear disadvantage of using basic standards is that the standards themselves may not be comparable with current conditions, and the individual variances may be virtually meaningless. The impact of inflation and changes in working practices will mean that the standard cannot be used as either a target or an estimate of expected cost levels. For these reasons basic standards are rarely used as the only standard by an organisation, but may be used alongside variance analysis which is based on more current data to obtain a longer term view of changes which have occurred.

INTERPRETING VARIANCES

The interpretation of variances, and the taking of appropriate action will be influenced by the way in which the standard was set. We will now examine some of the other issues that need to be considered in interpreting variances and taking appropriate action. The steps involved can be seen illustrated in the diagram on page 88.

is the variance significant? – control limits

The first issue to consider is whether the variance is significant enough for any action at all to be worthwhile. The idea of tolerance levels was mentioned earlier, and it is important to establish how large a variance should be in order to justify an investigation into its cause followed by appropriate action. Since any investigation or action will have a cost implication (at least in terms of management time), it would not make sense to do this unless there was an expected benefit that would justify it. **Control limits** within which a variance is acceptable may therefore be set by the organisation (see the diagram below). These limits will quickly identify the variances which need investigating.

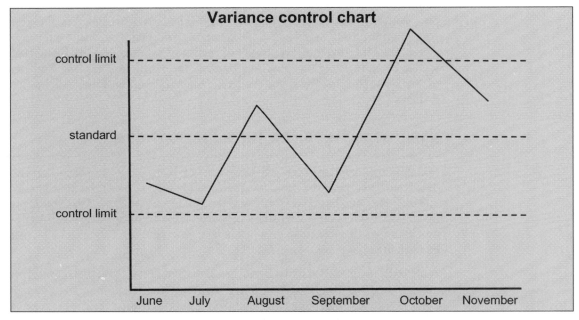

Variances are recorded chronologically from left to right on the chart, either individually or cumulatively. The control levels are agreed in advance. If a variance moves beyond these limits then investigation will be needed and appropriate action can be taken. In the chart shown here the control limit is exceeded in October.

The cumulative effects of variances must also be taken into account. The **trends** in variances that individually are small and may be considered immaterial may point to a situation that requires action. If, for example, efficiency levels amongst the direct labour force are very slowly decreasing then some action (perhaps retraining) will be needed to avoid excess costs occurring over a long period.

modifying standards

An important question to ask is:

'Is the variance due entirely to the way the standard was set, or is there a current situation that needs investigating?'

If a poorly set standard is creating a variance out of an otherwise acceptable situation, the most logical approach will be to amend the standard at the next opportunity. Resetting the standard will also be the most appropriate action if there is a long-term change to costs, otherwise 'false' variances will arise in future.

short-term changes

The cause of the variance will dictate whether or not action is required. If the variance is caused by a temporary change that will automatically right itself, then clearly no action is needed other than to check later to see that it has. Examples of this could be:

- a price variance caused by a change to another supplier because the normal supplier was temporarily out of stock
- a machine breakdown causing excess wastage of material

If, however, the variance is caused by some temporary change that may recur often enough to cause concern, then action should be taken either to prevent such changes or to alter the standard if the changes are uncontrollable.

An example of this could be individual batches of material that cause excessive wastage. A change of supplier may be a solution, but if all suppliers are having a similar quality problem due to some common situation then the issue may simply need to be acknowledged by monitoring the variances to ensure that they return to their expected level in future. If the material in this example were coffee beans that were affected by poor weather in the world's main coffee growing regions then it would clearly make some sense to monitor the situation over the coming seasons.

long-term changes

Sometimes variances are the result of situations that are potentially long term. Perhaps there has been a change in working practices or wage rates resulting in different costs, and if the managers consider the situation is acceptable then it would be logical to reset the standards. The same would apply to a general price change that is seen as reasonably permanent and uncontrollable. If, however, a price rise could be avoided by changing suppliers, then there would be no need to alter the standards, provided that managers considered that this was the best solution.

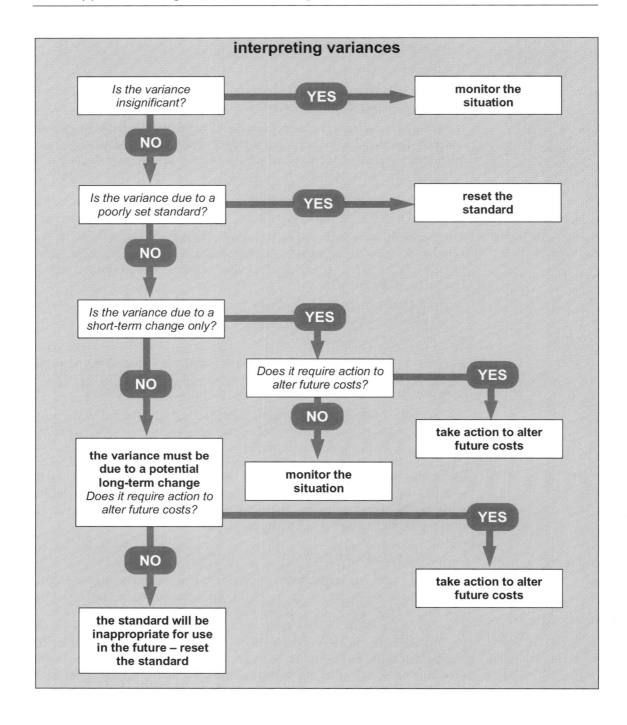

COMPOSITION OF STANDARD COSTS

elements of standard costs

The composition of standard costs – whether you are calculating the standard cost of a rubber washer, an aeroplane, or a hip replacement operation – can be analysed into common elements. These are the same elements of cost that you will be familiar with from your earlier studies:

Direct Costs	**Indirect Costs**
Direct Materials	Variable Overheads
Direct Labour	Fixed Overheads
Direct Expenses	

In this chapter we will concentrate on the standards and variances for direct materials and direct labour, and in the next chapter we will examine variable and fixed overheads. You do not need to study direct expense variances for this unit.

absorption costing and marginal costing models

The breakdown of costs into direct and indirect costs is based on the **absorption costing** model, where a suitable portion of all production costs (indirect as well as direct) is absorbed into the product's cost. A great many standard costing systems use this approach.

You should also be familiar with the **marginal costing** model. Here costs are analysed on the basis of the way they behave in relation to activity levels, and split into variable costs and fixed costs. This then gives the following alternative production cost breakdown:

ABSORPTION COSTING	**MARGINAL COSTING**
direct costs	**variable costs**
direct materials	variable direct materials
direct labour	variable direct labour
direct expenses	variable direct expenses
	variable overheads
indirect costs	**fixed costs**
variable overheads	fixed direct costs
fixed overheads	fixed overheads

Any category of direct or indirect costs could behave as either variable or fixed costs, but once the cost behaviour is established, standard marginal costing is very straightforward to use. The standard costs for direct materials and labour under absorption costing are developed in the same way as variable direct materials and labour under marginal costing.

standard direct material costs

You can assume when developing a standard direct material cost (and calculating variances) that this cost behaves as a variable cost. For example, it is reasonable to expect that the material cost for 2,000 items will be twice the cost of 1,000 of the same item. This assumption allows us to work out the standard cost for individual units, so that we can then multiply it by the quantity produced. It also explains why the absorption and marginal versions of these standards are effectively the same.

The standard direct material cost for a product comprises two elements:

■ the amount of the material, and

■ the cost of the material.

For example, a batch of 1,000 rubber washers may require 3 kilos of rubber, which costs £1.00 per kilo. If this data were accepted as the standard figures, then the standard direct material cost for each batch of washers would clearly be 3 kilos x £1.00 = £3.00.

The fact that the data needed to calculate a standard direct material cost is based on two elements determines:

■ where the information will come from, and

■ how the variances can be calculated.

standard direct labour costs

The composition of the standard direct labour cost for a cost unit is very similar to the material cost. It is also based on the implied assumption that this type of cost is variable, and so twice as many products will cost about twice as much. The standard direct labour cost for a product also consists of two elements:

■ the amount of labour time to be used, and

■ the labour cost per unit of time (the labour rate).

Using our example of a batch of rubber washers, if the standard direct labour time needed to manufacture them was two hours, and the standard labour cost was £12 per hour, then the standard direct labour cost would obviously be £24 per batch. Assuming there were no other direct costs, the total standard direct cost would be:

	£
Materials	3.00
Labour	24.00
	27.00 for one batch of washers

You will be familiar with this idea, and probably find the concept quite elementary, but it is a vital foundation for further understanding.

variable and fixed overheads

We will look in detail at how overheads can be dealt with in the next chapter. Variable overheads can be calculated by using an amount per unit. At this point we will show how fixed overheads could be incorporated into standard costs quite simply, by dividing the total fixed overheads by the expected number of units to be produced. The following Case Study shows how a 'standard cost card' could be completed using data for direct materials, direct labour and overheads to arrive at the total standard cost for one unit of output.

Case Study

STANDARD LIMITED: COMPLETING A STANDARD COST CARD

The following information has been calculated for the production of one unit of a product called 'Alpha'.

- Each unit will require 8 kilograms of direct material at a cost of £6.80 per kilogram.

- Each unit will require 3 hours of direct labour at a total cost of £33.

- Each unit will incur variable overheads of £5.

- Fixed overheads total £225,000, and the estimated output will be 7,500 units of Alpha.

required

Complete the standard cost card shown below. Note that the column headed 'cost per unit' refers to units of input (e.g. for materials it refers to cost per kilogram).

1 Unit of Alpha	Quantity	Cost per unit (£)	Total Cost (£)
Direct material	8 kg.	£6.80	£54.40
Direct labour	3 hrs	£11	£33
Variable overheads	1	£5	£5
Fixed overheads	1	£30	£30
Total			£122.40

solution

1 Unit of Alpha	Quantity	Cost per unit (£)	Total Cost (£)
Direct material	8	6.80	54.40
Direct labour	3	11.00	33.00
Variable overheads	1	5.00	5.00
Fixed overheads	1	30.00	30.00
Total			122.40

Note that:

- The hourly rate for direct labour is calculated by dividing the total labour cost by the number of hours.

- The fixed overhead per unit of Alpha is calculated by dividing the total overheads by the estimated output in units of Alpha.

THE CALCULATION OF DIRECT COST VARIANCES

One of the most important uses of standard costing is the calculation and interpretation of the variances between the standard costs of the actual production and the actual costs incurred.

There are four direct cost sub-variances that we need to be able to calculate; two relating to materials and two to labour, as well as a total material variance and a total labour variance.

DIRECT MATERIAL VARIANCES

Direct material variances consist of a total direct material variance that can be divided into two sub-variances.

total direct material variance

The total direct material variance =

the standard cost of materials for the actual production level	*minus*	the actual cost of materials for the actual production level

So it is simply measuring the difference between what the materials were expected to cost for the actual production level and what the materials did cost. Notice that we are using the **actual production level** in both cases; this is quite logical and also means that we are making a valid comparison by comparing 'like with like'.

The total **direct material variance** is exactly the same variance that would be calculated from comparing the **flexed budget** with the **actual direct material costs**. The standard costs would have been used to calculate the flexed budget, and we are using the actual production level for both the standard and the actual costs.

What standard costing allows us to do is to analyse this variance as follows to provide additional information.

The two sub-variances that relate to the cost of materials are:

■ the direct material **price** variance

■ the direct material **usage** variance

The **price** variance measures how much of the difference between the expected and actual cost of materials is due to paying a **price** for materials that is different to the standard.

The direct material **usage** variance measures how much of the difference between the expected and actual cost of materials is due to **using a different quantity** of materials.

Together these two variances will account for the whole difference between the expected and actual cost of the materials.

DIRECT MATERIAL PRICE VARIANCE

The direct material price variance =

the standard cost of the actual quantity of material used	*minus*	the actual cost of the actual quantity of material used

We are making a comparison between two values – the standard cost of the actual materials and the actual cost. Notice that both figures relate to the **actual materials used**, so that we are comparing two costs that both relate to the same actual quantity.

If the actual cost is less than the standard then the variance will be favourable; if it is more, the variance will be adverse.

If you carry out the calculation as outlined above, then a positive answer will be favourable and a negative one adverse.

direct material usage variance

The direct material usage variance =

| the standard quantity of material for actual production at standard price | *minus* | the actual quantity of material used at standard price |

With this usage variance we are also making a comparison between two values. This time the comparison is based on two quantities – the standard quantity for the actual production and the actual quantity used. These quantities are turned into values by costing them both at **standard price**.

remembering how to calculate direct variances

The key to calculating the variances accurately is remembering the basis of the formulas. One method that may help is the mnemonic 'PAUS', based on:

Price variances are based on

Actual quantities, but

Usage variances are based on

Standard prices.

One explanation why the variances are calculated in this way is that purchases are sometimes converted to standard price (and a price variance calculated) when the materials are bought. This price variance would relate to the actual materials bought. The materials in inventory (stock) would then be valued at standard price, and the usage variance would be calculated based on the amounts issued to production at standard price.

The two material sub-variances that we have looked at will account for the whole of any difference between the standard cost of the material used for the actual production level and the actual cost – the total direct material variance that was explained earlier. This provides a useful check that our calculations appear to be correct.

We will now demonstrate in a Case Study how the variances that we have looked at so far can be calculated in practice.

Case Study

THE PINE DOOR COMPANY: DIRECT MATERIAL VARIANCES

The Pine Door Company makes cottage doors from reclaimed pine. The company uses standard costing to plan and control its costs. The standard direct material cost for a door is as follows:

2.5 square metres of pine at £10.00 per square metre = £25 per door.

During the month of August, the company made 35 doors. The actual costs incurred were:

86 square metres of pine, costing £950 in total.

required

- Calculate the standard material cost of the August production of 35 doors.
- Calculate:
  - the total direct material variance
  - the direct material price variance
  - the direct material usage variance
- Check that, between them, the two sub-variances account for the total direct material variance.
- Explain what each of the variances tells us.

solution

The standard material cost of the 35 doors made in August is:

£25 per door x 35 doors = £875.

Notice that this amount is less than the actual cost of material.

The total direct material variance =

the standard cost of materials for the actual production level	*minus*	the actual cost of materials for the actual production level

£875 (calculated above) – £950 (from the data provided)

= £75 Adverse

This represents the difference between the standard cost of materials for 35 doors and the actual cost. It is adverse because the actual cost was greater (which is 'bad news').

The two sub-variances which will now be calculated should show how much is due to **prices** and how much is due to the **quantity** used.

The direct material price variance =

the standard cost of the actual quantity of materials used	*minus*	the actual cost of the actual quantity of materials used

86 square metres of pine were actually used, so the standard and the actual costs of this quantity of material can be compared as follows:

(86 sq metres x £10 per sq metre) – £950

£860 – £950 = £90 Adverse

The variance is adverse because the actual cost was more than the expected (standard) cost. This is confirmed by a negative numerical answer.

The direct material usage variance =

the standard quantity of materials for actual production at standard price	*minus*	the actual quantity of materials used at standard price

It was expected that 2.5 square metres of pine would be used for each of the 35 doors that were made. This gives a standard quantity of 87.5 sq metres for production. This standard quantity of 87.5 sq metres and the actual quantity of 86 square metres at the standard price of £10 per square metre are compared to calculate the variance.

(87.5 sq metres x £10) – (86 sq metres x £10)

£875 – £860 = £15 Favourable

Here the variance is favourable because less material was used than the standard quantity. This is confirmed by the fact that the numerical answer works out to a positive figure.

The calculation above could also be shown as:

£10 x (87.5 sq metres – 86 sq metres)

checking the overall position

Material price variance	£90 Adverse
Material usage variance	£15 Favourable
Total material cost variance	£75 Adverse

This is a useful check – although it is not a guarantee that the calculations are correct.

We can also use the sub variances to reconcile the standard cost of the actual production (the flexed budget) with the actual cost, as follows:

Standard cost of direct materials for actual production		£875
Add adverse material price variance	£90	
Less favourable material usage variance	£15	
		£75
Actual cost of direct materials		£950

what the variances tell us

The material price variance shows that a higher price than standard was paid for the pine that was used, and this cost £90 more than expected. Against that cost can be set the fact that slightly less pine was used than allowed for, and this saved £15. Overall, the material for the 35 doors that we made cost £75 more than planned.

DIRECT LABOUR VARIANCES

The approach for calculating direct labour variances is very similar to direct material variances.

Direct labour variances consist of a total direct labour variance that can be divided into sub-variances.

total direct labour variance

The total direct labour variance =

the standard cost of labour for the actual production level	*minus*	the actual cost of labour for the actual production level

It is measuring the difference between what labour was expected to cost for the actual production level and what labour actually cost. Notice that again we are using the **actual production level** in both cases.

The **total direct labour variance** is the same variance that would be calculated by comparing the direct labour costs in the **flexed budget** (which is developed from standard costs) with the **actual costs**. This works because we are using the actual production level for our comparisons.

The two most important sub-variances that relate to the cost of labour are:

■ the **direct labour rate variance**

■ the **direct labour efficiency variance**

The direct labour rate variance measures the labour cost difference due to the rate paid, and the direct labour efficiency variance measures the cost difference due to the amount of labour time used. The concept of labour 'rate' is similar to material 'price', and labour 'efficiency' is similar to material 'usage', as explained below. This makes remembering the calculation method and interpreting the variances much easier.

direct labour rate variance

The direct labour rate variance =

the standard cost of the actual labour hours used	*minus*	the actual cost of the actual labour hours used

We are again making a comparison between two values – the standard cost of the actual labour hours and the actual cost. Just like the material price variance, the labour rate variance is comparing two figures that both relate to an actual quantity – here the actual quantity is the **actual number of labour hours**.

direct labour efficiency variance

The direct labour efficiency variance =

standard labour hours for actual production at standard rate	*minus*	actual labour hours used at standard rate

This also has a strong resemblance to the material usage variance; we are simply considering the quantity of labour hours instead of the quantity of material.

Just like the material usage variance, we are using a standard figure to value these two quantities – this time it is the standard labour rate that is used. Although this variance is all about comparison of two amounts of time, we must remember to convert the answer into an amount of money by valuing the hours at the standard rate.

Provided we can remember the similarity of the labour variances to the material ones, there is probably no need to use any other memory aid. The direct labour variances must add up to the total difference in labour cost between standard and actual – the total direct labour variance.

| Case Study | # THE PINE DOOR COMPANY: DIRECT LABOUR VARIANCES |

The Pine Door Company (see earlier Case Study) makes cottage doors from reclaimed pine. The company uses standard costing to plan and control its costs. The standard direct labour cost for a door is as follows:

> 6 hours direct labour at £14.00 per hour = £84 per door.

During the month of August, the company made 35 doors. The actual costs incurred were:

> 200 hours direct labour costing £2,860 in total.

required

- Calculate the standard labour cost for the August production of 35 doors.

- Calculate
  - the total direct labour variance
  - the direct labour rate variance
  - the direct labour efficiency variance

- Check that, between them, the two sub-variances account for the total direct labour variance.

- Explain what each of the variances tells us.

solution

The standard labour cost of the 35 doors made in August is:

> £84 per door x 35 doors = £2,940

Notice that this amount is more than the actual cost of labour given as £2,860.

total direct labour variance =

the standard cost of labour for the actual production level	minus	the actual cost of labour for the actual production level

> £2,940 (calculated above) – £2,860 (from the data provided)
>
> = £80 Favourable

The two sub-variances which will now be calculated should show how much is due to rate and how much is due to the **amount of time** used.

direct labour rate variance =

| the standard cost of the actual labour hours used | *minus* | the actual cost of the actual labour hours used |

200 direct labour hours were actually used in August, so this is the basis of our comparison of costs for this variance.

(200 direct labour hours x £14) – £2,860 =

£2,800 – £2,860 = £60 Adverse

The numerical answer is negative because the actual cost of the direct labour hours used is greater than the standard cost of the same number of hours. This means that the hourly rate paid is greater than the standard hourly rate. This variance is therefore adverse.

direct labour efficiency variance =

| standard labour hours for actual production at standard rate | *minus* | the actual labour hours used at standard rate |

The standard labour time to make each of the 35 doors is 6 hours. This gives a standard labour time of 210 hours for production.

We will value both the standard hours and the actual 200 hours used at the standard rate of £14 per hour to calculate the variance.

(210 hours x £14) – (200 hours x £14)

£2,940 – £2,800 = £140 Favourable

Here the variance is favourable because we actually spent less time making the doors than the standard time – the labour force have been efficient. This is confirmed by the fact that the numerical answer works out to a positive figure.

The calculation above could also be shown as:
£14 x (210 hours – 200 hours)

checking the overall position

Labour rate variance	£60 Adverse
Labour efficiency variance	£140 Favourable
Total labour variance	£80 Favourable

As before, we can also use the sub variances to reconcile the standard cost of the actual production (the flexed budget) with the actual cost, as follows:

Standard cost of direct labour for actual production		£2,940
Add adverse labour rate variance	£60	
Less favourable labour efficiency variance	£140	
		£80
Actual cost of direct labour		£2,860

what each variance tells us

The labour rate variance shows that (on average) a little more was spent than the standard labour rate, and this cost an extra £60. However £140 was saved because the work was carried out more quickly than the standard time. Overall the labour cost for the 35 doors that were made was £80 less than planned.

idle time variance

We have seen that the total direct labour variance can be divided into two sub-variances – the direct labour rate variance and the direct labour efficiency variance. The direct labour efficiency variance values (at standard rate) the difference in time taken for the production between standard and actual.

In some circumstances this measurement of 'efficiency' may be considered misleading if it includes time where the labour force was 'idle' – being paid but not actually working on production. This could arise for a variety of reasons, for example a machine breakdown, and may not be within the control of the employees.

If this is the situation, and the amount of idle time is known, the original direct labour efficiency variance can be divided into two further sub-variances. These are the variance related to the idle time, and the remainder of the direct labour efficiency variance, which can now be considered as the efficiency variance.

The direct labour variance relating to idle time is (not surprisingly) known as the **direct labour idle time variance**.

The direct labour idle time variance =

actual **productive** labour hours used at standard rate	minus	**total** actual labour hours used at standard rate

The difference between 'productive' labour hours and total labour hours is equal to idle time, so a simpler way of expressing the idle time variance is:

actual idle time
at standard rate

This variance will always be adverse (or zero), since the total actual hours will never be less than the productive hours. If the productive hours are the same as the total actual hours then there is no idle time and the idle time variance will be zero.

Where there is an idle time variance calculated, the efficiency variance normally excludes the part caused by the idle time. This efficiency variance is based on comparing the standard time for the output with the actual productive time, as follows:

Where there is an idle time variance, the efficiency variance =

standard labour hours for actual production at standard rate	minus	actual **productive** labour hours used at standard rate

This efficiency variance, plus the idle time variance, will equal what the efficiency variance would have been calculated at if there had been no idle time.

We can use the earlier Case Study to demonstrate how this variance can be calculated.

Case Study

THE PINE DOOR COMPANY: IDLE TIME VARIANCE

The Pine Door Company (see earlier Case Studies) makes cottage doors from reclaimed pine. The company uses standard costing to plan and control its costs. The standard labour cost for a door is as follows:

6 hours direct labour at £14.00 per hour = £84 per door.

During the month of August the company made 35 doors. The actual labour costs incurred were:

200 hours direct labour costing £2,860 in total.

The original direct labour efficiency variance has already been calculated as £140 favourable.

Information just obtained reveals that in August there were 8 labour hours when the labour force were idle waiting for more material, leaving 192 productive hours.

required

- Calculate the direct labour idle time variance.

- Calculate the revised direct labour efficiency variance.

solution

- Calculation of variances

direct labour idle time variance =

actual **productive** labour hours used at standard rate	minus	**total** actual labour hours used at standard rate

(192 hours x £14.00) – (200 hours x £14.00) =

£2,688 – £2,800 = £112 Adverse

This is the same as:

actual idle time
at standard rate

8 hours x £14.00 = £112 Adverse

revised direct labour efficiency variance =

standard labour hours for actual production at standard rate	minus	actual **productive** labour hours used at standard rate

(35 doors x 6 hours x £14.00) – (192 hours x £14.00)

£2,940 – £2,688 = £252 favourable.

Note that the idle time variance of £112 adverse together with the revised efficiency variance of £252 favourable equals the £140 favourable efficiency variance that was originally calculated before the idle time was identified.

THE MAIN CAUSES OF DIRECT VARIANCES

It is important that we can not only calculate variances accurately, but also understand what has caused the individual variances.

This interpretation of variances is carried out by:

- identifying the possible range of causes for each variance, and then
- investigating the situation to establish the cause in the particular circumstances.

We will now look at the possible causes of the variances that we have studied so far.

If you are familiar with the sources of data for creating variances, and what each variance means, it should not be necessary to learn lists of possible causes of variances. Instead it should be possible to logically think your way through each situation to see its impact on variances. You may be given a scenario and asked to suggest the possible causes of variances. It is far better to use the facts given to you about the situation to develop a reasoned commentary, than to remember an 'all purpose' list of causes and simply regurgitate it.

Some situations may give rise to more than one variance. For example, purchasing cheaper material of lower quality could cause a favourable price variance but an adverse usage variance if there was higher wastage. This is often referred to as the interdependence of variances. It can result in unfair praise or blame if different managers are responsible for each variance.

Unfair comparisons may also arise from the use of an unrealistic or out of date standard.

The table below gives examples of possible causes of direct variances. Read it carefully, and ensure that you can appreciate the logic of including each item, and its effect.

There may be situations where you can envisage the cause creating further variances, since the table is not intended to be exhaustive.

'A' or 'F' refers to whether adverse or favourable variances may result.

DIRECT VARIANCE: Possible Cause	Material Price	Material Usage	Labour Rate	Labour Efficiency
Poorly set standard	A or F	A or F	A or F	A or F
Different material supplier	A or F			
Different material quality	A or F	A or F		A or F
Different currency exchange rate	A or F			
Poor training		A		A
Higher grade staff		F	A	F
Unexpected pay increase			A	
High general inflation	A		A	
Improved production machinery		F		F
Unexpected bulk discounts	F			
Low bonus payments			F	A
Machine breakdowns		A		A

INTERPRETING SPECIFIC DIRECT VARIANCES

At this stage it is worth looking back at the direct variances that we have examined, and making sure that we can link possible causes with each variance. We will now discuss each variance in turn. The total variances are not examined here, since the causes of these will be based on the causes of the appropriate sub-variances.

direct material price variance

The key to interpreting any variance is to remember what it is measuring. Here (as the variance title clearly tells us), the variance is concerned with the price of materials. We can therefore ignore any issues that are not related to price. Some of the reasons for price variances include:

- world-wide price changes (due to specific supply / demand issues or general inflation or deflation)

- change of supplier

- change of quality of material (better quality usually, but not always, costing more)

- changes in quantity purchased (obtaining better or worse quantity discounts)

Some of these reasons could also affect other variances. As noted earlier, these situations are sometimes referred to as the 'interdependence of variances'. The example often quoted is higher priced, better quality material creating an adverse material price variance, but also generating less wastage and therefore contributing to favourable material usage variances. Possibly even favourable labour efficiency variances could also arise if the material is easier to use.

direct material usage variance

Usage of material is concerned with how much material is used compared with the standard quantity that would be expected. Perhaps the most obvious example is the amount of wastage being higher or lower than expected. This could also be linked to material quality, or to skill level of labour or to poor machine maintenance.

However, the general assumption that a favourable variance is always 'good news' and that an adverse variance is always bad does not always apply for usage variances.

Sometimes any usage variance could be an indicator of a problem. For example, if making concrete products, a favourable usage variance for cement may mean that the mix is too weak and the final products will not be strong enough.

Another situation where a favourable variance could be an indicator of a problem is if the final product is undersize or underweight. This could occur in both manual operations and automated ones. For example, tins of paint may be only 95% filled by a machine that is poorly calibrated. The system would record a favourable usage variance, but legal action could result from the quantity of paint not being as described on the tin.

Sometimes usage variances are due to a deliberate decision made in response to the available material. For example, additional sugar may need to be added to a fruit drink mixture if the fruit used was less sweet than usual.

As with other variances, it is always important to examine the circumstances and any additional information provided before making a judgement.

direct labour rate variance

The labour rate variance is concerned with how much the rate of pay costs the organisation. Here the background splits into two main situations:

- using the planned labour force, but paying a different rate, and

- using a different labour force than planned, often causing a different rate to be paid.

When using the planned labour force, the cost of labour could be different to standard for any of the following reasons:

- a pay rate change (usually a rise) that was either not built into the standard, or is more or less than the expected pay rate change

- bonuses paid at more or less than the expected amount; if bonuses are included in the standard rate the amount will be based on an expected average level

- more or less overtime being paid than expected; this depends on whether the overtime premium is charged to direct costs or overheads – if it is charged to overheads it would not be reflected here

- a change in costs of employment – for example national costs like employers' national insurance contributions, which are normally incorporated in labour costs

Sometimes the labour rate variance will be linked to a change in the labour force being used, for example:

- a higher or lower grade of labour being used than planned, or trainees being used instead of fully trained operatives; this could also link to other variances including labour efficiency and material usage

- contractors or agency staff being used instead of the normal employees; these are often more flexible in terms of contracts, but usually cost a higher rate (including a charge to the agency where appropriate)

direct labour efficiency variance

This variance focuses on the time spent by the labour force in producing the output. More or less time spent could relate to how long individuals spend on the work, or to more or less people being used.

The amount of idle time that may have occurred will impact on the efficiency variance. This could be because no idle time is incorporated into the standard time (but some actually occurs), or because the actual idle time is more or less than expected. An idle time variance could be used to calculate the impact of idle time.

Although efficiency often appears to be entirely in the control of the labour force and their managers, there are also outside influences that can result in variances. The range of causes for labour efficiency variances includes:

- the level of training of staff

- the learning effect – individuals gradually become more efficient as they become more familiar with the work

- the quality of materials

- the availability of materials or components (for example awaiting a delivery)

- the efficiency of machinery including breakdowns (ranging from hand held tools to production lines)

- the working conditions (for example excessive heat or cold)

looking beyond the obvious

We saw that some causes can link to more than one variance – for example a cheap, poor quality material causing a favourable price variance but an adverse usage variance. However, quality is not always in line with the price. A cheap material may be of better quality than more expensive material, or the opposite may be true. You should also consider carefully comments made by managers who may be trying to avoid the blame for poor performance. A production manager could try to justify poor usage by blaming the quality of cheap materials (implying that the Purchasing Manager is at fault) whereas the problem may really be something else. You should therefore consider all possibilities.

Case Study

DRINK-COCOA LIMITED
CALCULATING AND INTERPRETING VARIANCES

Drink-Cocoa Limited manufactures and distributes cocoa. One of its main products is Chocco-Smooth, a cocoa blended from Foro and Trino beans. Chocco-Smooth is sold in 1 kilogram packs. Budgeted production is 10,000 one kilogram packs.

You work as an Accounting Technician reporting to the Finance Director.

The company operates an integrated standard cost system in which:
- purchases of materials are recorded at standard cost
- direct material costs are variable
- production overheads are fixed and absorbed on a unit basis
- production costs include labour costs for maintenance and setting up of the machines

The actual results for November are as follows:

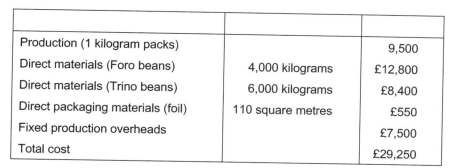

Production (1 kilogram packs)		9,500
Direct materials (Foro beans)	4,000 kilograms	£12,800
Direct materials (Trino beans)	6,000 kilograms	£8,400
Direct packaging materials (foil)	110 square metres	£550
Fixed production overheads		£7,500
Total cost		£29,250

The standard cost card for production of 1 kilogram of Chocco-Smooth cocoa is:

Product: 1 kilogram of Chocco- Smooth	Quantity	Unit price	Total cost
			£
Direct materials (Foro beans)	500 grams	£3 per kilogram	1.50
Direct materials (Trino beans)	500 grams	£1.50 per kilogram	0.75
Direct packaging materials (foil)	0.01 square metres	£10 per square metre	0.10
Fixed production overheads			0.65
Standard cost			3.00

required – part one

(a) Calculate the following variances for November:

    (1) direct material (Foro) price variance

    (2) direct material (Foro) usage variance

    (3) direct material (Trino) price variance

    (4) direct material (Trino) usage variance

    (5) direct packaging material (foil) price variance

    (6) direct packaging material (foil) usage variance

(b) Prepare an operating statement reconciling the actual material cost of producing 9,500 one kilogram packs of Chocco-Smooth with the standard material cost of producing 9,500 one kilogram packs.

solution – part one

(a)

    (1) Direct material (Foro) price variance

        Actual cost of £12,800 compared with standard cost of actual quantity purchased (4,000 x £3) = £800 adverse

    (2) Direct material (Foro) usage variance

        Standard cost per kg of Foro = £3

Total number of kgs used = 4,000

Total number of kgs which should have been used = 9,500 x 0.5 = 4,750 therefore variance = (4,750 – 4,000) x £3 = £2,250 favourable

(3)   Direct material (Trino) price variance

Actual cost of £8,400 compared with standard cost of actual quantity purchased (6,000 x £1.50) = £600 favourable

(4)   Direct material (Trino) usage variance

Standard cost per kg of Trino = £1.50

Total number of kgs used = 6,000

Total number of kgs which should have been used = 9,500 x 0.5 = 4,750 therefore variance = (4,750 – 6,000) x £1.50 = £1,875 adverse

(5)   Direct packaging material (foil) price variance

Actual cost of £550 compared with standard cost of actual quantity purchased (110 x £10) = £550 favourable

(6)   Direct packaging material (foil) usage variance

Standard cost per metre of foil = £10

Total number of square metres used = 110

Total number of square metres which should have been used = 9,500 x 0.01 = 95

therefore variance = (95 – 110) x £10 = £150 adverse

(b)

Actual total direct material cost			**£21,750**
Variances	Favourable	Adverse	
Direct materials (Foro) price		£800	
Direct materials (Foro) usage	£2,250		
Direct materials (Trino) price	£600		
Direct materials (Trino) usage		£1,875	
Direct materials (foil) price	£550		
Direct materials (foil) usage		£150	
Total variance	£3,400	£2,825	£575
Standard total direct material cost of actual production (working 1)			£22,325

Working 1

(£1.50 + £0.75 + £0.10) x 9,500 = £22,325

Additional data

You have been given the following information about Foro and Trino cocoa beans:

- Foro beans are a higher quality and provide a richer flavour whereas Trino beans are considered lower quality and tend to be bitter in taste. The cost of Foro beans is set by the market and recently the price has risen sharply due to a poor harvest. The purchaser has to take the price quoted on the market. The quality of the beans was as expected.

- An automated mixing machine broke down which led to more Trino beans being added to the mix. The breakdown has been blamed on the loss of maintenance personnel due to a lower than market pay rise.

- The price of Trino beans is set by the market and the price has recently fallen due to a good harvest. The purchaser has to take the price quoted on the market. The quality of the beans was as expected.

- In order to maintain the quality of the cocoa blend, the percentage of Foro beans should not fall below 45% of the weight of the blend.

r e q u i r e d – p a r t t w o

Using this information, prepare a report to the Production Director stating:

- Possible reasons for the Foro and Trino variances you calculated in part one.
- Whether the company could have taken any action and if so what action could have been taken.
- How the direct materials usage variances for Foro beans and Trino beans are linked.

solution – part two

To:	Production Director	From:	AAT student
Subject:	Reason for variances		

Direct material (Foro) price variance

The price variance for Foro beans is £800 adverse.

This is due to the market price of beans increasing due to the poor harvest, meaning there is lower supply therefore the price increases.

The company could not have taken any action as the market sets the price.

Direct material (Foro) usage variance

The usage variance for Foro beans is £2,250 favourable.

This has been caused by the mixing process making an error and adding a greater amount of Trino beans to the mix. The result is that the company has saved money on the purchase of the beans, but the mix is outside of the range recommended to produce an acceptable quality blend. Therefore the customers may be unhappy. The company could have secured the maintenance personnel by paying a market rate, or outsourcing the maintenance.

Direct material (Trino) price variance

The price variance for Trino beans is £600 favourable.

This is due to the market price of beans decreasing due to a good harvest meaning there is a larger supply, therefore the price reduces. The company could not have taken any action as the market sets the price.

Direct material (Trino) usage variance

The usage variance is £1,875 adverse because the company used more than expected. This was because of the automated mixing machine breaking down. The company could have ensured that maintenance was undertaken to prevent the machine breaking down. The Foro usage variance (2,250 favourable) is favourable which offsets the adverse Trino usage variance (1,875 adverse). In financial terms the overall position is a gain of £375. However the quality of the mix may be a problem as the percentage of Foro beans is below 45%. The company may therefore lose customers or have returned goods.

Chapter Summary

- Standard costing was developed in the manufacturing industry as a method of predicting the cost of products. When comparing actual costs with the expected (standard) costs, it enables variances to be calculated that help explain differences in the costs. There are various other benefits from setting up and using a standard costing system.

- Standards can be set at an Ideal, Attainable, or Basic level. There are also variations in attainable standards, called 'normal' standards and 'target' standards.

- The level at which a standard is set has implications for interpretation of variances, and the behaviour of employees.

- Actions to be taken resulting from variances will depend on materiality, whether the causes are short or long term, and how controllable they are.

- Actions to be taken can be divided into those that will change future costs or those that will require adjustment of the future standard.

- Standard costs can be used based on a traditional absorption costing system, or on a marginal costing system. The main difference arises in the treatment of fixed overhead variances: direct cost variances are calculated in the same way under both types of costing. The direct cost variances for materials and labour can be divided into variances based on the cost per unit of the resource (Price or Rate variances) and the quantity of resource used (Usage and Efficiency variances).

- Direct cost variances are calculated according to rules that help ensure uniformity.

- There can be many causes of variances, some influencing just one variance, while others affect several. The accurate calculation of a variance does not provide information on the cause itself, but the causes can often be deduced by examining the factors surrounding the situation.

Key Terms	**standard costing**	a formal method for predetermining the cost of cost units or products
	variance analysis	the comparison of actual costs with standard costs and the calculation of variances which account for differences in the costs
	marginal costing	a technique that values cost units based on variable costs only. Fixed costs are considered to relate only to the reporting period of time
	absorption costing	a technique that values cost units based on a suitable part of all the costs of production, whether fixed or variable in behaviour
	ideal standard	a standard set at a level that makes no allowance for losses, and which can only be attainable under the most favourable conditions
	attainable standard	a target or normal standard set at a level that assumes efficient levels of operation, but includes allowances for normal loss, waste, and machine downtime
	basic standard	a standard set some time ago which can be used to identify trends or develop other standards
	tolerance level	the range around the standard within which performance is considered acceptable and action does not need to be taken
	interdependence of variances	the fact that a single cause may create two or more separate variances
	total direct material variance	the difference between the standard material cost for the actual production and the actual material cost
	direct material price variance	the part of the total direct material variance due to differing material prices. It is based on the difference between standard and actual prices for the actual quantity of material used (or bought)

direct material usage variance the part of the total direct material variance due to differing quantities of material used. It is based on the difference between the standard quantity of material for the actual production, and the actual quantity of material used, valued at standard price

total direct labour variance the difference between the standard labour cost for the actual production and the actual labour cost

direct labour rate variance the part of the total direct labour variance due to differing labour rates. It is based on the difference between the actual labour hours at standard rate and the actual labour cost

direct labour efficiency variance the part of the total direct labour variance due to differing time being spent. It is based on the difference between the standard labour time for the actual production, and the actual labour time used, valued at standard rate

Activities

3.1 The following statements were compiled by a trainee accountant. State whether each of these statements is true or false.

		True	False
(a)	All variances should always be thoroughly investigated.		✓
(b)	Using standards set at a basic level may help to identify long-term trends in costs.	✓	
(c)	In order to motivate staff, standards should generally be challenging yet achievable.	✓	
(d)	One advantage of setting up a standard costing system is that an atmosphere of cost-consciousness is generated.	✓	
(e)	Responsibility accounting means that the accountant is responsible for calculating all the necessary variances.		✓
(f)	If a variance has been caused by a short-term change that will naturally right itself then there is probably no need to adjust the standards.	✓	
(g)	Interpretation problems arising through the interdependence of variances would not exist if variances were calculated accurately.		✓

3.2 A company manufactures a single product X, with the following direct inputs:

- 0.75kg direct materials which cost £10 per kg
- 12 minutes of direct labour, paid at a rate of £13 per hour

Fixed overheads totalling £140,000 are recovered on a unit basis. The estimated output is 20,000 units.

Required:

✻ 140000/20000

(a) Complete the standard cost card shown below:

One Unit of X	Quantity	Cost per unit of input £	Total cost £
Direct Materials	0.75 kg	£10.	£7.50
Direct Labour	0.2 hrs.	£13.	£2.60
Fixed Overheads	1	✻ £7	£7
Total			£17.10

(b) Calculate the total standard cost of 20,000 units.

£17.10 × 20000 = £342000

3.3 Grimley Limited has the following budgeted and actual direct cost and production data for the month of August.

	Budget	Budget	Actual	Actual
Production Units		20,000		19,000
		£		£
Direct Materials	40,000 kg	300,000	37,000 kg	278,000
Direct Labour	10,000 hrs	120,000	9,800 hrs	117,200
Total Costs		420,000		395,200

Required:

- Calculate the data for a standard cost card based on one unit.
- Calculate the relevant direct cost variances.

3.4 The glazing department of the Complete Window Company uses standard costs to monitor and control its output. The standard data for glazing one window are:

- 2 square metres glass at £25 per square metre
- 0.5 hours labour at £16.00 per hour

During one week in May, the department glazed 300 windows, with actual costs as follows:

- 610 square metres of glass, costing £15,400
- 145 labour hours, costing £2,440

Required:

Calculate the following variances for the glazing department:

(a) Direct material price variance.

(b) Direct material usage variance.

(c) Direct labour rate variance.

(d) Direct labour efficiency variance.

3.5 Marge Products Ltd uses marginal costing and has the following budgeted and actual variable cost and production data for the month of August.

	Budget	Budget	Actual	Actual
Production Units		30,000		32,000
		£		£
Variable Materials	3,000 kg	75,000	3,100 kg	81,000
Variable Labour	15,000 hrs	150,000	15,900 hrs	155,000
Total Variable Costs		225,000		236,000

Required:

- Calculate the standard cost data for one unit of production.
- Calculate the relevant variable cost variances.

3.6 Quango Limited has set its direct standard costs for one unit of its product, the quango, as follows:

Direct Materials: 96 kg @ £9.45 per kilo.
Direct Labour: 5 hours 6 minutes @ £12.60 per hour.

During week 13 the company produced 700 units of quango, and incurred direct costs as follows:

Direct Materials: 71.5 tonnes were used, costing a total of £678,700
Direct Labour: 3,850 hours were worked, costing a total of £48,440

Note: there are 1,000 kilos in a tonne.

Required:

Calculate the relevant direct cost variances.

3.7 A company purchases 5,000 kilograms of material at a cost of £53,000. The standard cost of material per kilogram is £10.

The material price variance is:

(a) £0.60 A	
(b) £3,000 F	
(c) £3,000 A	
(d) £6.00 A	

3.8 A company used 6,000 kilograms of material to produce 10,000 units. The budgeted production was 12,000 units, and the standard material for this output level was 6,600 kilograms at £2 per kilogram.

(a) The material usage variance is:

(a) 500 kilograms	
(b) £1,200	
(c) 600 kilograms	
(d) £1,000	

(b) State whether the variance is adverse or favourable.

3.9 The following direct cost operating statement has been accurately calculated and submitted to the Production Manager.

Standard Direct Cost of Production			£351,000
Variances	**Favourable**	**Adverse**	
Direct Material Price	£2,960		
Direct Material Usage		£5,350	
Direct Labour Rate		£9,260	
Direct Labour Efficiency		£5,150	
Total Direct Variances			£16,800
Actual Direct Cost of Production			£367,800

The following facts have been established:

- The actual production level was 15% greater than that originally envisaged in the budget.

- An anticipated labour pay rate increase was incorporated into the standard costs, but has not yet been paid.

- A machine worked slowly and caused excessive wastage, finally breaking down, and this led to unanticipated idle time, with overtime working needed once the machine was repaired.

- A new contract was agreed with the material supplier in which additional quantities were purchased in return for a discounted price.

Required:

Write an email to the Production Manager which outlines likely reasons for each of the variances.

3.10 The standard labour time to make one unit is 45 minutes. The standard labour rate is £10 per hour. Production was 5,000 units. Total labour time was 4,000 hours, of which 150 hours was idle time.

Required

Calculate the

- Labour efficiency variance (excluding the idle time)
- Labour idle time variance

3.11 The standard labour rate is £15.00 per hour. Each unit has a standard time of 6 minutes. The week 18 production of 6,950 units used 700 hours of productive labour plus 20 hours relating to idle time. The total labour cost for week 18 was £10,764.

Calculate the following variances and insert into the table.

	£	Adverse / Favourable
Labour rate variance		
Labour efficiency variance (excluding idle time)		
Idle time variance		

4 Standard costing – overheads and sales

this chapter covers...

In this chapter we will continue with our examination of standard costing, and look in detail at overheads.

We will start by looking at variable overheads and learn that their calculation is similar to the direct cost variances already studied.

We will then discuss why fixed overheads and their variances need a different approach to direct costs. The approach that is taken also depends on whether we are going to use marginal costing (and treat fixed costs as relating to a period of time), or absorption costing (and treat fixed overheads as part of the product cost).

We will then learn how to calculate fixed overhead variances and to understand how they are derived. The fixed overhead variances that we will examine are:

■ *expenditure variance*

■ *volume variance*

Then we will see how we can interpret the variances that we have calculated and examine possible causes.

Finally we will examine variances connected with sales: the total sales variance, the sales price variance, and the sales volume variance.

OVERHEAD VARIANCES

In the last chapter we examined direct cost variances and learned how they were calculated. In this chapter we will look at the variances for overheads (indirect costs). The two types of overhead that we need to deal with are variable overheads and fixed overheads. This distinction is based on the way that the overhead costs behave when the level of output changes.

The calculation of variances for variable and fixed overheads is entirely different, so we must be careful to use the correct methods. We will first examine variable overhead variances, before looking at fixed overhead variances.

VARIABLE OVERHEADS

Variable overheads are made up of indirect costs that tend to vary in total in proportion to activity levels. Variable overheads could include:

- indirect materials (for example cleaning materials)

- indirect labour (for example a supervisor's production-based bonus)

- indirect expenses (for example the cost of power to run machinery)

Variable overheads are often calculated at a standard rate per direct labour hour or per machine hour. It is assumed that the total cost of variable overheads will be in proportion to these hours. You will be familiar with the use of hourly rates as it is also commonly used as a basis for fixed overhead absorption.

The total standard variable overhead for a particular production level will be calculated as the standard hourly rate multiplied by the number of standard hours that the production should take.

The calculation of variable overhead variances is very similar to the calculation of direct labour variances. This is because:

- both direct labour costs and variable overheads use an hourly rate, and

- both direct labour costs and variable overheads are treated as variable costs

The total variable overhead variance is made up of two variances that we need to be able to calculate:

- the variable overhead price (or expenditure) variance

- the variable overhead efficiency variance

variable overhead price (or expenditure) variance

The variable overhead expenditure variance =

the standard variable overhead cost for the actual hours used	minus	the actual variable overhead cost incurred

This calculation can be used whether the hours refer to direct labour hours or machine hours.

The variance is calculated in a similar way to the direct labour rate variance. Here we are measuring how much of the total variable overhead variance is due to the hourly expenditure being different to the standard hourly rate.

Notice that (just like in the direct labour rate variance) we are using the actual hours to make our comparison.

variable overhead efficiency variance

The variable overhead efficiency variance =

standard hours for actual production at standard variable overhead rate	minus	actual hours used at standard variable overhead rate

This calculation can also be used whether the hours refer to direct labour hours or machine hours.

The variance is the equivalent of the direct labour efficiency variance. In fact if the variable overheads are charged using direct labour hours then this variance will be showing the impact of the labour efficiency on the variable overheads.

Notice that (just like in the direct labour efficiency variance) we are using a standard rate to value the difference between two amounts of time.

We will now illustrate the calculation of these variances by using the Case Study from the previous chapter with some additional information.

Case Study

THE PINE DOOR COMPANY:
VARIABLE OVERHEAD VARIANCES

The Pine Door Company makes cottage doors from reclaimed pine. The company uses standard costing to plan and control its costs. The company uses direct labour hours to charge the variable overheads. The standard variable overhead cost for a door is as follows:

6 direct labour hours at £2.00 per hour = £12 per door.

During the month of August, the company made 35 doors. The actual variable overhead costs incurred were £412 in total. 200 direct labour hours were worked during the month.

required

Calculate:

* The variable overhead price (or expenditure) variance.

* The variable overhead efficiency variance.

solution

The variable overhead price variance =

the standard variable overhead cost for the actual hours used	minus	the actual variable overhead cost incurred
(200 direct labour hours x £2)	–	£412
£400	–	£412

= £12 Adverse

The variable overhead efficiency variance =

standard hours for actual production at standard variable overhead rate	minus	actual hours used at standard variable overhead rate
(6 hours per door x 35 doors x £2)	–	(200 hours x £2)
£420	–	£400

= £20 Favourable

Notice that because direct labour hours are being used to charge variable overheads this calculation is very similar to the direct labour efficiency variance shown earlier, and both result in favourable variances. The only difference is that here we have used the standard variable overhead rate of £2 per hour. To calculate the direct labour efficiency variance the direct labour rate of £7 per hour was used.

FIXED OVERHEADS

We will now turn our attention to dealing with fixed overheads and the related variances. The way fixed overheads are tackled depends on whether absorption costing or marginal costing is being used, so we will start with a reminder of how these systems operate.

fixed costs: absorption or marginal costing?

When fixed costs are involved in costing products there are two traditional schools of thought about how they should be dealt with.

Absorption costing attempts to incorporate fixed costs into the cost of the product by absorbing a suitable part of the expected fixed cost into each unit produced.

Marginal costing views fixed costs as time-based rather than product based, and therefore does not attempt to incorporate these costs into each unit produced. Instead it costs each unit based on only the variable costs, and deals with the fixed costs in the statement of profit or loss for the appropriate reporting period.

using absorption costing for fixed costs

One advantage that standard absorption costing can claim is that the standard cost for a product will be a 'full' cost, and incorporate a portion of all the costs of production. Therefore, provided the actual production level is close to the projected level, and all cost estimates are reasonably accurate, the standard cost of the product will be close to the actual full cost. However, the standard will give an inaccurate forecast of product cost:

- if the costs are not as expected, and/or

- if the production volume is not in line with expectations

For this reason the fixed overhead variances produced under standard absorption costing need to take account of:

- overhead costs

- production volumes

using marginal costing for fixed costs

With marginal costing, by contrast, the volume of production will not affect the standard marginal cost of a product, because the only costs contained in the standard are variable costs – fixed costs are excluded. As fixed costs are dealt with by comparing the expected fixed cost for the period with the actual fixed cost, the only fixed overhead variance that needs to be calculated under marginal standard costing is simply the difference between these two figures.

We will now look in detail at the treatment of fixed overhead variances using marginal costing.

FIXED OVERHEAD VARIANCES – MARGINAL COSTING

fixed overhead expenditure variance

Under standard marginal costing the only fixed overhead variance is usually called the **fixed overhead expenditure variance**. It is very simple to calculate, as follows:

Budgeted Fixed Overhead for period	*minus*	Actual Fixed Overhead for period

The variance would therefore be calculated for the week, month, quarter or other reporting period, and the number of items produced would not form part of the calculation.

If the actual cost was **lower** than the budgeted amount the variance would be **favourable**, and if it was **higher**, it would be considered **adverse**. The variance could be used as part of a reconciliation between actual and standard costs for the production in a period of time.

Case Study

WENSHAM WHEELBARROWS: FIXED OVERHEAD VARIANCES – MARGINAL COSTING

Wensham Wheelbarrows manufactures a single product – the 'Wensham' wheelbarrow. The company had the following results for their third quarter. The company used standard marginal costing. Both direct materials and direct labour are considered to behave as variable costs. There are no variable overheads.

	Budgeted	Actual
Number of Units	10,000	12,000
Direct Materials	£50,000	£65,000
Direct Labour	£80,000	£94,000
Fixed Overheads	£75,000	£81,000
Total Costs	£205,000	£240,000

The direct variances have already been calculated (based on information not shown) as follows:

Direct material price variance	£6,000 A
Direct material usage variance	£1,000 F
Direct labour rate variance	£4,000 F
Direct labour efficiency variance	£2,000 A

required

1 Calculate the fixed overhead expenditure variance.

2 Calculate the standard cost of the actual production.

3 Reconcile the standard cost of the actual production with the actual cost of the production.

solution

Step 1

Fixed overhead expenditure variance

= Budgeted Fixed Overhead for period – Actual Fixed Overhead for period

= £75,000 – £81,000

= £6,000 A

This variance can logically be confirmed as adverse since the fixed overheads actually cost more than the amount that was budgeted.

Step 2

At first glance the direct variances that have been given in the Case Study do not seem to fit in with the rest of the data. This is because the budgeted production level is different to the actual level. To see how the direct variances would reconcile we must acknowledge that the standard variable cost must be based on the actual production level, as follows:

Standard Variable Cost of Actual Production:

Direct Materials (£50,000 ÷ 10,000) x 12,000	£60,000
Direct Labour (£80,000 ÷ 10,000) x 12,000	£96,000
Total	£156,000

Step 3

We can then reconcile the figures as follows:

Budgeted / Standard variable cost for actual production			£156,000
Budgeted fixed costs			£75,000
Variances	**Favourable**	**Adverse**	
Direct materials price		£6,000	
Direct materials usage	£1,000		
Direct labour rate	£4,000		
Direct labour efficiency		£2,000	
Fixed overhead expenditure		£6,000	
Total variance		£9,000	£9,000
Actual cost of actual production			£240,000

FIXED OVERHEAD VARIANCES – ABSORPTION COSTING

The fixed overhead variances under standard absorption costing are more complicated than under marginal costing. As mentioned earlier they attempt to take account of:

- differences arising due to cost

- differences resulting from the volume of production.

The variances analyse the differences between the amount of fixed overhead absorbed by a standard absorption costing system, and the actual cost of the fixed overheads.

total fixed overhead variances and expenditure and volume variances

The absorption rate is agreed before the period starts, and is arranged so that the planned level of output will cause enough overhead absorption to exactly match the expected overheads. If the absorption base is units, then the output will be measured in units, but if the absorption base is labour hours or machine hours, then we must also measure the output in standard labour or machine hours.

If everything goes to plan there will be no under-absorption or over-absorption, and no fixed overhead variances! The plan could be illustrated as shown on the next page.

This diagram is based on the planned figures and so they will always agree. It would not make sense to plan for any other situation!

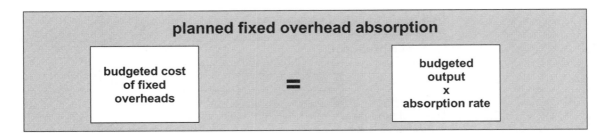

will the plan work? – possible imbalances

When actual figures are used there may be an imbalance – ie they may not always agree. This could be due to either:

■ the fixed overheads not costing what was expected, or

■ the output not turning out to be as planned, or (as usually happens)

■ a combination of the two.

Since the absorption rate is worked out in advance and used throughout, the rate itself will not be a source of any imbalance.

Once the results for the period are known, then the **planned** figures on the diagram shown above can be replaced by the **actual** figures in the diagram below.

The following diagram represents the actual figures. The total of the two boxes may not agree because of the possible differences explained on the previous page. The difference between the amounts in the two boxes will form the total fixed overhead variance – the amount by which the fixed overheads are either under-absorbed or over-absorbed.

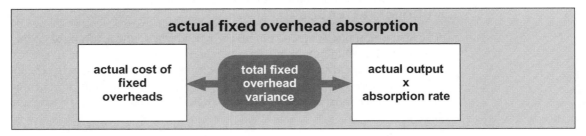

Total **fixed overhead variance** therefore equals:

Fixed Overhead Absorbed – Actual Cost of Fixed Overhead

If the actual cost of fixed overheads is more than the actual output multiplied by the absorption rate then not enough cost has been absorbed by the output – we have **under absorption**. This will give an **adverse** total fixed overhead variance.

fixed overhead expenditure and volume variances

The difference shown in the diagram on the previous page measures the **total fixed overhead variance** – this is due to the difference between the plan and what actually happens. There are two reasons why the actual results could be different from the plan, and these two reasons combine together to result in the total fixed overhead variance. They are:

1   The actual amount **spent** on fixed overheads may not be the same as the planned (or budgeted) fixed overheads. In the diagram, the left-hand box – the actual cost – will be different from the planned figure. This difference is measured by the **fixed overhead expenditure variance**.

2   The actual **volume of output** may not be the same as the planned level of output. This will cause a different amount of fixed overhead to be absorbed than was expected. In the diagrams the figures in the right-hand box will differ. This difference is measured by the **fixed overhead volume variance**.

The actual figures to be used in the diagram on the opposite page are likely to be different from the plan because of changes in expenditure and output volume levels. It is the **combination** of these two differences/variances which will result in an overall **total fixed overhead variance**.

The main variances can be summarised when we bring the two diagrams together like this:

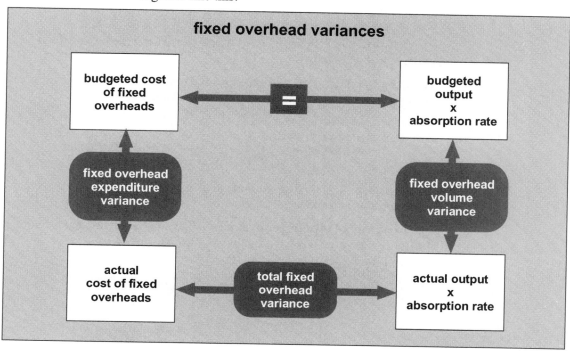

the absorption base

Remember that the amount of fixed overhead absorbed will be based on the actual output multiplied by the absorption rate. The way that the output is measured here will depend on the way that absorption is to take place (the absorption base). If the absorption base is production units, then the output needs to be measured in that form.

If the absorption base is direct labour hours, then the output must be measured in standard labour hours (ie the standard direct labour hours for the actual output). This is often a source of confusion. Remember that what we are measuring is the output; the standard hours for that output is sometimes a convenient way of expressing it.

The same principle will apply if the absorption base is machine hours. The actual output would then need to be expressed in standard machine hours.

Where standard hours are used as an absorption base it is vital to appreciate that absorption will normally take place based on the standard hours for the actual production level, not the actual time taken.

This is so that every identical item produced will absorb the same amount of fixed overhead – even if it took a bit more or less time to make. This will give us a uniform standard amount of overhead that will be absorbed for each identical product, that can be added to the standard material, labour and variable overhead costs to provide the standard absorption cost of that product.

calculation of fixed overhead expenditure and volume variances

The **fixed overhead expenditure variance** is shown on the left-hand side of the diagram on the previous page, and is calculated as follows:

Budgeted Cost of Fixed Overheads	*minus*	Actual Cost of Fixed Overheads

If the actual cost is less than the budgeted cost the variance is favourable, and if it is greater the variance is adverse.

The **fixed overhead volume variance** is shown on the right-hand side of the diagram on the previous page, and is calculated as follows:

Actual Output x Absorption Rate	*minus*	Budgeted Output x Absorption Rate

If the actual output is greater than the budgeted output, the calculation will result in a favourable variance. This is because producing more than planned will reduce costs per unit – which is a good thing.

As mentioned above in relation to the total fixed overhead variance, the form in which the output needs to be expressed will depend on the form of the absorption rate. If the absorption rate is expressed in an amount per unit, then the output should also be in units. If the absorption base is some form of standard hours, then the output must be expressed in standard hours, and the volume variance can be written as:

Standard Hours for Actual Output x Absorption Rate	*minus*	Standard Hours for Budgeted Output x Absorption Rate

The volume variance is therefore a straight comparison of the overheads that would be absorbed by the two output levels (actual and planned).

Some form of standard hours is often used to help measure output because:

- it can be used to convert different kinds of output into a common form – eg a carpenter who produces both tables and chairs, and,

- it enables further analysis of costs – eg by dividing the fixed overhead volume variance.

If an organisation makes a single product then the fixed overhead variances discussed so far will be identical whichever absorption base is used, as illustrated in the Case Study that follows.

Case Study

NODGE LIMITED: FIXED OVERHEAD VARIANCES

Nodge Limited manufactures a single product – the 'nodge'. The company had the following budgeted and actual data for the first year of production. Each unit was budgeted to take four direct labour hours to produce, two of which would be using manned machines.

	Budget	Actual
Production Units	20,000	23,000
Standard Direct Labour Hours	80,000	
Standard Machine Hours	40,000	
Fixed Overheads	£200,000	£195,000

r e q u i r e d

Calculate the total fixed overhead variance, and the breakdown into expenditure and volume, assuming the overhead absorption base is:

1   Units

2   Standard direct labour hours

3   Standard machine hours

s o l u t i o n

1   Absorption base of Units

The absorption rate would be £200,000 ÷ 20,000 units = £10 per unit

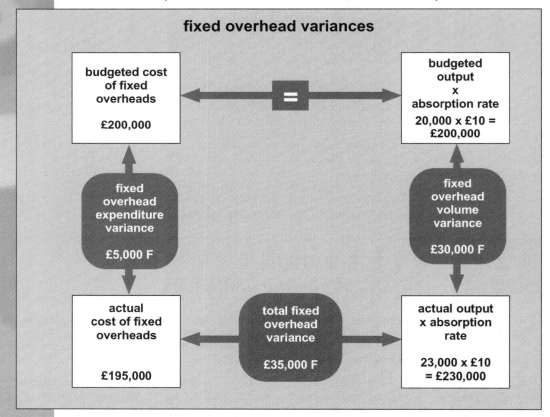

Here, the combination of the higher volume achieved and lower actual cost of overheads has resulted in over-absorption and a favourable total fixed overhead variance.

2 Absorption base of Standard Direct Labour Hours

The absorption rate would be £200,000 ÷ 80,000 = £2.50

The standard direct labour hours for the actual production would be:

23,000 units x 4 hours = 92,000.

The total fixed overhead variance equals:

Fixed Overhead Absorbed – Actual Cost of Fixed Overhead

(£2.50 x 92,000) – £195,000 = £35,000 F

The volume variance equals:

Absorption Rate x (Actual Output – Budgeted Output)

Since we are measuring outputs in standard direct labour hours, we will insert the following figures:

Actual Output (in standard direct labour hours) is 92,000 (as calculated above)

Budgeted Output (in standard direct labour hours) is 80,000 (the figure given in the Case Study)

The volume variance therefore equals:

£2.50 x (92,000 – 80,000) = £30,000 F

This is the same result that is achieved when we use units as an absorption base. The expenditure variance is also unchanged at £5,000 F.

3 Absorption base of Standard Machine Hours

The absorption rate would be £200,000 ÷ 40,000 = £5.00

The standard machine hours for the actual production would be:

23,000 units x 2 hours = 46,000

The total fixed overhead variance equals:

Fixed Overhead Absorbed – Actual Cost of Fixed Overhead

(£5.00 x 46,000) – £195,000 = £35,000 F

The volume variance equals:

Absorption Rate x (Actual Output – Budgeted Output)

Since we are measuring outputs in standard machine hours, we will insert the following figures:

Actual Output (in standard machine hours) is 46,000 (as calculated above)

Budgeted Output (in standard machine hours) is 40,000 (the figure given in the Case Study)

The volume variance therefore equals

£5.00 x (46,000 – 40,000) = £30,000 F

This is again the same result that is achieved when we use units as an absorption base.

The expenditure variance is again unchanged at £5,000 F.

The fixed overhead variances that we have calculated can be shown in the form of a reconciliation statement (similar to the ones that we used in the last chapter for direct costs). This statement reconciles budgeted fixed overheads for actual production with actual fixed overheads. It uses the same information as the boxes in the diagram used earlier in this Case Study.

	Favourable	Adverse	
Budgeted / Standard fixed cost for actual production			£230,000*
Variances	**Favourable**	**Adverse**	
Fixed overhead expenditure	£5,000		
Fixed overhead volume	£30,000		
Total variance	£35,000		–£35,000
Actual fixed cost for actual production			£195,000

Working

Actual output x absorption rate per unit (as calculated in 1 above)
    23,000 units x £10 per unit = £230,000

Calculation on other absorption bases gives same result.

**Case
Study**

WALMER LIMITED:
OVERHEAD VARIANCES AND SUB-VARIANCES

The Finance Department of Walmer Limited has recorded the following data:

- The budgeted production level is 5,000 standard hours. This will enable the absorption rate of £3.00 per hour to absorb the budgeted fixed overheads of £15,000

- Actual fixed overheads amount to £13,000

- Actual output is 5,800 standard hours

required

Calculate the Total Fixed Overhead Variance, and analyse it into the sub-variances.

solution

We can either use the diagram to help with the calculation, or use the formulae.

using the diagram

Using the diagram, and inserting first the known figures – and then the variances as differences – gives this result:

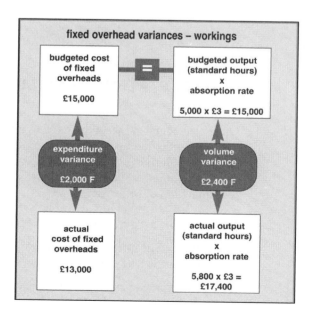

Using the formulas

Using the formulas we can confirm the results shown in the diagram.

The Expenditure Variance equals:

Budgeted Cost of Fixed Overheads – Actual Cost of Fixed Overheads.

£15,000 – £13,000 = £2,000 F

The Volume Variance equals:

Absorption Rate x (Standard Hours for Actual Output – Standard Hours for Budgeted Output)

£3 x (5,800 – 5,000) = £2,400 F

The Total Fixed Overhead Variance equals:

Fixed Overhead Absorbed – Actual Cost of Fixed Overhead

(£3 x 5,800) – £13,000 = £4,400 F

A full summary of the overhead variances reads:

Fixed Overhead Expenditure Variance	£2000 F
Fixed Overhead Volume Variance	£2400 F
Total Fixed Overhead Variance	£4400 F

INTERPRETATION OF FIXED OVERHEAD VARIANCES

Once we understand what the fixed overhead variances are trying to measure, their interpretation becomes quite straightforward. There may be a variety of different underlying causes for these variances in the same way that there are for direct variances, but the individual variances are always trying to measure the same kind of differences.

fixed overhead expenditure variance

The fixed overhead expenditure variance shows whether actual spending on fixed overheads was more or less than the budgeted amount.

The fixed overhead expenditure variance is measuring the difference between the budgeted cost of the fixed overheads and the actual cost. An adverse variance indicates that the actual cost is more than was expected, and a favourable variance that the actual cost is less. The reasons for the variances could include poor budgeting, or the fact that actual costs are different due to unforeseen price changes. The costs of these overheads are not expected to change because of differing output levels since they are defined as 'fixed' costs so any difference in output is irrelevant in the interpretation of this variance.

fixed overhead volume variance

The fixed overhead volume variance shows the difference between the overheads that would be absorbed by the planned volume of output and the amount absorbed by the actual volume of output.

The fixed overhead volume variance is measuring how much more or less fixed overheads have been absorbed compared to the planned amount of absorption. As the variance name indicates, this is entirely concerned with how the actual volume of output compares with the planned volume. The reason for this is because the system attempts to cost a set amount of overhead onto each unit of output. When the actual output is different to that which was planned, a volume variance will arise.

The effect of lower actual output than was planned would be an amount of overhead that has been left over and not accounted for as part of the output cost. This would mean that ideally (if adjustments could have been made in time) a larger amount of overhead should have been added to each unit. As this is not possible after the event there is an amount of unabsorbed overhead, which needs to be written off in the accounts. This is why low output causes an adverse variance that results in a further cost to be written off (debited) in the accounts.

output volume differs from budgeted volume?

If the actual output is greater than expected, the volume variance will be favourable, representing an amount which can be credited to the accounts to compensate for more overhead being absorbed than was planned.

The reasons behind a volume variance will be concerned with either:

■ the setting of the budgeted level of output (eg unrealistically high output or output set at too conservative a level), or

■ something which caused the actual output to differ from the budget, (eg a shortage or additional levels of some resource, or machine breakdown)

WALMER LIMITED (continued):
INTERPRETATION OF FIXED OVERHEAD VARIANCES

solution

Using the data in the last Case Study, the following interpretation could be put on the numerical results.

- The fixed overheads actually cost less than the budgeted amount by £2,000. This was demonstrated in the expenditure variance. We do not have any evidence as to whether this was caused by poor estimation of costs, or by changes in the overhead cost structure that occurred after the budget was prepared.

- The actual volume of output achieved was greater than was budgeted, and this caused £2,400 more fixed overhead to be absorbed than was planned.

- In all, through the combination of lower cost and greater output a total of £4,400 more fixed overhead was absorbed than the fixed overheads actually cost. This over-absorption is represented by the total favourable variance, which will be credited to the accounts.

In Chapter 3 we examined direct cost variances, and we have now seen how both fixed and variable overhead variances can be calculated. The following Case Study illustrates how all these calculations can be carried out and reconciled.

DELTA PRODUCTS LIMITED: VARIANCE ANALYSIS

Delta Products Limited manufactures a single product, and uses standard absorption costing for planning and monitoring costs. The standard cost of each unit produced is as follows, based on the budgeted production level of 5,000 units per month.

Direct Materials	150 litres @ £1.25 per litre
Direct Labour	5 hours @ £16.00 per hour
Variable Overheads	5 hours @ £2.00 per hour
Fixed Overheads	5 hours @ £8.50 per hour

The variable and fixed overheads are absorbed based on the standard direct labour hours for the production level achieved.

In September the following data is available on actual production level and costs incurred:

Production Level	5,500 units produced
Direct Materials	820,000 litres were used, costing £1,020,000 in total
Direct Labour	26,000 hours were taken, costing £416,000 in total
Variable Overheads	Total expenditure on variable overheads was £53,500
Fixed Overheads	Total expenditure on fixed overheads was £222,800

required

1   Calculate the standard cost of the actual production of 5,500 units.

2   Calculate the following variances, and use them to reconcile the actual costs incurred with the standard cost of the actual production.

- Direct Material Price Variance
- Direct Material Usage Variance
- Direct Labour Rate Variance
- Direct Labour Efficiency Variance
- Variable Overhead Expenditure Variance
- Variable Overhead Efficiency Variance
- Fixed Overhead Expenditure Variance
- Fixed Overhead Volume Variance

solution

1   Standard cost of one unit

Direct Materials	150 litres @ £1.25 per litre =	£187.50
Direct Labour	5 hours @ £16.00 per hour =	£80.00
Variable Overheads	5 hours @ £2.00 per hour =	£10.00
Fixed Overheads	5 hours @ £8.50 per hour =	£42.50
		£320.00

Standard cost of 5,500 units £320.00 x 5,500 units =   £1,760,000.

2   The direct cost variances can be calculated as follows:

*   Direct Material Price Variance

    (820,000 litres x £1.25) – £1,020,000   =   £5,000 FAV

*   Direct Material Usage Variance

    £1.25 x ([150 litres x 5,500 units] – 820,000 litres)   =   £6,250 FAV

*   Direct Labour Rate Variance

    (26,000 hours x £16.00) – £416,000   =   £0

*   Direct Labour Efficiency Variance

    £16.00 x ([5 hours x 5,500 units] – 26,000 hours)   =   £24,000 FAV

*   Variable Overhead Expenditure Variance

    (26,000 hours x £2.00) – £53,500   =   £1,500 ADV

*   Variable Overhead Efficiency Variance

    £2.00 x ([5 hours x 5,500 units] – 26,000 hours)   =   £3,000 FAV

Using the format explained earlier to calculate the fixed overhead variances, the diagram appears as shown below:

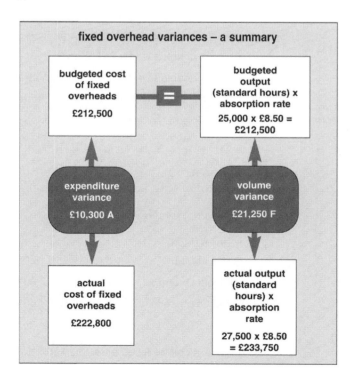

Reconciliation

	£	£	£
Standard cost of production of 5,500 units			1,760,000
Direct Variances:			
Direct Material Price Variance		(5,000) F	
Direct Material Usage Variance		(6,250) F	
Direct Labour Rate Variance		0	
Direct Labour Efficiency Variance		(24,000) F	
			(35,250)
Variable Overhead Variances:			
Expenditure Variance		1,500 A	
Efficiency Variance		(3,000) F	
			(1,500)
Fixed Overhead Variances:			
Expenditure Variance		10,300 A	
Volume Variance		(21,250) F	
			(10,950)
Actual Cost of Production			
(£1,020,000 + £416,000 + £53,500 + £222,800)			£1,712,300

SALES VARIANCES

In Chapter 3 we saw how direct variances for materials and labour are used, and how they can be calculated. So far in this chapter we have looked at overhead variances under both marginal and absorption costing. We will now examine variances that are concerned with the impact of changes in our sales, rather than our costs.

When standard costing is used in an organisation it can either concentrate on costs, as we have already studied, or be used for both costs and revenues (sales) so that variances will explain the whole of any difference in profit between the planned figure and what actually happened. This is the situation that we are now going to look at with the introduction of:

- the sales price variance, and

- the sales volume variance, and the total of these two

- the total sales variance.

In the same way that the cost of direct materials is determined by the price and the quantity, total sales revenue is made up of selling price (for each item) and the quantity of items sold.

For example, if a company plans to sell its product for £50 each, and it intends to sell 3,000 of these products in the month, then its expected sales revenue will be £50 x 3,000 = £150,000. If either the selling price or the quantity sold (sales volume) changes then this will have an impact on both the sales revenue and profit.

sales price variance

The sales price variance shows how much impact there has been on profit due to selling goods at a different price than the one planned (budgeted).

The sales price variance =

the actual sales revenue from the actual quantity of goods sold	*minus*	the standard sales revenue from the actual quantity of goods sold

It can also be expressed as:

actual quantity x (actual selling price – standard selling price)

You should notice the following points about the sales price variance:

■ the variance is based on the **actual quantity of sales** (i.e. the actual sales volume) this is a similar idea to how the material price variance is calculated.

■ the format is similar to the direct material price variance, although here we are using selling prices, and deducting the standard price from the actual price. This is so that a positive numerical answer will mean that we are selling our products for more money than we planned – this will generate additional profits and is therefore a favourable variance. A negative numerical answer will denote an adverse variance.

---

worked example

The budget was to sell 3,000 items at a standard £50 each (as above), but we actually sold 2,900 items at £55 each.

The sales price variance would be:

(2,900 units x £55)   minus   (2,900 units x £50)

= £14,500 Favourable.

Notice that

• we use the actual sales quantity, and

• the variance here is favourable because the actual selling price is greater than the standard selling price

• the profit will be £14,500 greater than planned just because of the difference in the selling price

sales volume variance

The sales volume variance shows how much impact there has been due to selling more or less goods than originally planned.

To see the impact on profit caused by the volume difference, we can multiply the difference in sales volume by either:

- standard contribution per unit (if we are using marginal costing), or

- standard profit (margin) per unit (if we are using absorption costing)

These alternative versions of the sales volume variance are calculated as follows:

■ **Sales Volume Variance – Marginal Costing**

The sales volume variance (using standard contribution) =

the actual quantity of goods sold multiplied by standard contribution per unit	*minus*	the budgeted quantity of goods sold multiplied by standard contribution per unit

worked example

The budget was to sell 3,000 items at a standard £50 each (as above), but we actually sold 2,900 items at £55 each.

The standard contribution is £30 per unit.

The sales volume variance (using standard contribution) would be:

(2,900 units x £30)   minus   (3,000 units x £30)

= £3,000 Adverse

This variance, together with the sales price variance would account for the difference in **contribution** between the budgeted / standard figures and the actual figures. This assumes that the actual variable costs are in line with the standard.

Budgeted contribution	3,000 x £30 = £90,000
Sales price variance	£14,500 Favourable
Sales volume variance	£3,000 Adverse
Total sales variance	£11,500 Favourable
Actual contribution (2,900 x £35)	£101,500

■ Sales Volume Variance – Absorption Costing

The sales volume variance (using standard profit) =

the actual quantity of goods sold multiplied by standard profit per unit	*minus*	the budgeted quantity of goods sold multiplied by standard profit per unit

worked example

The budget was to sell 3,000 items at a standard £50 each (as above), but we actually sold 2,900 items at £55 each.

The standard profit is £14 per unit.

The sales volume variance (using standard profit) would be:

(2,900 units x £14)   minus   (3,000 units x £14)

= £1,400 Adverse

This variance, together with the sales price variance would account for the difference in **profit** between the budgeted / standard figures and the actual figures. This assumes that the actual costs are in line with the standard.

Budgeted profit	3,000 x £14 =	£42,000
Sales price variance	£14,500 Favourable	
Sales volume variance	£1,400 Adverse	
Total sales variance		£13,100 Favourable
Actual profit (2,900 x £19)	£55,100	

Case Study

STANDARD SAILS: SALES VARIANCES

Standard Sails is a company that manufactures and sells yacht sails. The company uses standard absorption costing. One of its products is the 'Premier' that has standard data as follows:

	£
Selling Price	500
Direct Costs	200
Fixed Overheads	180

The budget for May was to make and sell 200 Premier Sails.

The actual number sold in May was 195, and the sales revenue from these transactions totalled £99,450. Costs were in line with standard costs.

required

Calculate the sales price variance and the sales volume variance, and show how these account for the profit difference.

solution

Since we are provided with the actual sales revenue in total rather than per unit, we can calculate the variance as follows.

The sales price variance is:

the actual sales revenue from the actual quantity of goods sold

minus

the standard sales revenue from the actual quantity of goods sold

£99,450 – (195 x £500)   = £1,950 Favourable

The sales volume variance is calculated using the standard profit per unit. This is £500 – (£200 + £180) = £120.

The variance can be calculated as:

standard profit per unit x (actual sales volume – budgeted sales volume)

£120 x (195 – 200)   = £600 Adverse

If we compare the budgeted and actual profits (since costs are in line with the standard) we get the following result:

	Budget		**Actual**	
Sales	(200 x £500)	£100,000		£ 99,450
less				
Direct Costs	(200 x £200)	£ 40,000	(195 x £200)	£ 39,000
Overheads				
Absorbed	(200 x £180)	£ 36,000	(195 x £180)	£ 35,100
Profit		£ 24,000		£ 25,350

The improvement in profit of £1,350 is accounted for by the sales price variance of £1,950 (favourable) and the sales volume variance of £600 (adverse).

Chapter Summary

■ Variable overhead variances are calculated in a similar way to direct cost variances. Two main variable overhead variances can be calculated – the variable overhead expenditure variance and the variable overhead efficiency variance.

■ Fixed overhead variances differ from other variances due to the way that fixed costs behave and the way the chosen costing system deals with them.

■ When marginal costing is used, fixed costs are considered time-based, and are not absorbed by the output. The fixed overhead variance under this system is a simple measurement of more or less expenditure than planned.

■ When absorption costing is used, fixed overheads are absorbed into the output based on a predetermined rate. The total fixed overhead variance is the amount by which the amount of overhead absorbed differs from the overhead actually incurred. This can be due to the expenditure on overhead being different to what was planned, or the volume of output being different, or both.

■ Fixed overhead variances can be calculated either using a diagram or learning traditional formulas. Whatever method is used care must be taken to avoid errors.

■ Sales variances measure the effect on profit from differences in selling price or volume.

Key Terms		
	variable overheads	indirect costs which vary in proportion to the volume of production or other output
	variable overhead expenditure variance	measures how much of the variable overhead variance is caused by the hourly cost differing from the standard hourly rate
	variable overhead efficiency variance	measures how much of the variable overhead variance is caused by the amount of hours (labour or machine) used differing from standard
	fixed overheads	indirect costs which do not vary in proportion to the volume of production or other output
	marginal costing	a technique that values cost units based on variable costs only. Fixed costs are considered to relate only to the reporting period of time
	fixed overhead expenditure variance (marginal costing)	the only fixed overhead variance generated using marginal costing. It measures the difference between the budgeted expenditure and the actual expenditure on fixed overheads in a reporting period
	absorption costing	a technique that values cost units based on a suitable part of all the costs of production, whether fixed or variable in behaviour
	absorption base	the mechanism by which absorption costing absorbs indirect costs into cost units. It may be simply per cost unit, or (for example) per standard labour or machine hour
	total fixed overhead variance (absorption costing)	the difference between the actual expenditure on fixed overheads, and the amount of fixed overhead absorbed by the actual output. The expenditure and volume variances will combine in this total variance
	fixed overhead expenditure variance (absorption costing)	the difference between the budgeted expenditure and the actual expenditure on fixed overheads in a reporting period
	fixed overhead volume variance (absorption costing)	the difference between the fixed overhead which would have been absorbed by the budgeted output and the fixed overhead which was absorbed by the actual output.
	sales price variance	the difference in profit caused by selling goods at a different price from standard
	sales volume variance	the difference in profit caused by selling a different volume of goods than budgeted
	total sales variance	the total of the sales price variance and the sales volume variance

Activities

4.1 A company uses direct labour hours to charge variable overheads. The standard labour hours per unit produced is 5 hours, and the standard hourly charge is £1.50. During the month 500 units were produced, using 2,420 direct labour hours. The actual variable overheads for the month were £3,910.

Required:

$(2420 \times £1.50) - 3910 = 280 (Adverse)$

Calculate:

(a) The variable overhead expenditure variance.

(b) The variable overhead efficiency variance.

$$\underset{3750}{(5 \times 500 \times 1.50)} - \underset{3630}{(2420 \times 1.50)} = 120 \; (Favourable.)$$

4.2 A company uses machine hours to charge variable overheads. The standard machine hours per unit produced is 1.5 hours, and the total standard variable overhead cost per unit is £30.

During the month 1,250 units were produced, using 1,900 machine hours. The actual variable overheads for the month were £38,600.

$\times$ Standard hourly rate $= 30/1.5 \; £20$

Required:

$(1900 \times 20) - 38600 = 600 \; (Adverse)$

Calculate:

(a) The variable overhead expenditure variance.

(b) The variable overhead efficiency variance.

$$\underset{37500}{(1.5 \times 1250 \times 20)} - \underset{38000}{(1900 \times 20)} = 500 \; (Adverse)$$

4.3 You have been provided with the following information:

- Budgeted fixed overheads are £500,000

- Budgeted output is 25,000 units

- Actual output is 30,000 units

- Actual fixed overheads are £480,000

Required:

Calculate: $OAR = £20$

(a) The fixed overhead volume variance.

$$\underset{600\,000}{(30000 \times 20)} - \underset{500000}{(25000 \times 20)} = £100,000 (F)$$

(b) The fixed overhead expenditure variance.

$\hookrightarrow 500,000 - 480,000 = £20,000 \; (F)$

4.4   You have been provided with the following information:

- Budgeted fixed overheads are £60,000
- Budgeted output is 5,000 units and 500 labour hours
- Actual output is 3,500 units and 430 labour hours
- Actual fixed overheads are £58,000

Required: OAR = 60,000 – 5,000 = £12.

Calculate:

60,000 – 58,000 = £2,000 (F)

(a)   The fixed overhead expenditure variance.

(b)   The fixed overhead volume variance.   12 × (3500 – 5000) = -£18000 (A)

4.5   Sofa-so-Good Limited manufactures sofas and sells them to furniture shops. The company uses standard absorption costing, with an absorption rate of £200 per sofa for fixed overheads.

The budget for the year was to manufacture 2,200 sofas and incur £440,000 of fixed overheads.   OAR

The actual production for the year was 2,150 sofas, and the actual fixed overheads incurred amounted to £428,000.

Required:

(a)   Calculate the following variances:

440,000 – 428,000 = £12,000 (F)

- Fixed overhead expenditure variance
- Fixed overhead volume variance   ⇒ 200 × (2150 – 2200) = -£10,000 (A)

(b)   Explain one disadvantage that Sofa-so-Good Limited may experience by absorbing overheads on a per-sofa basis.

(c)   Complete the following reconciliation between budgeted fixed overheads for actual production and actual fixed overheads.

Budgeted / Standard fixed cost for actual production			£440,000
Variances	**Favourable**	**Adverse**	
Fixed overhead expenditure	£12,000		
Fixed overhead volume		£10,000	
Total variance	£2,000		-£2000
Actual fixed cost for actual production			£428,000

4.6 Zorbant Ltd absorbs fixed overheads based on the budgeted fixed overheads of £94,600, and the budgeted number of standard direct labour hours to be worked of 2,200.

The actual output for the period turned out to be 2,500 standard hours. The actual fixed overheads for the period were £99,000.

Required:

(a) Calculate the fixed overhead absorption rate. = 94600 ÷ 2200 = £43.

(b) Calculate the fixed overhead variances. 94 600 - 99000 = -£4,400 (Adverse)

(c) State which of the following comments are valid, based on the above data:

1 The expenditure variance is adverse due to the increased volume of output which has been produced.

2 The expenditure variance is favourable since the actual fixed overheads are less than were budgeted for.

③ The expenditure variance is adverse since the actual fixed overheads are more than were budgeted for.

④ The favourable volume variance reflects the fact that more output was achieved than was budgeted for.

5 The favourable volume variance is due to the overheads being less than anticipated.

6 The adverse volume variance is due to more output being achieved than was budgeted for.

4.7 G Loop Manufacturing Limited makes a single product, the Gloop, and absorbs fixed overheads on the basis of standard labour hours.

For the year it had budgeted to make 2,000 Gloops, and take 14,000 standard labour hours to do so. It budgeted that its fixed overheads would amount to £448,000.

During the year the company actually made 1,800 Gloops.

The fixed overheads for the year actually amounted to £455,000.

Required:

(a) Calculate the budgeted absorption rate per standard hour.

(b) Calculate the standard hours to make one Gloop.

(c) Calculate the standard hours to make the actual output of 1,800 Gloops.

(d) Calculate:

The fixed overhead expenditure (or price) variance, and

The fixed overhead volume variance.

(e) Reconcile the overhead absorbed by the standard hours for the actual production of 1,800 Gloops, with the actual fixed overheads using the above variances.

4.8   The Maxima Office Furniture Company manufactures a range of desks and chairs and sells them to furniture shops.

The company uses standard absorption costing, using standard direct labour hours as an absorption base.

Each desk takes 5 standard hours to produce, and each chair takes 2 standard hours.

The budget for the year was to utilise 40,000 direct labour hours by making 5,000 desks and 7,500 chairs.

The budget for fixed overheads for the year was £600,000.

The actual production for the year was 5,100 desks and 7,000 chairs. The actual fixed overheads incurred amounted to £603,500.

Required:

(a)   Calculate the standard direct labour hours for the actual production.

(b)   Calculate the fixed overhead absorption rate per standard direct labour hour.

(c)   Calculate the following variances:

- Fixed overhead expenditure variance
- Fixed overhead volume variance
- Total fixed overhead variance

4.9 The following table shows various unrelated situations that may contribute to adverse or favourable fixed overhead variances. Place ticks in the appropriate columns to show which variances are likely to be affected or if there is no impact on these variances.

Situation	Fixed Overhead Expenditure Variance			Fixed Overhead Volume Variance		
	Adverse	Favourable	No impact	Adverse	Favourable	No impact
Production manager awarded a pay increase						
Unplanned additional day's holiday shut down						
Additional direct labour staff used to increase production						
Unplanned pay rise given to direct labour staff						
New maintenance contract implemented with reduced costs						
Additional shift working (including supervisors) used to increase production						

4.10 A company that uses standard marginal costing has the following standard unit data for one of its products:

Standard selling price	£130
Standard variable costs	£50
Standard Contribution	£80

During the month the budgeted sales were 10,600, and the actual sales were 10,000, generating actual sales revenue of £1,350,000.

Required

Calculate the

- Sales price variance
- Sales volume variance
- Total sales variance

5 Cost management techniques

this chapter covers...

This chapter commences with an examination of activity based costing (ABC), and shows how it works and when it is most appropriate and beneficial.

Next is an examination of value engineering and value analysis which was created out of issues caused by shortages. In these techniques every aspect of a product or component is examined to establish whether it is necessary and if so whether the function can be achieved more efficiently.

Target costing is considered next, which takes the selling price as a starting point for design to ensure that costs are planned to ensure profitability.

The next section in this chapter deals with lifecycle costing as it applies to products. The use of discounted cash flow in this context is also explored.

The final section in this chapter looks at the impact of specific emerging technologies on operational control. Here we discuss cloud accounting, artificial intelligence, data analytics and visualisation techniques.

ACTIVITY BASED COSTING (ABC)

background to ABC

Activity based costing was developed in the 1970s and 1980s as an alternative to absorption costing. Since the time when absorption costing was initially developed (at the time of the Industrial Revolution), many aspects of manufacture had changed, and it was felt that absorption costing was not providing information of sufficient quality. The points that were made by advocates of ABC were:

Overheads (indirect costs) typically now account for the major part of product costs, and should therefore be accounted for in a less arbitrary way than they would under absorption costing. For example, simply absorbing overheads based on just one basis (e.g. direct labour hours) does not acknowledge the complexity of costs that can make up overheads.

Both production methods and batch sizes can have a major impact on product costs, yet these are largely ignored by absorption costing. For example, the cost involved in setting up equipment will be far greater per unit of output for small production runs than for large ones.

Modern production methods do not lend themselves to the use of absorption rates such as direct labour hours or machine hours. Integrated production systems can often operate with minimal human intervention.

cost pools and cost drivers

ABC works by identifying the indirect activities, and grouping their costs into 'cost pools', one for each major activity. For each cost pool there must be a factor that drives the costs and causes those costs to change. This 'cost driver' is identified and its rate calculated. The rate is then used to charge the output with cost, based on the output's use of the activity.

For example in a stores department (which would typically form one service cost centre under absorption costing), the activities could be determined as:

1 Receiving goods inwards, and

2 Issuing goods to production.

The costs of running the stores department would be analysed into the costs for carrying out each of these activities – the 'cost pools'. The cost drivers might be agreed as:

1 Number of Deliveries Received (for receiving goods inward), and

2 Number of Requisitions (for issuing goods).

The rate per cost driver would then be calculated by dividing the cost pool by the cost driver for that pool.

Using this technique, a product that required many different components that were delivered separately and then issued frequently to production, would be charged with a high cost from the activities in the stores department. In comparison, a product that was made from components delivered together and issued to production in bulk would incur fewer costs.

Using a suitable analysis of costs and their drivers, an organisation can adapt the system to its own circumstances. Each different product will then be charged with a more accurate cost based on its use of the activities than if absorption costing had been used.

The diagram below shows how the system works. Study it and then read the two Case Studies that follow. They both illustrate the application of activity based costing, the first in a manufacturing company and the second to a college operating in the service sector.

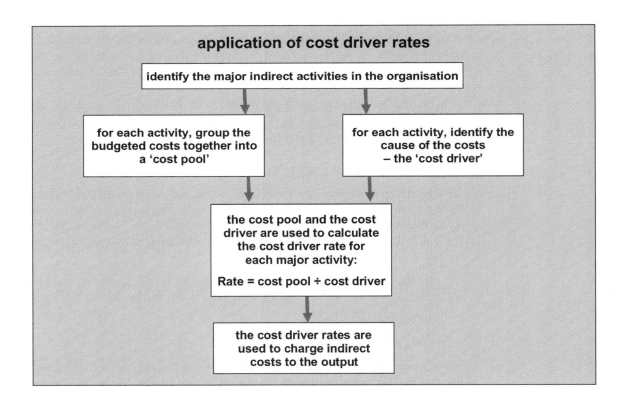

Case Study

ABC COMPANY:
ACTIVITY BASED COSTING

The ABC Company has introduced activity based costing to cost its output. It makes several products on mechanised production lines, including AB, and BC. AB is a product that is usually made in large batches of 1,000 units, since it sells in large quantities. BC is a specialised product selling to a niche market, and is therefore made in small batches of 20 units.

As a part of the introduction of ABC the company has identified one major activity as 'setting up the production equipment'. The cost associated with this activity in a financial year is budgeted at £250,000, and therefore this amount forms the cost pool for setting up production equipment.

The company has identified the cost driver of this activity as 'number of set-ups performed', since if the number increases the cost will be proportionally greater. One batch of any product requires one set-up to be performed.

The budgeted figure of £250,000 was based on an estimated 500 set-ups in the financial year.

The unit costs for AB and BC have already been calculated excluding the set-up costs, as follows:

AB   £50.00 per unit
BC   £55.00 per unit

required

Calculate the total cost per unit of AB and BC, including set-up costs.

solution

The cost driver rate for set-ups = £250,000 ÷ 500 = £500 per set-up

Charging at this rate:

One unit of AB would incur set-up cost of £500 ÷ 1,000 = £0.50

One unit of BC would incur set-up cost of £500 ÷ 20 = £25.00

Incorporating this into the previous costs gives per unit costs of:

	AB	BC
	£	£
Costs excluding set-ups	50.00	55.00
Cost of set-ups	0.50	25.00
Total Cost	50.50	80.00

In this Case Study set-ups account for approximately 1% of the total cost of a unit of AB, compared to 31% of the total cost of a unit of BC. These differences would not be identified using a traditional absorption costing system that treated set-ups as a part of general overheads.

ABC COLLEGE:
ACTIVITY BASED COSTING IN THE SERVICE SECTOR

The ABC College is a small private college, providing a variety of part-time business related courses. The college has determined that there are four major activities that are undertaken, that have the following cost pools for the financial year and cost drivers.

Activity	Cost pool	Cost driver information
Teaching	£500,000	Teaching Hours (25,000 in year)
Course Preparation	£300,000	New Courses (30 in year)
Lesson Preparation	£100,000	Teaching Hours (25,000 in year)
Student Administration	£100,000	Number of Students (1,000 in year)

The costs for two separate courses are to be calculated using ABC.

The first is the Advanced Marketing Course. This course will run for 250 teaching hours, and should attract 20 students. The course has been run previously.

The second is a new course in Taxation for Exporters to Scandinavia. The course will run for 100 teaching hours, and there are 5 prospective students.

required

Calculate the cost per course and cost per student for each of the two courses.

solution

First the cost driver rates need to be established:

Teaching	£500,000 ÷ 25,000	=	£20 per teaching hour
Course Preparation	£300,000 ÷ 30	=	£10,000 per new course
Lesson Preparation	£100,000 ÷ 25,000	=	£4 per teaching hour
Student Administration	£100,000 ÷ 1,000	=	£100 per student

Secondly, these rates are applied to the courses according to their demand for the activities:

1 Advanced Marketing Course

Teaching	£20 x 250 =	£5,000
Course Preparation	(existing course)	-
Lesson Preparation	£4 x 250 =	£1,000
Student Administration	£100 x 20 =	£2,000
Cost for course		£8,000
Cost per student	£8,000 ÷ 20 =	£400

2 Taxation for Exporters to Scandinavia

Teaching	£20 x 100 =	£2,000
Course Preparation	£10,000 x 1 =	£10,000
Lesson Preparation	£4 x 100 =	£400
Student Administration	£100 x 5 =	£500
Cost for course		£12,900
Cost per student	£12,900 ÷ 5 =	£2,580

Although the two Case Studies were for very different organisations, the same logic applies to the absorption of overheads in each situation. In the first Case Study it can be clearly seen that the short production runs for the 'BC' product resulted in much greater set up costs being incurred for each unit produced. Similarly, in the second Case Study the 'course preparation' cost is mainly responsible for the much higher cost per student attending the 'taxation for exporters to Scandinavia' course.

In both these Case Studies, if activity based costing had not been used then all overhead costs (including set-ups etc) would have been absorbed on the same basis to all the outputs. This would mean that some products would absorb too little cost, while others would absorb an unfairly large amount.

implementing activity based costing

If an activity based costing system is to be introduced, then the benefits of the system must outweigh the costs. The benefits of the system will include more accurate product costs, which should lead to better pricing and better decision-making generally. The costs of introducing the system will include software, and management and staff training. There is also the high cost and time involved in developing the system to be considered. It may be necessary to bring in experts as consultants to develop and implement the system, and this will be both expensive and time consuming. It can take several years to bring an ABC system into operation in a large organisation.

The type of organisation that is most likely to benefit from the introduction of an activity based costing system is one where:

- a large proportion of operating costs are indirect

- there is a diverse range of products or services that consume the organisation's resources in different ways

- the organisation operates in a competitive environment where accurate decisions are vital.

A higher proportion of the organisations that have implemented ABC are in the service sector, including financial services, compared to traditional manufacturing.

Organisations with a standardised product or service range, relatively low indirect costs, and that operate in a less competitive market are less likely to benefit from the introduction of ABC.

VALUE ENGINEERING AND VALUE ANALYSIS

Whereas general cost reduction programmes concentrate on producing existing products more efficiently and cheaply, a more focussed approach can be used. This technique was developed during the resource shortages during the Second World War, and examines each component to ensure that it contributes to the value of the product. Components that can be made from cheaper materials or in different ways without compromising the value to the user of the final product will be changed.

In order to ensure that value is maintained, what constitutes that value must be analysed:

- before production starts (this is **value engineering**)

- or when the product or service is already on the market (**value analysis**).

definitions of value engineering and value analysis

value engineering Ensuring that new products or services are designed for quality but at low cost, by analysing how every part of the design enhances value.

value analysis Analysing the value of every part of the design of an existing product or service, and questioning whether its function can be achieved some other way at lower cost.

The aim of both these processes is to build quality into the design of the product or service, while keeping the costs down. Relevant specialists in engineering, design and technology will be consulted.

Clearly it is easier to make alterations at the design stage than afterwards, the aim being to build in value but at lower cost. At the design stage, each part or feature of the product or system is looked at to check that it is necessary and that it contributes value.

In existing products or services, it is possible to analyse the value provided to the customer, and decide whether that level of quality can be kept or improved, when costs are reduced.

For example, the exact colour of a disposable razor may be of no importance to customers, whereas the exact colour of a sofa may be part of its value. Cheaper raw materials which may show colour variations may be acceptable for some products but not others.

The term 'value added' is used to describe activities or manufacturing processes that create an aspect of the product that customers are willing to pay for. Some writers describe value added activities as those that change the 'form, fit, or function' of a product.

Value engineering and value analysis attempt to eliminate activities that are 'non-value added'. These are the wasteful activities that do not contribute to the value of the product. As well as more obvious examples like idle time while waiting for materials, or moving part-finished products to the next stage in production, it can also include the inspection activity if it doesn't contribute to the quality of the product.

Businesses that have mainly eliminated non-value added activities may be said to be 'lean' organisations.

Ethical values should also be considered when making changes to the design of products. Packaging should be minimised and made environmentally friendly. The end life of the product should be considered so that the maximum amount of components can be recycled efficiently. Ethical and commercial considerations will converge when a component which is found to be unnecessary can be entirely eliminated.

practical aspects of value engineering and value analysis

Value engineering and value analysis must look at each product or service in great detail. Typical questions to be asked include:

- Can the function of this product or component be achieved some other way?

- Are all the functions of the product or service essential?

- Can the product be made lighter or smaller, thus using less material? (This may enhance its value.)

- Can components be standardised across a range of products?

- Can the design of the product or the processes involved in a service be modified to save time?

advantages of value engineering and value analysis

The potential advantages of these techniques to the producer or provider are:

- continuous improvements in design and methods

- more efficient use of resources

- higher profits

- enhanced reputation

- extended product life

- improved customer service through standardisation of components
- improved employee motivation

The potential advantages of these techniques to the customer are:

- prices may be reduced without loss of quality
- better design based on satisfying users' needs
- improved performance and reliability
- quicker delivery
- standard components for servicing

We have seen that cost reduction programmes should be planned for the long term. Value engineering and value analysis can be used as part of these programmes, so that the value of products or services to users is maintained or increased, even when costs are reduced.

examples of cost reduction and value analysis

- In a hospital outpatients' clinic, the original system meant that each consultant remained in one room, seeing a succession of patients. Time was wasted while patients were prepared for the consultation. The system was changed to one in which two rooms were used and the consultant moved between them. While the consultant saw one patient, the next could be prepared in the other room. The service to patients was improved at reduced cost.

- In a factory manufacturing cheap pottery mugs, the handles for the mugs were made separately and attached to the mugs before firing. A moulding process was then developed which allowed the mug to be produced with the handle. This speeded up production and reduced the number of rejects.

- Products such as radios and telephones are often produced in a range of exterior designs but offering the same functions. The basic product can then be exactly the same, but housed in different casings. Costs can be reduced by manufacturing the working parts in large numbers, and the value to customers is maintained. This is an example of 'variety reduction'.

TARGET COSTING

During the 1960s many new management and cost management techniques were developed, particularly by the Japanese. One of these was the concept of 'target costing'.

Where selling prices are determined by market forces it is often possible to anticipate what an ideal selling price is before the product is designed. In this way the whole design can be driven by the target price, so that all the materials, labour and expenses meet the requirements of the product and its profitability.

The steps involved in **target costing** are:

- decide the level of **market share** the organisation wants to achieve for the product and the level of **profit** expected

- estimate the target **selling price** at which the product would be expected to achieve the desired market share

- subtract the organisation's required level of profit from the target selling price to give the **target cost**

- compare the actual costs with the target. For a product in the design stage, the projected cost would be compared with the target cost. If the costs are too high and there is a '**cost gap**', then cost reductions must be found in order to meet the target. Alternative methods of production may have to be considered. Value engineering and value analysis may be used

- if it is impossible to reduce costs to the target level without affecting quality, then it can be seen that the product is not viable at the chosen selling price and profit level

Target costing can only be used in situations where there is sufficient information available about the market for the product or service. It must be possible to link selling prices with market share. The organisation must also have a specific target for contribution or profit as a percentage of sales.

Target costing may be used with activity based costing. In activity based costing, overheads are charged to a specific product according to how much use it makes of the activities within the organisation. Required cost reductions would be concentrated on the activities most used by the product in question. This method should result in real cost savings for that product. In contrast, charging overheads to products using apportionment and absorption does not give a realistic view of how the costs (and therefore any reductions in those costs) relate to a particular product.

Target costing should take account of ethical considerations in the design process. For example, it may be possible to use board created from wood waste as an alternative to plastic in the construction of some products. This may be of equivalent cost and yet meet the requirements of being sourced sustainably and have the ability to be recycled easily at the end of the product's life.

advantages of target costing

The potential advantages of target costing to the producer or provider are:

- improved sales volumes and market share through competitive pricing

- good relationships with customers through consultation and a team-based approach

- achievement of a planned level of profit

- more efficient use of resources

- improvements in production methods

- involvement of all sections of the organisation, resulting in better coordination of functions

The potential advantages of target costing to the customer are:

- the required product or service obtainable at the right price
- more reliable service from the supplier resulting from better relationships
- prices reduced without loss of quality

All the advantages of value engineering and value analysis are relevant if these methods are being used to achieve the target cost.

Case Study

METTLE PLC: TARGET COSTING

situation

Mettle plc is a manufacturer of components for heavy goods vehicles. The market for these products is limited to a small number of large companies, which manufacture the vehicles. Mettle plc currently supplies only three customers and the loss of a single customer would therefore be a serious problem. Mettle plc will lose sales if its prices for components are not competitive.

The sales manager of Mettle plc has established a maximum price for a particular component, C34, above which the vehicle manufacturers will not buy from Mettle plc. This price is £350 per unit of C34. At this price, sales demand for the next year is expected to be 6,000 units of C34. Mettle plc has a target level of 18% operating profit on sales.

Note: here we are using target 'operating profit', which means that the 'total costs' will include non-production costs. In other cases, the 'target profit' may be based on a required level of contribution or of gross profit, depending on the costing method being used in the organisation.

required

Calculate:

(a) The expected total sales revenue from component C34 for the next year.

(b) The target operating profit required by Mettle plc from the total sales of C34.

(c) The total target cost for C34 for the next year.

(d) The target operating profit per unit of C34.

(e) The target cost per unit of C34.

solution

(a) Expected total sales revenue from C34 = £350 x 6,000 = £2,100,000

(b) Target operating profit from C34 = 18% x £2,100,000 = £378,000

(c) Total target cost for C34 = £2,100,000 – £378,000 = £1,722,000

(d) Target operating profit per unit of C34 = £378,000/6,000 = £63

(e) Target cost per unit of C34 = £350 – £63 = £287

target costing and value engineering

We have seen that value engineering is used to ensure that quality is built into the design of new products without incurring unnecessary costs. Unnecessary costs are those which do not add value to the product. As a result of value engineering, the lowest cost for a particular design should be established. This technique is clearly a useful tool if target costing is being used. If the lowest cost for the design meets the target cost, then that design is acceptable. If not, then it is necessary to re-think the whole design and carry out value engineering again or to reconsider the original product specifications. Care must be taken to avoid wasting resources on a lengthy design process in which too many alternatives are considered.

Success is achieved using a combination of target costing and value engineering if the resulting product satisfies the needs of both the customer and the producer:

- the product satisfies the user's requirements (value in use and prestige value)
- the selling price is at a level that customers are prepared to pay
- the selling price attracts sufficient customers to meet the producer's target market share
- the costs are reduced to the target level, so that the producer's target profit level is reached

The following diagram illustrates the links between value engineering and the steps of target costing.

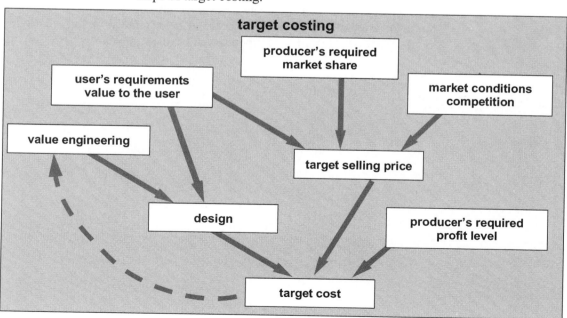

LIFE CYCLE COSTING

In Chapter 2 we looked at the impact of the product life cycle on forecasting. Here we will examine life cycle costing.

The life cycle of a product is a sequence of stages through which it passes, from the start of its development to the point at which it is no longer sold or supported by customer services. We use the term 'product life cycle' throughout this section, but all the ideas could equally well be applied to services.

Products typically go through a number of distinct stages between conception and finally being withdrawn from sale. The stages are:

- development
- launch
- growth
- maturity
- decline

These stages are shown on the graph below.

Life cycle costing can also be applied to decisions relating to non-current assets (for example machinery). In that situation we would examine costs and savings over the life of the asset.

The length of a product life cycle can vary from a few years to 50 years or more. For example, products and services in hi-tech industries have short life cycles, whereas standard food products sell for many years.

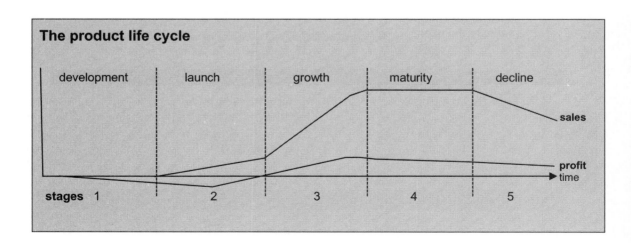

Life cycle costing involves considering costs for the whole life cycle of a product instead of the usual short time periods. Target selling prices and target costs may result from a planning process covering the life cycle of the product.

As the product life cycle progresses, costs are accumulated in:

- research, development and design

- production

- selling and distribution

- customer services

When all these costs are considered, for many products, the costs of production represent a small proportion of the total. Research and development, followed by the detailed design of the product, may build up a very large part of the costs. Examples of such products include medicines, computer software and cars. In some cases, heavy costs are incurred at the end of the life cycle, when sales have ceased, for example in decommissioning nuclear power stations.

Life cycle costing aims to collect together the costs of a single product over its entire life cycle. This means accounting for costs over a period of several years instead of a single year or less. Life cycle budgeting similarly involves planning for all the costs and revenues associated with the whole life cycle of the product.

life cycle costing and decision making

Research, development and design take place before the product goes into production. They also have a major influence on the other life cycle costs. Money spent on value engineering at the design stage can reduce production, marketing and customer service costs. On the other hand, a badly designed product will be more difficult to make, to sell and to maintain. This interdependence between the different stages of the life cycle is the main argument in favour of looking at the total cost of all the stages, rather than concentrating on just the production costs.

Budgeted life cycle costs and forecast sales volumes may be used for pricing decisions. The demand for a product will vary over its life cycle and the total sales revenue must cover the total life cycle costs. Forecasts of sales demands at different possible selling prices and expected costs for several years in advance are necessary to carry out the calculations for deciding on the best selling price. The chosen selling price, together with a required profit percentage, may be used for target costing. On the other hand, life cycle budget calculations may show that the product will not be profitable and therefore that expensive research and development work should not be carried out.

Economies of scale will need to be considered alongside pricing decisions. Generally, the lower the selling price, the higher the sales volume that can be sustained. Higher sales volume will result in fixed costs being shared over a greater number of units and sometimes variable costs can be reduced by bulk discounts. The learning effect may also have an impact as practice improves efficiency. The degree of mechanisation will also depend partly on the expected volumes and whether it is worthwhile to incur heavy capital costs in exchange for lower production costs. This idea is explored later when we examine the use of Discounted Cash Flow techniques.

The proportion of costs that are fixed and variable will change over the product life cycle. At the initial stages of development, launch and growth the majority of costs will be fixed costs (for example costs of design, product development and marketing). As the life cycle continues, a lower level of fixed costs will usually be needed to sustain the product through maturity as customers are aware of the product and marketing can be reduced to a certain extent.

If life cycle budgeting and costing is being used, the accounting systems of the organisation must be designed to collect the relevant information. The costs of:

- research, development and design

- production

- selling and distribution

- customer services

must be collected separately for each product over its life, rather than being split down into monthly totals, for example. Of the costing methods studied in this book, activity based costing is likely to be the most appropriate. It can be seen that the four stages listed above represent groups of activities. Each one could be broken down into a number of separate activities, each with an appropriate cost driver. A particular product could then be charged for its usage of each activity.

Once the life cycle of a product is completed, the actual costs and revenues can be compared with the life cycle budget in order to obtain information to help with future planning and decision making.

Case Study

AEROCAR PLC: LIFE CYCLE COSTING

situation

The managers of Aerocar plc are considering the possible development of a revolutionary kind of engine. The following forecasts have been made for the life cycle of this engine:

- research, development and design would take 3 years and cost £3million per year

- production and sales would take place over the following 4 years

- production costs would be £2million per year for 4 years plus £3,000 per engine

- selling and distribution costs would be £1 million per year plus £1,000 per engine

- customer services would have to continue for 6 years and would cost £1.2 million per year

- the total sales demand for the engine over the whole of its life cycle has been estimated for two possible selling prices:

    Case 1: 12,000 engines at a selling price of £7,000 each

    Case 2: 15,000 engines at a selling price of £6,000 each

required

(a) Calculate the total life cycle sales revenue at each of the possible selling prices.

(b) Calculate the total life cycle costs for:

    Case 1: 12,000 engines

    Case 2: 15,000 engines

(c) Calculate the total profit from the engine and the percentage profit on sales over its life cycle for each of the two possible selling prices.

    Hint: Set out your answer in £millions, correct to 1 decimal place.

solution

(a) Sales revenue

12,000 engines at a selling price of £7,000 each gives sales revenue of

12,000 x £7,000 = £84,000,000 or £84.0million.

15,000 engines at a selling price of £6,000 each gives sales revenue of

15,000 x £6,000 = £90,000,000 or £90.0million.

(b) Life cycle costs

Case 1: 12,000 engines

	£million	£million
Research, development and design		
£3million per year for 3 years		9.0
Production		
£2million per year for 4 years	8.0	
12,000 engines at £3,000 each	36.0	44.0
Selling and distribution		
£1 million per year for 4 years	4.0	
12,000 engines at £1,000 each	12.0	16.0
Customer services		
£1.2million per year for 6 years		7.2
		76.2

Case 2: 15,000 engines

	£million	£million
Research, development and design		
£3million per year for 3 years		9.0
Production		
£2million per year for 4 years	8.0	
15,000 engines at £3,000 each	45.0	53.0
Selling and distribution		
£1 million per year for 4 years	4.0	
15,000 engines at £1,000 each	15.0	19.0
Customer services		
£1.2million per year for 6 years		7.2
		88.2

(c) Life cycle summary and profit calculation:

Selling price per engine	£7,000	£6,000
Total sales demand	12,000	15,000
	£million	£million
Total sales revenue	84.0	90.0
Life cycle costs	76.2	88.2
Life cycle profit	7.8	1.8
Profit percentage on sales	9.3%	2.0%

Notes:

It can be seen that, according to these forecasts, the selling price of £7,000 per engine would be the more profitable option.

Suppose Aerocar plc uses target costing in conjunction with life cycle budgeting and costing, with a required profit percentage of 15% on sales. If the decision were made to use the selling price of £7,000 per engine, then the required profit would be 15% of the total sales revenue.

15% x £84million = £12.6million

Target total cost = £84million – £12.6million = £71.4million

Forecast total cost = £76.2million

The managers of Aerocar plc would have to look for £4.8million in cost reductions (the 'cost gap') in order to meet this target. They would have to bear in mind that, if they cut back on the research phase, for example, the engine might cost more to produce. New forecasts for all the costs would need to be prepared.

LIFE CYCLE COSTING AND DISCOUNTED CASH FLOW

Discounted cash flow (DCF) is a technique that can be used to help with long term decision making. It uses discount factors, which are multiplied by future cash flows, to convert the cash flows into their 'present values'. This enables fair comparisons to be made between cash flows that occur at different times. The discount factors are based on assumed interest rates or cost of capital.

The technique is explained further in the next chapter (page 204 onwards) when we look at long term decision making. At this point, we will concentrate on how DCF can be used specifically for life cycle costing.

When we use DCF to make decisions we are usually making comparisons between two situations. In order to make valid comparisons we must bring the appropriate cost figures into our calculations. These are often called relevant costs. One way to remember what costs are relevant to any decision is that they are future incremental cash flows.

This means the costs are:

- future (not those costs that have already been incurred and cannot be changed by our decision),

- incremental (these are just the extra costs or savings resulting from the decision), and

- cash flows (always ignore non-cash items like depreciation).

Sometimes we can use just one DCF calculation to make our decision. This approach often suits situations where we are deciding to simply do something or not to do it. The Case Study that follows takes this approach, and is based on developing (or not developing) a new product.

The alternative approach is to use two DCF calculations. This is useful when we want to compare doing something in one of two ways.

LIFE CYCLE PRODUCT COSTING

A company is considering developing and launching a new product into a fast moving market. The following data has been estimated, based on the project going ahead.

- Product development and testing would cost £6m immediately and a further £6m in one year's time.

- Marketing would cost £0.5m in one year's time, and a further £0.2m for each of the next two years.

- Variable unit costs would be £4, and each unit would sell for £10.

- Fixed production costs that relate only to this product would be £0.5m for each year of production. Production and sales will take place in the same year.

- The company already incurs fixed costs of £5m related to other products and these costs will continue.

- Sales will be as follows (based on the start of the project being year 0):

  Year 2   1m units

  Year 3   2m units

  Year 4   0.5m units

  There will be no sales after year 4.

The company's cost of capital is 5% and relevant discount factors are:

Year	Discount Factor
0	1.000
1	0.952
2	0.907
3	0.864
4	0.823

r e q u i r e d

Using DCF, calculate whether the new product is worthwhile. Carry out calculations in £ thousands.

solution

The cash flows and present values are set out in the following table.

Year	Details	Cash inflow £000	Cash outflow £000	Discount factor	Present value £000
0	Product development		6,000	1.000	(6,000)
1	Product development		6,000		
	Marketing		500		
	Net total year 1		6,500	0.952	(6,188)
2	Marketing		200		
	Sales Revenue	10,000			
	Variable costs		4,000		
	Fixed costs		500		
	Net total year 2	5,300		0.907	4,807
3	Marketing		200		
	Sales Revenue	20,000			
	Variable costs		8,000		
	Fixed costs		500		
	Net total year 3	11,300		0.864	9,763
4	Sales Revenue	5,000			
	Variable costs		2,000		
	Fixed costs		500		
	Net total year 4	2,500		0.823	2,057
				Net Present Value	4,439

Notice that the fixed costs that are already incurred are not relevant and are therefore not brought into the calculation. This is because they would not be altered by the decision on the new product – they remain the same regardless.

Based on the data given, the net present value is positive, so the project appears to be worthwhile.

THE IMPACT OF TECHNOLOGY

The collection and use of data for operational control is being changed by rapidly evolving technology. There are many opportunities now to use technological advances that were impossible only a decade or two ago. We will now discuss some of these processes, and see how they can benefit organisations, as well as the challenges that they present.

cloud accounting

Cloud accounting (which is also known as web-based accounting) is where the software and the data for an organisation is held remotely by an external IT provider. This means that (subject to security checks) that system can be accessed from anywhere that has internet access, and this makes working from a variety of locations (including home working) for staff more achievable. Software available will include (for example) activity based costing systems, and information should be available in real time. Cloud accounting will normally provide automatic software updates. The number of (and cost of employing) IT specialists within the organisation will be reduced.

Operating a cloud accounting system will have costs associated with it. The contract with the external IT provider could be a simple monthly subscription, or it may be based on usage of the system. However, the capital costs which would otherwise be incurred on servers and software will be avoided.

One possible implication of using cloud accounting is the security of the data being held outside of the organisation. Although IT providers will always promise total security, there have been well publicised examples in recent years of hacking and data breaches.

artificial intelligence (AI)

Artificial intelligence is based on computers 'learning' how to tackle jobs more efficiently and effectively by using the data previously gathered to improve. One common example of fairly limited (also known as 'narrow') artificial intelligence is software that is used as a search engine. By examining previous searches, the software is able to predict possible requirements of the search, and to provide the most popular results. Organisations that use their own search engines for customers to find what they are looking for can utilise software that will be able to 'know' alternative names for product groups and avoid suggestions that do not make sense. However, there are sometimes reports of online stores making bizarre substitutions to customers' shopping when the software does not work as expected.

Artificial intelligence is used in a wide range of applications, including email spam filters, manufacturing robots, image recognition and self-driving vehicles. One development that could be of use to many commercial organisations is 'chat-bots' that can interact with customer queries either online or through voice recognition. However, the frustration of customers and the loss of goodwill when such systems do not work well is something to be carefully considered before implementation.

data analytics

Data is routinely analysed by management accountants, and a large part of this unit is concerned with using data to provide useful information. This data is mainly 'structured', so is in a form that lends itself to easy analysis. For example, accounting and cost data is numerical and can be extracted through spreadsheets and other software.

Data analytics includes the analysis of 'unstructured' data, from both inside and outside the organisation. This will require more sophisticated software (possibly incorporating artificial intelligence) that can look beyond numerical data and make sense of a wider range of data. Examples of unstructured data from inside the organisation include email messages and online enquiries, as well as telephone conversations. For retail organisations it could also include data on the routes taken by shoppers through stores, and this could be linked with successful sales patterns. Outside the organisation there is a wealth of possible data ranging from vehicle traffic flows to shopping habits and online browsing.

Organisations must choose carefully what information they require in order to reach their goals. Although there are enormous strategic advantages to be gained from data analytics, there is clearly a cost to be considered. There are also ethical considerations. For example, it must be considered to what extent is it ethical (or even legal) to use face recognition technology to track customers through retail stores, or even outside in the high street. There is clearly a difference between using face recognition technology and simply using data from customer loyalty programs to offer customised promotions.

visualisation

One of the key skills related to management accountancy is the communication of information. We have become used to using simple graphs and pie charts to represent data, and the concept of visualisation takes this idea further through the use of software that can provide more sophisticated images.

A simple example would be using maps superimposed with colours representing customer data (for example frequency of orders or average spend). Graphics can be animated to show changes over time (historical and forecast) and the result presented as a short video. This is often a more engaging result than simply relying on using time as one axis on a graph.

There are many examples of visualisation available online, and the concept will become much clearer once you have examined the ways that data can be communicated visually and the huge range of options available.

Chapter Summary

- Activity based costing (ABC) is a development of absorption costing that uses activities to drive costs rather than arbitrary absorption methods. This should provide more accurate costs for pricing and decision making when used in appropriate circumstances.

- In value engineering (for new designs) and value analysis (for existing designs), the question: 'Can the same (or better) value to the user be achieved some other, cheaper way?' is asked about every part of the design. If this can be done, then:
  - the organisation should be able to increase its sales and profitability
  - customers will benefit from the availability of more efficiently designed products and services

- Target costs are calculated by starting from the chosen selling price for the product and deducting the organisation's required profit. If it proves impossible to plan costs at the target level without affecting quality, then the product is not viable at this selling price.

- When using target costing, the chosen selling price for the product may be decided by considering the market value, taking into account the market share that the producer hopes to obtain.

- Life cycle costing can be used to examine and quantify the costs throughout the life cycle stages of a product. At various stages during the life cycle the proportion of fixed and variable costs will alter considerably.

- Discounted cash flow techniques can be used in conjunction with life cycle costing. They can be used to analyse the net present value (or cost) of products.

- The impact of technology on operational control includes cloud accounting, artificial intelligence, data analytics, and visualisation.

**Key
Terms**

activity based costing	this is a development of absorption costing, and uses a more sophisticated system to deal with the indirect costs. This involves examining indirect costs to determine what causes them, and using this information to charge the costs to the units of output in an appropriate manner
value engineering	ensuring that new products or services are designed for quality but at low cost, by analysing how every part of the design enhances value
value analysis	analysing the value of every part of the design of an existing product or service, and questioning whether its function can be achieved some other way at lower cost
value added activities	those activities that create an aspect of a product or service that customers are willing to pay for
non-value added activities	wasteful activities that do not contribute to the value of the product or service
lean organisations	those organisations that have mainly eliminated non-value added activities
target costing	setting targets for costs as selling price less required profit and if necessary using cost reduction to meet the target cost
life cycle costing	accounting for the costs of a product over its entire life from the start of development to the end of customer support
cloud accounting	the use of an external IT provider to store accounting data and software, that can then be accessed remotely via the internet
artificial Intelligence	the ability of software to 'learn' from historical data to become more efficient and effective
data analytics	the analysis of structured and unstructured data from inside and outside the organisation to provide information
visualisation	the use of graphics, pictures and animation to present data for easier understanding

Activities

5.1 XYZ Ltd is considering introducing activity based costing (ABC) to replace the absorption costing system that it currently uses.

The Stores section is initially being trialled to determine what difference ABC would make to product costs compared to the current system.

The total budgeted cost of running the Stores section is £120,000 per year.

The two main activities of the Stores section have been identified as:

- Receiving goods inwards (costing £20,000 per year), and

- Issuing goods to production (costing £100,000 per year).

The cost drivers for the stores section have been agreed as:

- Number of deliveries received of 500 per year (for receiving goods)

- Number of issues to production of 500,000 per year (for issuing goods)

Two of the current products are the Simplex and the Complex, with unit costs calculated under absorption costing as follows:

	Simplex	Complex
	£	£
Total Unit Costs	70.00	145.50
Annual production	2,000 units	200 units

Under the current absorption system, the Simplex unit total costs include £5.00 overhead related to the Stores section, and the Complex total costs include £10.00.

The Simplex direct material is delivered to stores 10 times per year. This material is then issued to production 100 times per year.

The Complex direct material comes from several different suppliers, and deliveries total 200 per year. There are 1,000 issues of material per year.

Required

Calculate the rate per cost driver for receiving goods, and for issuing goods.

Calculate how much of each activity is used per year by each product.

Calculate the revised unit cost of the Simplex and the Complex by using ABC for the Stores section instead of the current method.

5.2 The following table shows activities in separate manufacturing organisations. Identify which activities add value to the end product and which are non-added value.

		Added value	Non-added value
(a)	Moving engines made in one location to another factory for installing in cars		
(b)	Holding meeting to decide on the colour of paint to use on new range of products		
(c)	Applying several coats of paint to prestige products		
(d)	Fitting strings to electric guitars by a musical instrument manufacturer		
(e)	Waiting by production workers for materials to be delivered		
(f)	Clearing waste materials away from production area		

5.3 The managers of Snaps plc expect to achieve sales next year of 25,000 units of a digital camera, the Digisnap. They have established a market price of £480 per unit. Snaps plc has a target level of 22% operating profit on sales.

Required:

Calculate:

(a) The expected total sales revenue from the Digisnap for the next year.

(b) The target operating profit required by Snaps plc from the total sales of Digisnap.

(c) The total target cost for Digisnap for the next year.

(d) The target operating profit per unit of Digisnap.

(e) The target cost per unit of Digisnap.

5.4 Delta Limited is considering designing a new product, and will use target costing to arrive at the target cost of the product. You have been given the following information and asked to calculate the target cost for materials so that the purchasing manager can use this as a target in her negotiations with suppliers.

- The price at which the product will be sold is £50

- The company has firm orders for 20,000 units at a price of £50

- The fixed costs per unit are £16 per unit

- The labour requirement is 20 minutes at a cost of £18 per hour

- The required profit margin is 40%

- The material requirement is 200 grams per unit (ie 0.2 kilogram)

(a) Calculate the target cost per kilogram for the materials component of the product.

	£
Sales price per unit	
Profit margin	
Total costs	
Fixed cost per unit	
Labour cost per unit	
Maximum material cost per unit	
Target cost per kilogram	

(b) Complete the following statement:

The trade price per kilogram quoted on the supplier's price list is £50 per kilogram. The purchasing manager has negotiated a discount of 15%. The discount should be **accepted / rejected** because the £50 reduces to £ [ ] which is **above / below** the Target cost. The cost gap is £ [ ] per kilogram.

(c) The minimum percentage discount needed to achieve the Target cost is:

[ ]

5.5 Clever Technologies Ltd is considering developing a new product. It will consist of a mobile phone charger that will use a combination of solar power and generated kinetic energy. Through wireless technology the device will enable any phone within range to be kept fully charged continually.

The following data has been collected regarding this new product.

Development costs (including creating prototypes) are expected to be £1,900,000 in each of years 0, 1 and 2.

Production unit numbers and sales numbers are planned as follows:

	Production	Sales
Year 2	50,000	0
Year 3	90,000	80,000
Year 4	100,000	110,000
Year 5	0	50,000

No production or sales are expected after year 5.

Variable costs of production are budgeted at £15 per unit. Fixed production costs are budgeted at £2,000,000 for each of the years 2 to 4.

Selling prices are planned at £70 per unit.

The company's cost of capital is 10%, and this is reflected in the discount factors given below.

Complete the following table to calculate both the non-discounted and discounted life-cycle cash flows for the product. Round to the nearest £000.

Year	Cash Inflow £000	Cash Outflow £000	Net Cash Flow £000	Discount Factor	Present Value £000
0				1.000	
1				0.909	
2				0.826	
3				0.751	
4				0.683	
5				0.621	
	Totals				

5.6 The Radical Company produces a variety of goods, according to customers' demands. Some items have been produced to the same specification for many years, while others are constantly updated to meet the needs of the consumers. Some products have long production runs, while others are produced in small batches for specific customers.

Explain whether you believe that Absorption Costing, Marginal Costing, or Activity Based Costing would appear to be most appropriate for this company.

6 Decision making techniques

this chapter covers...

This chapter starts with a summary of the key differences between short-term and long-term decision making. We then examine the costs that are relevant for decision making.

We then go on to look at short-term decisions, starting with make or buy decisions and the associated problem of product discontinuation and segment closure. We also consider similar decisions based on services instead of products.

We then consider how to deal with scarce resources, in particular:

■ *more than one constraint for a single product,*

■ *a single constraint affecting two or more products, and*

■ *the use of linear programming where there are multiple constraints affecting two products.*

The next section deals with the use of discounted cash flow and net present value calculations to appraise long-term projects. This is followed by a discussion of how other methods can also be used (payback period, discounted payback period, internal rate of return, and accounting rate of return). Calculation involving these methods is explained, along with a commentary on their strengths and weaknesses for appraisal.

SHORT-TERM AND LONG-TERM DECISION MAKING

In this chapter we are going to consider some techniques for either short-term or long-term decision making. Before we do so it is important that we can appreciate the key differences.

- **time frame**

    Short-term decisions are generally considered to be those that effect a period of up to one year, often starting almost immediately. You will probably be familiar with some of the simpler techniques, like break-even analysis, from your earlier studies. Long-term decisions are those that affect planning for several years.

- **capital investment**

    Short-term decisions will often involve little or no capital investment, and these will be operational decisions. Long-term decisions will typically involve significant capital investment, often at the start of the period, but possibly later on as well.

- **risk**

    Short-term decisions can sometimes be reversed, and they are therefore often less risky than long-term decisions. Both the timescale and the size of the capital investment mean that long-term decisions are inherently risky. They are difficult to change once set in motion, and they rely on future events that are uncertain. A key component in calculating the viability of long-term projects is the organisation's cost of capital. This can change over time, and therefore the further into the future that the decisions affect, the more chance there is that the cost of capital will alter and affect viability.

RELEVANT COSTS FOR DECISION MAKING

In this chapter we are going to examine various techniques and situations related to decision making. When looking at costs and benefits for any kind of decision making the key is to only use relevant costs (and sometimes income) in the calculations.

What is relevant will depend on the decision that is being considered, but will always be simply the costs or income that will change depending on the outcome of the decision. There is no point in thinking about costs that will be the same no matter what decision is made. For example, if a machine replacement is being considered, but both the new and the existing machines have the same maintenance costs, then these maintenance costs are not relevant to the decision.

Since relevant costs will always be those that can be affected by the decision, they must always be costs that can occur in the future. Costs that have already been incurred cannot be changed whatever is decided, and so should be ignored. These past costs that are not relevant are sometimes known as 'sunk costs'.

We must also be careful not to be swayed by notional costs, like depreciation, that are based on past activities. We are really only interested in income and costs that are based on future flows of cash.

One way to think of relevant costs is to use the idea of them being 'future incremental cash flows'. Let's look at that phrase in more detail.

Future	**not past** transactions that cannot be changed
Incremental	the **extra** cost or income that derives directly from the decision being considered
Cash flows	movements of **real money**, not notional book entries

Suppose a company has a machine that is no longer in day to day use, but is only used for special orders that occur about once a year. A decision is being made about whether to keep the machine, or to sell it and hire in a machine to deal with the special orders when necessary. Here, the only **relevant** figures are:

- the amount that the machine could be sold for, and

- the cost of hiring a machine to deal with the special orders.

Notice that both these figures pass our test of being 'future incremental cash flows'.

The following amounts are irrelevant and can be ignored for the purposes of the decision:

- original cost of the machine, since it is a sunk cost

- the depreciation being charged on the machine and it's written down value

- any costs that do not change whichever machine is used

An idea that fits neatly within this concept is opportunity cost. This is the income avoided by the course of action taken, and is a relevant cost. This means that the relevant cost that should be applied when considering using a resource is the income that could otherwise be generated from that resource. If the resource could be used in various alternative ways then the opportunity cost would be the highest amount of income that it could generate – because logically that is the best use.

For example, suppose a company has a material in stock that could be used for the project that we are trying to evaluate. There are no plans to use the material for anything else. The material originally cost £1,000, but could be returned to the supplier in exchange for £500. Alternatively, it could be sold to another organisation for £700.

In this situation, the relevant cost of using the material in the project would be £700, since this is the highest income that we would be avoiding by using the material. We would not logically choose to return it to the supplier for less than we could sell it for. The figure of £1,000 is not relevant since it is sunk cost.

The same idea could be applied to labour. If a project that is being evaluated involves taking labour away from an existing job, then the contribution that is being lost will form an opportunity cost that is part of the relevant cost.

The general concept of relevant costs fits in with the application of marginal costing, and can be applied to various situations. These will be illustrated in the rest of this chapter.

MAKE OR BUY DECISIONS

One of the situations where decisions need to be made concerns the possible outsourcing of production. This means having products made for you by an outside organisation instead of making them in-house.

If production was outsourced savings would normally be made of various manufacturing costs, but of course the cost of buying in a ready made product would be much greater than simply buying raw material. Great care must be taken to calculate which costs would be saved and which would remain.

variable costs

The general rule would be that any variable costs relating to the production that would not be taking place in-house would be saved, although any variable non-production costs (for example selling costs) would remain.

fixed costs

It is possible that some fixed costs may also be saved if they relate entirely to the production of the products to be made elsewhere. However fixed production costs that relate to several products, some of which continue to be made on site would not be saved in the short term. This is because if one product was no longer made on site these shared fixed costs would not change in total and would then need to be covered by the existing products.

other issues to consider

If a decision is to be made about outsourcing then various other commercial issues will need to be considered. These include:

- price – the agreed price must be guaranteed for an acceptable period of time, with any future increases within agreed limits
- quality – there needs to be sufficient reassurance that quality will be maintained when the production is in the control of another organisation

■ supply – the manufacturing company must be able to offer guaranteed continuity of supply and timely deliveries

■ commercial sensitivity – some products may be made to a 'secret' formula, or a company may wish to protect its brand by implying that its products are not made by anyone else

Once a decision has been made to cease manufacture of a product in-house it may be difficult to reverse in the future, especially if skilled staff and / or specialised equipment are required.

TOUCAN LIMITED: MAKE OR BUY DECISION

situation

Toucan Limited, a soft drink manufacturer, currently makes two products in its factory. The first product is 'Wings', a high energy drink, and the second is 'SSSh', a calming and relaxing drink.

The following budgeted operating statement relates to the next year, and assumes that both products will be manufactured in-house. It is based on making and selling 1,000,000 units of Wings, and 1,000,000 units of SSSh.

	£000	£000	£000
	Wings	**SSSh**	**Total**
Sales	750	500	1,250
Variable costs of production	200	230	430
Direct fixed costs of production	150	110	260
Shared fixed costs of production	150	100	250
Gross profit	250	60	310
Administration costs			80
Selling and Distribution costs			100
Operating profit			130

Consideration is being given to an option to buy in ready made SSSh units at £0.30 per unit. This would save both the variable costs of production and the direct fixed costs of production of that product. Shared fixed costs of production would remain the same in total. The number of units of SSSh sold would be unchanged.

If the decision were made to buy in the SSSh units, then the released manufacturing space could be used to increase the manufacture and sales of Wings to 1,200,000 units. The direct fixed costs of Wings production would be unchanged by this. Additional selling and distribution costs of £20,000 would be incurred by this increase in volume of Wings.

required

(a) Calculate the following data for each product, based on the current plan to manufacture both products in-house:
- Selling price per unit
- Variable production cost per unit
- Gross profit per unit

(b) Draft a revised budgeted Operating Statement, based on buying in ready-made units of SSSh and increasing the volume of Wings units made and sold.

(c) Recommend whether, on the basis of your figures, the decision should be made to buy in SSSh. Note any factors that may risk the future business remaining in line with the budget if your recommendation were to be followed.

solution

(a)

Selling price per unit

Wings	£750,000 / 1,000,000	= £0.75 per unit
SSSh	£500,000 / 1,000,000	= £0.50 per unit

Variable costs per unit

Wings	£200,000 / 1,000,000	= £0.20 per unit
SSSh	£230,000 / 1,000,000	= £0.23 per unit

Gross profit per unit

Wings	£250,000 / 1,000,000	= £0.25 per unit
SSSh	£60,000 / 1,000,000	= £0.06 per unit

(b)

Revised Operating Statement

	£000	£000	£000
	Wings	**SSSh**	**Total**
Sales	900	500	1,400
Variable costs of production / buy-in	240	300	540
Direct fixed costs of production	150		150
Shared fixed costs of production	250		250
Gross profit	260	200	460
Administration costs			80
Selling and Distribution costs			120
Operating profit			260

(c)

Recommendation

From the calculations, the total operating profit would increase from £130,000 to £260,000, and therefore the units of SSSh should be outsourced. However, factors that may make the business riskier in future include:

- whether sales of Wings can be increased by 20% as assumed
- whether the quality of SSSh can be assured
- whether the long-term continuity of supply and price of SSSh can be assured

CLOSURE OF A BUSINESS SEGMENT

The closure of an uneconomic part of a business requires careful planning. Particular attention must be paid to the cost savings that will be made, especially if there are costs which are currently apportioned to more than one part of the business. It will often be the case that all or part of these costs will continue after closure, and therefore need to be set against the income of the remaining part of the business.

If closure is undertaken then redundancy costs of employees will need to be calculated and taken into consideration. As these are a 'one-off' cost, the exact way that these are accounted for in the management accounts would depend on the company policy.

It is possible that the operation could be relocated overseas to make it more economic. This could relate to a manufacturing activity, and the products could then be transported to be sold to the same or new markets. This could either be based on outsourcing to an established foreign business, or by setting up an in-house operation in the new location.

The outsourcing model would be similar to the 'make or buy' decision that was discussed earlier in this chapter. The added risk factor would be currency exchange movements that could rapidly change or eliminate any profits.

Setting up a new operation in a foreign country would be a complicated project, although the planning would follow the normal procedures. The added complications of language, legal systems, tax and currency would have to be considered carefully.

Case Study

MINUTEMAN LIMITED: CLOSURE OF A BUSINESS SEGMENT AND MAKE OR BUY

Minuteman Limited is a watch manufacturer located in the UK. It currently manufactures two ranges of watches; a craftsman made traditional precision watch that sells to the premium market for £450, and an electronic fashion watch that is assembled from bought-in components and sells for £40.

The manager is concerned about the lack of profitability of the electronic watch division.

The current factory is used for the manufacture of both watch ranges, and there is no likelihood of another use for the part currently used for assembly of the electronic watches.

The operating statement for the last quarter was as follows:

	Premium Watch	Electronic Watch	Total
	£000	£000	£000
Sales	225	160	385
Materials and components	15	64	79
Direct labour	75	60	135
Fixed Factory Costs	45	32	77
Administration Costs	20	20	40
Selling and Distribution Costs	10	20	30
Operating Profit / (Loss)	60	(36)	24

The following information has been established:

- Materials and components and direct labour are variable costs
- Fixed factory costs relate to the whole factory, and have been apportioned based on sales value
- Administration costs are fixed costs and would remain if the electronic watches were no longer made
- Selling and distribution costs are variable costs
- Redundancy costs can be ignored
- This level of sales of both watches is expected to continue

required

CLOSURE OF A BUSINESS SEGMENT

- Restate the operating statement in a marginal costing format, showing clearly the contribution of each division to company fixed costs.

- Recommend whether the electronic watch division should be closed in the short term.

MAKE OR BUY DECISION

- The manager has obtained quotations from the Far East where these watches could be made for £15 each (including delivery). The existing variable selling and distribution costs would apply to the bought in watches.

- Prepare a budgeted operating statement in a marginal costing format based on ceasing to manufacture the electronic watches in the factory, but buying them in ready made from the Far East.

solution

CLOSURE OF A BUSINESS SEGMENT

Operating Statement – Marginal Costing Format

	Premium Watch	Electronic Watch	Total
	£000	£000	£000
Sales	225	160	385
Variable Costs:			
Materials and components	15	64	79
Direct labour	75	60	135
Selling and distribution costs	10	20	30
Contribution	125	16	141
Fixed Costs:			
Fixed Factory Costs			77
Administration Costs			40
Operating Profit / (Loss)			24

The operating statement in this format clearly shows that the electronic watch division is making a contribution to overall fixed costs of £16,000. If the electronic watches were to be discontinued the overall profit would therefore be reduced to £8,000.

MAKE OR BUY DECISION

Budgeted Operating Statement – Marginal Costing Format

	Premium Watch £000	Electronic Watch £000	Total £000
Sales	225	160	385
Variable Costs:			
Materials and components	15		15
Bought in watches		60	60
Direct labour	75		75
Selling and Distribution Costs	10	20	30
Contribution	125	80	205
Fixed Costs:			
Fixed Factory Costs			77
Administration Costs			40
Operating Profit / (Loss)			88

The contribution from the Electronic Watch Division would increase from £16,000 to £80,000. The overall profit would increase from £24,000 to £88,000.

However additional risks in terms of currency movements, price stability and quality control would need to be considered.

DECISIONS FOR SERVICES

Most of the techniques that we have just used for make or buy decisions and continue or discontinue products or divisions can also be applied to services. The following Case Study will provide an example of a 'supply or buy-in services' decision.

Case Study

MEALS FOR YOU
SUPPLY OR BUY-IN SERVICES

situation

Meals for You is a fast food outlet that currently offers both a take-away and a delivery service. The following is a summarised operating statement for the last month.

	£	£
Revenue	41,250	
Food	12,000	
Delivery	3,000	
		15,000
Fixed Costs:		
Labour	10,000	
Other	8,000	
		18,000
Operating Profit		8,250

The following information has been established about the current situation. The firm sells 1,500 orders per month, at an average price of £25 per order. Half of these are delivered by freelance drivers who are paid £1 per mile. Each delivery involves an average trip of 4 miles.

The organisation is considering changing its delivery service. It has been approached by a national company, Delivermee, who would carry out the deliveries instead of the current freelancers.

Delivermee would charge a fixed cost of £5,000 per month, plus a delivery charge of £3 per delivery. Due to the extensive advertising that Delivermee carry out, it is estimated that the number of orders placed for delivery would increase by 20%, without affecting the number of take away orders. The current labour employed by 'Meals For You' (shown as a fixed cost) would be able to manage the additional orders. The delivery charge made to customers would be unchanged from the current level per order.

required

Complete the two following tables, analysing the revenue and costs into 'Food Sales' (take away and delivered) and 'Delivery Service' based on (1) the current position, and (2) the position if the contract with Delivermee is taken up. Comment briefly on whether the contract with Delivermee should be taken up.

(1) Current Position   Monthly Operating Statement

	Total £	Food Sales £	Delivery Service £
Revenue			
Variable Costs			
Food			
Delivery			
Fixed Costs			
Labour			
Other			
Operating Profit			

(2) Proposed Position   Monthly Operating Statement

	Total £	Food Sales £	Delivery Service £
Revenue			
Variable Costs			
Food			
Delivery			
Fixed Costs			
Labour			
Other			
Operating Profit			

solution

(1) Current Position   Monthly Operating Statement

	Total £	Food Sales £	Delivery Service £
Revenue	41,250	37,500	3,750
Variable Costs			
Food	12,000	12,000	
Delivery	3,000		3,000
Fixed Costs			
Labour	10,000	10,000	
Other	8,000	8,000	
Operating Profit	8,250	7,500	750

Notes on workings

Food Sales Revenue   1,500 orders x £25 = £37,500

Delivery Service Revenue   £41,250 – £37,500 = £3,750. Equivalent to £5 per order, based on 1,500 / 2 = 750 orders delivered

(2) Proposed Position   Monthly Operating Statement

	Total £	Food Sales £	Delivery Service £
Revenue	45,750	41,250	4,500
Variable Costs			
Food	13,200	13,200	
Delivery	2,700		2,700
Fixed Costs			
Labour	15,000	10,000	5,000
Other	8,000	8,000	
Operating Profit	6,850	10,050	–3,200

Notes on workings

Food Sales Revenue	(1,500 + (750 x 20%)) = 1,650 orders x £25 = £41,250
Delivery Service Revenue	(750 x 120%) = 900 orders x £5 delivery charge = £4,500

Comments

The contract with Delivermee should not be taken up. Although the variable costs per delivery are cheaper (£3 compared with £4), the additional fixed monthly charge of £5,000 makes the proposition unviable. The additional sales generated by the contract do not provide sufficient additional contribution to cover this monthly charge.

We will now use a further Case Study that illustrates how relevant revenues and costs can be used to decide whether to discontinue a service.

Case Study

ALLSERVE LTD: DISCOUNTINUE SERVICE DECISION

situation

Allserve Ltd has a high street premises where it offers a range of services, including shoe repairs, key cutting and dry cleaning.

One of the services that it provides is a photographic printing service to produce large high-quality prints from digital cameras and smart phones. Each large print has a sales price of £1, and it has variable costs in the form of photographic paper and inks.

The specialist printing machine that carries out the printing is leased from Kadoc, and the lease has a renewal clause that needs to be decided upon. If the lease is renewed for a further year, the lease charge will be £500 per month. If the lease is not renewed there will a termination charge payable by Allserve Ltd of three months' normal lease charge.

There has been a gradual decline in the sales of prints over the last few years, as more customers carry out printing at home, or keep their pictures in digital format. It is forecast that the coming year would see sales of a total of 3,000 prints. After that the demand is expected to be minimal.

Allserve Ltd currently owns photographic paper and inks that originally cost £400 when it bought them from Kadoc. If the contract is renewed these supplies will be sufficient for 2,000 prints, and a further £200 will need to be spent for the remaining 1,000 prints forecast. If the contract with Kadoc is not renewed it will have no use for the current supplies, but it could sell them back to Kadoc for £180.

required

Show a comparison of relevant revenues and costs if the lease contract is renewed or cancelled.

Comment briefly on the result of the calculations.

solution

Renew Lease Contract		Cancel Lease Contract	
	£		£
Sales Revenue	3,000	Sale of Supplies	180
Additional Supplies	−200	Termination Fee	−1,500
Lease Costs	−6,000		
Net Cost	**−3,200**	**Net Cost**	**−1,320**

Although both options have a net cost, the cancellation of the contract has the lower net cost, and therefore the lease should be cancelled.

LIMITING FACTOR DECISIONS

You may need to deal with situations where production is reduced because of one or more 'limiting factors'. These could be, for example:

- shortage of materials – a short or longer term issue that may restrict production; tactics for dealing with this situation range from changing supplier to using up inventories, or even changing the product that is being made

- shortage of labour – this could restrict production, especially if the labour force is skilled; this could be tackled by overtime working, subcontracting or outsourcing

- limited production capacity – based on the size or maximum throughput of the organisation's manufacturing plant; while long-term solutions include outsourcing or investing in property and equipment, short-term issues can sometimes be resolved by shift working or manipulating inventory levels

Dealing with one factor alone is relatively straightforward if there is only one product, and a given scenario should contain clear information on the calculations required. The next two topics to examine are:

- more than one constraint for a single product

- product choice when there is one limiting factor

dealing with a combination of limitations

There may be occasions when there is a limit on not just one resource, but a combination of two or more. This can also form the basis for an examination task, so you should make sure that you are able to carry out the necessary calculations.

The first technique that we are going to use here is quite logical. We will calculate which one of the limitations on our output is going to limit production most severely, and concentrate on that problem.

For example, if we originally planned to make 5,000 units, but find that we only have sufficient labour for 4,800 units, and enough materials for 4,000 units, then materials is the most pressing problem. It would not make sense to bring in temporary staff while there was still a material shortage. If we can solve the material shortage problem, only then should we turn our attention to the labour limitation. The issue that most constrains the output (as materials does in this example) is sometimes known as the binding constraint.

Later in this chapter we will examine the use of linear programming to deal with the problem of multiple scarce resources.

product choice when there are limited resources

The next situation that we must be able to deal with when there are limited resources concerns selecting the most profitable products. The situation arises when it was originally planned to make a number of different products, but a shortage of some resource now makes the plan impossible. The resource that is preventing normal output is known as the limiting factor. The most common limiting factors are either materials or labour.

What we must do in these circumstances is calculate which of our products gives us the most profitable use of the limited resources. The technique relies on marginal costing techniques, and even if the data is provided in a different form, you must first identify the variable costs for each product.

The full procedure to be adopted is as follows:

- Using marginal costing, calculate the contribution per unit that each different product generates. This is carried out by subtracting the variable costs per unit from the selling price per unit. Fixed costs are ignored.

- Identify the resource that is in short supply (the limiting factor), and how much of that resource is needed to make one unit of each different product. Divide the contribution per unit already calculated by the quantity of limited resource required to make a unit. This gives the contribution per unit of limiting factor.

- Rank the possible products according to the value of the contribution per unit of limiting factor. Starting with the product ranked highest, schedule the production so that the expected demand is met for this product. Then schedule the next highest-ranking product, and so on until the limited resources are used up.

The procedure is based on the idea of opportunity cost. By concentrating on the products that have the highest contribution per unit of limited resource we are ensuring that the opportunity cost is minimised. This is because we are continually avoiding income from less profitable uses of that resource.

This technique will ensure that the quantities of different products manufactured will make the most profit from the limited resources. This does mean that some products will be made in reduced quantities, or not made at all. This will leave the demand from some customers unsatisfied, and the technique does not address any further implications of this policy. For example, a customer of a product that may have production suspended could also be a valuable customer of other products. Suspension of manufacture could result in the customer cancelling their orders and finding an alternative supplier for all their requirements.

The two Case Studies that follow show how the technique is used to schedule production so that the profit from using limited resources is maximised.

**Case
Study**

THE THREE COUNTIES COMPANY:
CONTRIBUTION PER UNIT OF LIMITING FACTOR

The Three Counties Company manufactures three products, each using the same material. The budget data for quarter 2 (the next quarter) is as follows. (There is no budgeted finished goods inventory at the beginning or end of any quarter.)

Product	Demand	Costs per unit		
	(units)	Materials	Labour	Overheads
Gloucester	10,000	£25.00	£30.00	£60.00
Worcester	15,000	£50.00	£30.00	£60.00
Hereford	12,000	£15.00	£20.00	£40.00

The material costs £5.00 per kilo. Due to its short shelf life it must be used in the period that it is bought. The labour force is employed on a fixed contract that entitles them to a weekly pay of £350 for a guaranteed 40-hour week. The contract prohibits any overtime working. The overheads are a fixed cost.

The Gloucester sells for £125 per unit, the Worcester for £150 per unit, and the Hereford for £90 per unit.

It has just been discovered that there is a limit on the quantity of material that can be purchased in quarter 2 of 180,000 kilos.

required

Produce a revised production budget in units for quarter 2 that maximises profit.

solution

Since the labour force is paid a guaranteed week, the cost of labour behaves as a fixed cost in this Case Study. Because overheads are also fixed, the only variable cost is material. This gives contributions per unit calculations as follows:

	Gloucester	Worcester	Hereford
	£	£	£
Selling Price per unit	125	150	90
less variable costs	25	50	15
contribution per unit	100	100	75

The quantity of material used for each product can be calculated by dividing the cost of material for a unit by the cost per kilo of £5.00. This quantity is then used to calculate the contribution per kilo of material (the limiting factor).

	Gloucester	Worcester	Hereford
Quantity of material per unit	5 kg	10 kg	3 kg
Contribution per kilo of material	£100 / 5	£100 / 10	£75 / 3
	= £20	= £10	= £25
Ranking	2	3	1

The ranking is derived directly from the contribution per kilo of material. Note that this ranking is different from both the contribution per unit and from the profit per unit if calculated under absorption costing. We now use the ranking to produce up to the demand level of first the Hereford, followed by the Gloucester, and finally the Worcester, using up the material until there is none left.

Product	Ranking	Production (units)	Material Required (kilos)		
Hereford	1	12,000	12,000 x 3 kg	=	36,000
Gloucester	2	10,000	10,000 x 5 kg	=	50,000
Worcester	3	9,400*	9,400 x 10 kg	=	94,000
					180,000

* The quantity of Worcester that can be produced is calculated as follows: First, the remaining quantity of material is calculated in kilos:

(180,000 – 36,000 – 50,000 = 94,000)

Then the number of units of Worcester that can be produced with that material is calculated: (94,000 kg / 10 kg each unit = 9,400 units).

In the next Case Study we will see how labour can be a limiting factor, and how we will tackle the problem.

THE TWO CITIES COMPANY:
CONTRIBUTION PER UNIT OF LIMITING FACTOR

The Two Cities Company manufactures two products, each using the same material and the same direct labour force.

The original budget data for month 6 is as follows. There is no budgeted finished goods inventory at the beginning or end of any month.

Product	Demand	Costs per unit		
	(units)	Materials	Labour	Overheads
Bristol	2,000	£70.00	£18.00	£80.00
Cardiff	2,500	£60.00	£12.00	£40.00

The material costs £10.00 per kilo. The labour force is paid on an hourly basis at £6 per hour, and can be called in to work as appropriate. They have no minimum agreed working week, and will be sent home if there is no work available. Because of the nature of the contract there is no overtime premium payable. The overheads are a fixed cost.

The Bristol sells for £178 per unit, and the Cardiff for £150 per unit.

Following negotiations with the company management regarding conditions of employment, a number of the direct labour workers have decided to withdraw their labour. This leaves a reduced number of employees willing to work normally. It is estimated that the maximum number of working hours available from those working normally is 7,100 hours in month 6.

required

Produce a revised production budget in units for month 6 that maximises profit.

solution

Due to the conditions under which the labour force operates, the labour cost behaves as a variable cost. The material cost is also a variable cost, since it will always vary in proportion to production levels. Note that even though there is no shortage of material, its cost is still used to determine the contribution figures. This gives contributions per unit calculations as follows:

	Bristol	Cardiff
	£	£
Selling price per unit	178	150
less variable costs:		
materials	70	60
labour	18	12
contribution per unit	90	78

The amount of labour time used for each product can be calculated by dividing the cost of labour for a unit by the labour hourly rate of £6.00. The direct labour time

is then used to calculate the contribution per hour of direct labour (the limiting factor).

	Bristol	**Cardiff**
Labour time per unit	3 hours	2 hours
Contribution per direct labour hour	£90 / 3 = £30	£78 / 2 = £39
Ranking	2	1

We now use the ranking to produce up to the demand level of first the Cardiff, followed by the Bristol, using up the labour hours until there is none left.

Product	Ranking	Production (units)	Labour Hours Required		
Cardiff	1	2,500	2,500 x 2 hours	=	5,000
Bristol	2	700	700 x 3 hours	=	2,100
					7,100

This results in the following contribution:

Product	Production (units)	Contribution per unit	Total contribution
Cardiff	2,500	£78	£195,000
Bristol	700	£90	£63,000
			£258,000

LIMITING FACTORS AND BUY-IN DECISIONS

We saw earlier in this chapter how we can use relevant costs to help with make or buy decisions, and we have just learned how to rank products when there is a limited resource.

Sometimes we may have a situation where, as well as a limiting resource, we have the option to buy-in some finished products. This would often be a way of managing the limited resource, because buying in a finished product would avoid using our own manufacturing resources.

Typically, buying in finished goods in these circumstances, will generate a lower contribution than making in-house. The object will be to minimise the lost contribution, and we do this by calculating the lost contribution per unit of the limiting factor. This shows us the cost we will incur for every unit of limited resource that we avoid using.

The technique has similarities to the limited resource calculations that we have just used. It also provides a ranking that we can use to plan production, and the number of units to buy in.

We will now extend the last Case Study to demonstrate how to carry out this process.

Case Study

THE TWO CITIES COMPANY: LIMITING FACTOR AND BUY-IN DECISIONS

The Two Cities Company manufactures two products, each using the same material and labour force, as explained earlier. The data shown earlier remains valid.

Following the information about the limited number of 7,100 labour hours available in month 6, the company has found another company that could make either or both the current products. The buy-in price would be £163 per unit for the Bristol, and £120 per unit for the Cardiff.

required

Produce a further revised plan that shows the manufacture of each product, together with any items bought in ready-made, and the total contribution.

solution

The first stage is to calculate the lost contribution from buying in each product compared with making in-house. This can then be used to calculate the lost contribution per labour hour avoided, and to rank the products for buy-in purposes.

	Bristol	Cardiff
Selling Price per unit	£178	£150
Buy-in Price per unit	£163	£120
Contribution per unit (buy-in)	£15	£30
Contribution per unit (make)	£90	£78
Lost contribution (cost) to buy-in	£75	£48
Hours of labour per unit avoided	3	2
Lost contribution per labour hour	£25	£24
Ranking (lowest is best)	2	1

This shows that buying in units of Cardiff will be more beneficial than buying in units of Bristol to avoid using the limited resource of labour hours.

We can now construct a plan for units to make and buy-in. We will use our labour hours to first manufacture units of Bristol (because these are less beneficial to buy-in), and then use any remaining hours to make units of Cardiff. Any shortfall will be filled with buy-in units.

	Units	Labour Hours	Contribution / unit	Total Contribution
Bristol (make)	2,000	6,000	£90	£180,000
Cardiff (make)	550*	1,100	£78	£42,900
Cardiff (buy)	1,950	-	£30	£58,500
		7,100		£281,400

*The 1,100 labour hours remaining after making units of Bristol, is sufficient to make 550 units of Cardiff, based on 2 hours per unit.

Notice that although this version of the Case Study reduces the contribution from making products in house (compared with the original plan), the overall total contribution of £281,400 exceeds the total of £258,000 calculated when there was no option to buy in.

USING LINEAR PROGRAMMING

When we have a situation where there are two products and two or more limited resources, we can use linear programming to help us to work out the optimum production plan to maximise contribution.

Linear programming involves representing data by a straight line either on a graph or in formulas. The assumptions that are necessary to use this technique to manage limited resources are:

- the contribution per unit of each product remains the same regardless of volume produced
- the amount of resources per unit of each product remains the same regardless of volume produced
- the resources used and units produced are divisible.

This third point means that we may get solutions incorporating fractions of a unit, which in the real world are not possible. We may therefore have to adjust our answers very slightly to make sure that they work in whole numbers without exceeding the maximum resources.

Using linear programming can be a little complicated, so we will work through an example, explaining as we go. It can be carried out by using a graph, or by using simultaneous equations. This example will use both methods.

worked example

A company makes two products, the Aye and the Bee, both using the same materials and labour. For the next period, the total material is limited to 5,050 kilos, and the labour is limited to 3,000 hours. There is no limit on the demand for the Aye or the Bee. The company wishes to maximise the total contribution from the products.

The unit data for the products is as follows:

		Aye		Bee
		£		£
Selling price		113		105
Materials	(4 kilos)	20	(5 kilos)	25
Labour	(3 hours)	45	(2 hours)	30
Unit contribution		48		50

The first step is to calculate the contribution per kilo of material and per labour hour for each product, as follows:

	Aye	Bee
Contribution per kilo of material	£48 / 4 = £12	£50 / 5 = £10
Contribution per labour hour	£48 / 3 = £16	£50 / 2 = £25

We can see that Aye has the higher contribution per kilo of material, but Bee has the higher contribution per labour hour. Therefore, we will need to use linear programming to decide the best production combination. If the same product had the highest contribution per kilo of material and per labour hour, then we would simply make as many as possible of that product, and none of the other.

The total contribution that we need to maximise can be expressed as 48A + 50B where A is the number of Ayes, and B is the number of Bees, and they are multiplied by their unit contributions. We will come back to this idea later in the example.

graphical method

Using the same letters, the material constraint can be expressed as

4A + 5B = 5,050 kilos

This is using the number of units multiplied by the material needed per unit.

Using this equation:

If we did not make any units of A, then A = 0, and B = 5,050 / 5 =1,010 units

If we did not make any units of B, then B = 0, and A = 5,050 / 4 =1,262 units rounded

This gives us two points between which we can draw a straight line on a graph. This is the line that represents the material constraint.

If we take the same approach with the labour hours constraint, we get the equation

3A + 2B = 3,000 hours

Similarly, using this equation:

If we did not make any units of A, then A = 0, and B = 3,000 / 2 =1,500 units

If we did not make any units of B, then B = 0, and A = 3,000 / 3 =1,000 units

This gives us another two points between which we can draw a further straight line on a graph. This is the line that represents the labour constraint.

The graph would then look as follows:

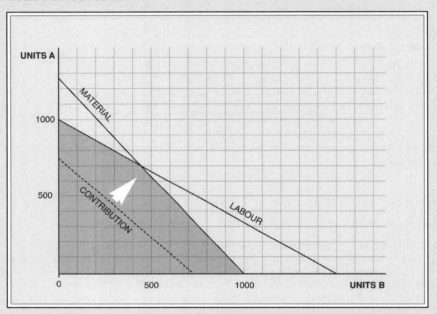

The shaded area on the graph shows the possible combinations of production for A and B. The point where the two constraint lines cross will give us the optimum position, where contribution is maximised.

We can see from the graph that the point where the lines cross is equivalent to about 700 Ayes and 450 Bees. The answer using the graphical method will depend on how clear and accurate the graph is.

We can confirm that the point where the lines cross is the maximum contribution by using a contribution line. This can be based on an assumed total contribution. The dotted line on the graph shows the total contribution of £36,000, but a different number could have been chosen. This is using the total contribution equation that we created at the beginning of the example.

48A + 50B = 36,000.

This gives us points of   A = 0 and B = 720,

and   B = 0 and A = 750

It is the gradient of this line that is important. We now imagine moving this line in the direction of the arrow, but still keeping the same gradient. We will see that the furthest it can go, with at least some of the line in the shaded area is when it touches the point where the two constraints cross.

This can be important where there are more than two constraints, and so there is more than one point where lines cross. Then using the contribution line gradient will determine where the optimum point is.

simultaneous equations method

The same result can be arrived at by using simultaneous equations to find the point where the two constraint lines cross. This avoids any inaccuracy from reading data from a graph, but it can sometimes lead to answers that are not in whole numbers, so need adjusting.

The material constraint was earlier shown as $4A + 5B = 5,050$

and the labour constraint as $\qquad$ $3A + 2B = 3,000$

To find the point where the lines cross, we must use these equations together. If we multiply the materials equation by 2, and the labour equation by 5, each equation is still valid, but we can now easily deduct one from the other.

Material equation x 2 gives $\qquad$ $8A + 10B = 10,100$

Labour equation x 5 gives $\qquad$ $15A + 10B = 15,000$

Deducting the first from the second: $\quad 7A = 4,900$

Therefore $A = 4,900 / 7 = 700$

If we then use $A = 700$ in either equation we can find B.

Using the labour equation: $\qquad (3 \times 700) + 2B = 3,000$

Therefore $B = (3,000 - 2,100) / 2 \qquad = 450.$

This is telling us that we should produce **700 Ayes and 450 Bees** to maximise total contribution, as follows:

	Production (units)	Materials (kilos)	Labour (hours)	Contribution £
Ayes	700	2,800	2,100	33,600
Bees	450	2,250	900	22,500
Total	1,150	5,050	3,000	56,100

This is the same answer that we estimated from the graph. This solution works perfectly to use up all the resources, and it does not need any adjustment due to rounding.

The example that we have just used to demonstrate linear programming is quite comprehensive, but you should be aware that the technique could also deal with the following further complications:

- there may be more than two scarce resources to deal with – for example limited material, limited labour, and limited machine time. This would be demonstrated by an additional constraint line on the graph, and it could make the shape of the feasible area more complicated. In this case the line representing the total contribution should be used to determine which intersection of lines would maximise contribution.

- there could also be a maximum limit on the number of one of the products being considered (or possibly both). This would be shown on the graph as a vertical or horizontal line, which may reduce the feasible area.

TECHNIQUES USING DISCOUNTED CASH FLOW (DCF)

We looked briefly at discounted cash flow (DCF) in the last chapter when we applied it to life cycle costing. Here, we will explain the technique in further detail, so that we can apply it to other long-term decisions.

DCF is used to help with long-term decision making, by taking account of the 'time-value' of money when comparing cash flows. It works by using factors to multiply by the actual future cash flows to convert them into 'present value' cash flows. Once all future cash flows have been converted into their equivalent present values, they can be added or subtracted from each other since they are all now comparable.

The logic of DCF is that future incoming cash flows have less value than current ones because we have to wait to receive the money. If we had received it immediately then it could have been invested to grow in value. For example, £751 invested now at 10% interest per year would grow to £1,000 after 3 years. This calculation is based on compound interest – check the figures yourself. In the language of DCF we would say that £1,000 in 3 years' time has a 'present value' of £751.

The further into the future the cash flow occurs (and the greater the assumed interest rate) the greater the difference between the actual future cash flow and its present value. We would be provided with 'discount factors' to convert the cash flows into present values. For example the discount factor for three years based on 10% is 0.751, and for five years at the same rate is 0.621. The interest rate used for discount factors is often the cost of capital to the organisation.

We use the term 'net present value' to describe the net result of comparing the present values of all the relevant future cash flows – deducting negative flows from positive ones. If the result is positive, this shows that even after taking account of the 'time-value' of the cash flows, the incoming flows are greater than the outgoing flows. This usually means that the situation or project that the figures are based on is worthwhile.

Now we will use a fairly simple Case Study to demonstrate how DCF works.

Case Study

SOLAR SAVINGS:
CALCULATING NET PRESENT VALUE

situation

A company is considering installing solar panels on the roof of a block of flats that it is building to provide hot water for all the tenants. The solar panels will cost £30,000 to purchase and install, and have an expected useful life of 6 years. The total received from tenants would increase from the normal rental income of £45,000 per year to £52,400 per year if they were to be supplied with solar powered hot water. The company's cost of capital is 10%, and this rate is to be used for the DCF calculation.

required

Using the following discount factors, calculate whether the installation of solar panels is likely to be worthwhile.

Year	Discount factor
1	0.909
2	0.826
3	0.751
4	0.683
5	0.621
6	0.564

solution

Year	Detail	Cash flow £	Discount factor	Present value £
0	Purchase and installation	(30,000)	1.000	(30,000)
1	Increased	7,400	0.909	6,727
2	receipts from	7,400	0.826	6,112
3	tenants	7,400	0.751	5,557
4		7,400	0.683	5,054
5		7,400	0.621	4,595
6		7,400	0.564	4,174
Net Present Value				2,219

The net present value of £2,219 is positive, so the installation of solar panels appears worthwhile based on these figures.

When using DCF to make a comparison – for example automation or no automation, we can:

- ignore costs that are the same in both cases
- ignore non-cash costs like depreciation
- include both capital and revenue receipts and payments

We can use a further Case Study to illustrate the techniques.

Case Study

EDDY'S READIES:
DISCOUNTED CASH FLOW AND AUTOMATION

situation

Eddy's Readies Limited makes a range of prepared meals that are ready to be heated and eaten. The operation is currently labour intensive, and a large number of people are employed to prepare the meals in the factory, using traditional cooking techniques. These employees are brought in to work according to demand, and are therefore treated as a variable cost.

The manager has been investigating the purchase of automated production line equipment that would eliminate the need for the majority of employees. The purchase and installation of the equipment would cost £1,000,000, and would be depreciated at £200,000 per year.

The following income statement is based on the next year's operation, assuming the current working practices, and production of 1 million meals.

	£000
Sales	3,950
less:	
variable material cost	1,800
variable labour cost	700
Contribution	1,450
less:	
fixed production costs	150
fixed administration costs	320
Operating profit	980

The net operating assets of the business are currently £1,500,000.

If the automated production line is installed:

- labour costs will reduce to £250,000 per year, regardless of the production level

- fixed production costs will increase by £160,000 per year, in addition to the depreciation expense

- other costs will be unchanged

The company's cost of capital is 5%, and discount factors over the five year life of the project are as follows:

Year	Discount factor 5%	Year	Discount factor 5%
0	1.00	3	0.864
1	0.952	4	0.823
2	0.907	5	0.784

The automated production line will be paid for immediately and have no value at the end of the five year project. Assume that sales and costs remain at the same level for each of the five years, and occur at the end of each year.

required

Using the following table, calculate the net present value of the automation project.

Year	Cash outflow £000	Cash savings £000	Discount factor	Present value £000
0				
1				
2				
3				
4				
5				
	Net Present Value			

solution

Working:

Annual cash savings	Labour £700,000 – £250,000	£450,000
	Less additional production costs	£160,000
	Net cash savings	£290,000

Year	Cash outflow £000	Cash savings £000	Discount factor	Present value £000
0	1,000		1.000	(1,000)
1		290	0.952	276
2		290	0.907	263
3		290	0.864	251
4		290	0.823	239
5		290	0.784	227
	Net Present Value			256

The net present value is a positive amount of £256,000, which means that based on these figures the automation project appears to be worthwhile.

Note that in the calculation only cash figures which arise directly from the decision to automate (or not) are used. The Case Study therefore provided lots of data that was not needed for this technique. You may need to carefully select the data that you need to use in a DCF calculation.

FURTHER LONG-TERM APPRAISAL METHODS

We have examined discounted cash flow and how it can be used to appraise long-term projects using the calculation of net present value. We will now look at some other appraisal methods and see how useful they are.

payback period

This is the simplest method of appraisal. It uses the same actual cash flows as are used in the DCF method, and simply asks 'how long will it take to get the initial investment back?'. The answer is worked out by adding together the cash inflows from the first year going forward until the cumulative total reaches the amount invested. The assumption is that the quicker the return, the better.

To give a simple example, a business is considering a project that will involve an initial investment of £20,000. The cash inflows are expected as follows:

Year 1   £4,000

Year 2   £6,000

Years 3 to 6 £5,000 per year

The payback period would be 4 years, based on (£4,000 + £6,000 + £5,000 + £5,000).

If the figures did not work out exactly, then the last year could be expressed as a fraction of a year.

For example, a business is considering a project that will involve an initial investment of £20,000. The cash inflows are expected to be £6,000 per year for years 1 to 6.

The payback period could be expressed as roughly 3 years + 1/3 year, based on (£6,000 + £6,000 + £6,000 + (£6,000/3)).

Payback is quite a common method of initial appraisal in the business world, since it is easy to understand. It emphasises that a quick payback reduces risk, based on the idea that the longer projects go on, the riskier it is.

There are, however, many disadvantages to using payback, particularly if it is not used in combination with other appraisal techniques:

■ it ignores the time-value of money, and it treats early inflows the same as late inflows, provided they are within the payback period.

■ it ignores any cash flows outside the payback period. For example, two projects that both had a payback of four years would be considered of equal value, but one may have no cash inflows after the fourth year and the other may have cash inflows for several more years.

■ it does not distinguish between projects requiring a large investment and those needing only a small outlay, making some comparisons difficult.

discounted payback period

Discounted payback operates in a similar way to the non-discounted version just discussed. Instead of using the actual cash figures, it uses the cash figures after discounting by using a discount factor based on the organisation's cost of capital. It therefore uses the same figures that are used to calculate net present value.

Discounted payback therefore takes account of the time-value of money. However, the remaining disadvantages of the normal payback method still apply to this method.

internal rate of return (IRR)

The internal rate of return (IRR) is the discount rate that, when applied to a project, results in a net present value (NPV) of zero. It can be thought of as the 'break-even' percentage cost of capital. This helps to give us an understanding of the riskiness of a project should interest rates rise.

Establishing the IRR can be achieved by calculating the NPV at a variety of different costs of capital (discount %s). When a pair of percentages are found, one that gives a positive NPV, and the other a negative NPV, then the IRR must be in between these two rates.

The closer the two rates are, the more accurately we can estimate the IRR. For example, if we obtain a positive NPV using 10%, but a negative one when using 25%, then we know the IRR must be in between, but any estimate will be rather inaccurate. Alternatively, if we obtain a positive NPV using 15% and a negative one using 20%, an estimate will be much more accurate.

The technique to estimate the IRR between two rates is known as interpolation. Although plotting NPV against discount % on a graph gives a slightly curved line, the way we estimate the IRR assumes that the line is straight (i.e. it assumes 'linearity'). This is why we can only obtain an estimate, and that the closer the points on the curve that are chosen, the closer the estimated straight line will be to the curve. The formula to calculate the IRR may be presented using various letters. We will first show it using words, and then show a version using letters. You may prefer one format over the other.

IRR = Low % Rate + (NPV using Low % Rate / NPV difference) x % Rate Difference

Using the following letters, we will then restate the formula.

A = low discount % rate

B = high discount % rate

C = NPV using low discount % rate

D = NPV using high discount % rate

IRR = A + ((C / (C – D)) x (B – A)

Although the formula may look complicated, it is simply using the known NPVs and discount rates to estimate where the IRR will occur between the two rates.

worked example

The following table shows the cash flows from a project, together with the present values using discount rates of 15% and 20%.

Year	Cash Flow £	Discount 15%	Discounted Cash Flow	Discount 20%	Discounted Cash Flow
0	−88,000	1.000	−88,000	1.000	−88,000
1	+30,000	0.870	+26,100	0.833	+24,990
2	+35,000	0.756	+26,460	0.694	+24,290
3	+35,000	0.658	+23,030	0.579	+20,265
4	+35,000	0.572	+20,020	0.482	+16,870
Net present values			+7,610		−1,585

Inserting the data into the formula gives the following:

IRR = 15% + (7,610 / 9,195) x 5%

IRR = 19.1% approximately

One issue to be careful about is that the difference between the NPVs is

(7,610 − (−1,585)), which is the same as (7,610 + 1,585) = 9,195

The internal rate of return is useful because it can be compared with the organisation's cost of capital and provide an easy to understand percentage difference. It can also be thought of as the maximum cost of capital at which the project would be (just) viable.

Using the interpolation method can only ever give an estimate, but it is normally accurate enough for comparison purposes, both with the organisation's cost of capital and with alternative projects.

Unlike the payback method, it takes account of all the cash flows, and it also takes account of the time-value of money.

One disadvantage is that it does not distinguish between projects needing a large investment and those requiring only a small amount. It does not provide the same result as the accounting rate of return (considered next), and this can lead to confusion.

accounting rate of return (ARR)

Unlike all the appraisal methods examined so far, the accounting rate of return (ARR) is based on accounting profits, not cash flows. The accounting rate of return is also known as the return on investment, and it is equivalent to the return on capital employed of a project.

The formula for calculating the ARR is:

(Average annual accounting profits / investment) x 100%

Note that the average accounting profit is based on the **profits after depreciation charges** – remember that depreciation is ignored in the other appraisal methods, which are cash-based.

The investment figure used can be either:

- the initial investment, or

- the average investment

Be careful that you follow any guidance as to which version of ARR you are asked to use.

The average investment, where the project has no final or scrap value, will normally be **half of the initial investment.** This is because the investment is diminishing each year, as the non-current assets are depreciated, and will reach zero at the end of the project. The average investment will therefore be half-way between the initial investment and zero. If there is a projected scrap value at the end of the project, then this will be added to the initial investment, and half of the total calculated.

---

worked example

A project is expected to last five years, with an initial investment of £100,000, and no residual value. The annual profits are expected to be as follows:

Annual revenue	£65,000
Annual Depreciation	£20,000
Other Annual Costs	£25,000
Annual Profit	£20,000

The average investment would be £100,000 / 2 = £50,000.

ARR = (£20,000 / £50,000) x 100% = 40%

If the annual profits were not identical, then the average would be calculated by totalling them, and then dividing by the number of years.

You will see that the accounting rate of return takes a totally different approach to the other methods that we have examined. It does not take account of the time-value of money, but it does incorporate every years' results (unlike payback).

Due to its similarity with return on capital employed (ROCE), it is widely understood, and is popular with some managers. It can help understanding of whether a new project could be incorporated into a business, by comparing the project's ARR with the existing ROCE (or target ROCE) of the business.

comparison of methods

The following table summarises the main features of each of the appraisal methods that we have examined. You may wish to discuss some of these points further, and then you can consider which are the most important.

	Payback Period	Discounted Payback Period	Net Present Value (NPV)	Internal Rate of Return (IRR)	Accounting Rate of Return (ARR)
Simple to calculate	✔				✔
Easy to understand	✔				✔
Uses cash flows	✔	✔	✔	✔	
Favours quick returns	✔	✔	✔	✔	
Uses accounting profits					✔
Includes all years' results			✔	✔	✔
Uses time-value of money		✔	✔	✔	
Result is comparable with cost of capital				✔	
Result is comparable with ROCE					✔

Chapter Summary

■ Decision making is often carried out by examining relevant costs. These are the financial changes that arise directly out of the decision being considered.

■ Short-term decision making calculations focus on maximising total contribution or total profits after deducting relevant costs. We can ignore the timing of receipts and payments in our work because there will be no significant differences in timing between the cash flows. We can also treat the receipts and payments as being estimated with equal accuracy. With long-term decisions we can't use the same approach, £1 received today is not of equal value to £1 received in five years time and an estimate of sales this year is much more likely to be accurate than an estimate for four years in the future. So we use a range of techniques to evaluate long-term decisions which reflect the different risks.

■ Make or buy decisions involve using marginal costing to examine all costs and establish which ones would remain if the goods were outsourced. Other non-financial issues would also need to be considered.

■ Discontinuation of a product or a business segment also uses relevant costs, as do problems regarding services.

■ Scarce resources can be dealt with by considering the binding constraint, ranking according to contribution per limited factor, or by using linear programming.

■ Discounted cash flow net present value is a valuable tool for appraising long-term decisions. Other methods include payback period, discounted payback, internal rate of return, and accounting rate of return. Each method has strengths and drawbacks.

Key Terms	**relevant cost**	a cost that arises directly from a decision; these are often future incremental cash flows
	contribution	the difference between sales and variable costs; this can be calculated per period or per unit
	linear programming	a technique that can be used to maximise contribution when there are two products and multiple constraints
	net present value	the net result of cash inflows and outflows at different points in time, converted into present value terms by using discount factors
	net present cost	the net result of cash inflows and outflows at different points in time, converted into present cost terms by using discount factors; net present cost is always a net outflow
	cost of capital	the interest rate that represents the cost to the organisation of using its own funds or obtaining further funds (for example by borrowing)
	internal rate of return (IRR)	the discount rate that when applied to the cash flows in a project results in a net present value of zero
	interpolation	a technique that can be used to estimate the internal rate of return
	payback period	the time it takes for the cash inflows from a project to equal the original investment
	discounted payback period	the time it takes for the discounted cash inflows from a project to equal the original investment
	accounting rate of return (ARR)	the average profit from a project, expressed as a percentage of the investment

Activities

6.1 A company produces and sells premium baked beans in 400 gram cans. It is considering also producing and selling the same product in 200 gram cans. The smaller cans will be sold at more than half the current price, although there will be an impact on the sales volume of the current product. The following information is available.

- Current sales volume is 7.0 million units of the 400 gram cans and this is expected to reduce to 6.0 million units if the smaller cans are also produced.

- Current fixed production costs are £0.85 million per year.

- Current labour cost per unit is £0.05, which is completely variable.

- Current material cost per unit is £0.11 (including can), which is completely variable.

- Current selling price is £0.80 per unit.

- The new product would have variable material costs (including can) of £0.07 per unit.

- The new product would have a variable labour cost of £0.03 per unit.

- The total fixed costs per year would increase by £0.11 million.

- Selling price of the existing product would be unaffected, but the new product would sell for £0.55 per unit, with expected sales of 2.2 million units.

As an alternative to making their own 200 gram cans of beans, the company has an offer from another company to supply complete 200 gram cans of beans. The product would be identical to those that could be made in house.

The cost of buying in the cans of beans would be 20p per can. Under this option there would be no additional material or labour cost, but there would be additional fixed costs of £15,000 per year to cover warehousing compared with the current situation.

If this option were chosen there would still be a reduction in sales of the 400 gram cans as outlined above.

Required:

(1) Complete the following table to calculate the changes in revenue and costs if the new product were to be produced alongside the existing product. Show negative amounts in the total column with minus signs.

	Units	Per Unit £	Total £
Lost contribution on 400 gram can sales			
200 gram can sales:			
Additional revenue			
Material cost			
Labour cost			
Increase fixed costs			
Net increase / (reduction) in profit			

(2) Complete the following table to calculate the changes in costs and revenues if the new product were bought in. Show negative amounts in the total column as minus amounts.

	Units	Per Unit £	Total £
Lost contribution on 400 gram can sales			
200 gram can sales:			
Additional revenue			
Buy-in cost			
Increase fixed costs			
Net increase / (reduction) in profit			

(3) State whether, based on your calculations, the company should produce the 200 gram cans in house, or buy them in, or maintain the current position.

6.2 Duo-active is a manufacturer located in the UK. It currently manufactures two products in its factory, Aye and Bee.

The manager is concerned about the lack of profitability of the Bee product.

The current factory is used for the manufacture of both products, and there is no likelihood of another use for the part currently used for the manufacture of the Bee product.

The operating statement for the last quarter was as follows:

	Aye	Bee	Total
	£000	£000	£000
Sales	320	160	480
Direct materials	40	35	75
Direct labour	115	60	175
Fixed Factory Costs	85	75	160
Selling and Distribution Costs	10	5	15
Administration Costs	10	10	20
Operating Profit / (Loss)	60	(25)	35

The following information has been established:

- Materials and direct labour are variable costs.
- Fixed factory costs relate to the whole factory, apart from £25,000 which relates specifically to supervision costs in production of Aye and £15,000 which relates to supervision costs in production of Bee. The remaining costs have been apportioned equally.
- Administration costs are fixed costs and would remain if either of the products were discontinued.
- Selling and distribution costs are variable costs.
- Redundancy costs can be ignored.
- This level of sales of both products is expected to continue.

Required:

Complete the table below to show the performance of each product in marginal costing format.

	Aye	Bee	Total
	£000	£000	£000
Sales			
Total variable costs			
Fixed costs related to products			
Product contribution			
Whole business fixed costs			
Operating Profit			

Recommend whether the Bee product should be discontinued.

6.3 A company produces two products, the Shiver and the Shake from the same material, with revenues, variable costs and weekly demand as follows:

	Shiver	Shake
Selling price	£50	£60
Direct materials (at £10 per kg)	£20	£25
Direct labour	£12	£16
Demand	12,000 units	15,000 units

Weekly production capacity is restricted to a maximum of total 25,000 units.

(a) Assuming that there is no shortage of resources, complete the following table to show the optimum production level for each product and the resulting contribution.

	Shiver	Shake	Total
Production (units)			
Total contribution £			

(b) In the coming week there is a shortage of raw materials and only 36,000 kg will be available. Complete the following table to show the various contributions, and the optimum production and material usage quantities for the week.

	Shiver	Shake	Total
Contribution per kg of material £			
Production (units)			
Material usage (kg)			
Total contribution £			

6.4 A company makes two products, the Exe and the Wye, both using the same materials and the same labour.

The key details are as follows:

	Exe	Wye
Contribution per unit	£40	£25
Materials per unit	2 kg	2 kg
Labour time per unit	1 hour	0.5 hour

For the coming period, there will be a maximum amount of material available of 10,000 kg. The maximum labour available will be 3,500 hours.

Required:

• Calculate the contribution per kg of material and the contribution per labour hour for each product, using the following table.

	Exe	Wye
Contribution per kg material		
Contribution per labour hour		

• Using simultaneous equations, calculate the production of Exe and Wye that will maximise total contribution

• Sketch a graph that illustrates the optimum production (you do not need to show a total contribution line).

• Complete the following table to show the production, the materials required, the labour hours required, and the total contribution for each product and in total.

	Exe	Wye	Total
Production (units)			
Materials required (kg)			
Labour required (hours)			
Contribution			

6.5 A company is considering purchasing machinery that will result in savings in labour costs. The machinery will cost £60,000 and last for three years with no residual value. The labour savings if the machine is acquired are expected to be £25,000 per year. The company's cost of capital is 10%. Savings can be considered as being generated at the end of each year.

Complete the following table to calculate the net present value of the proposal to purchase the machinery:

	Year 0	Year 1	Year 2	Year 3
Net cash flows £				
Discount factor	1.000	0.909	0.826	0.751
Present values £				
Net present value £				

6.6 A company is considering purchasing machinery that will result in savings in labour costs. The machinery will cost £70,000, plus installation costs of £4,500, and last for three years with scrap value of £1,000. The running costs of the machinery will be £1,500 per year, payable at the end of each year. In addition, the machinery will need to be serviced at the end of year 2, costing £8,000. The labour savings if the machine is acquired are expected to be £38,500 per year. The company's cost of capital is 10%. Savings can be considered as being generated at the end of each year.

Complete the table on the next page to calculate the net present value of the proposal to purchase the machinery:

	Year 0	Year 1	Year 2	Year 3
Cash inflows £				
Cash outflows £				
Net cash flows £				
Discount factor	1.000	0.909	0.826	0.751
Present values £				
Net present value £				

6.7   A company is considering investing in a project that will require an initial cash investment of £1,200,000 to purchase non-current assets. The assets will last six years, with no residual value. The annual profits are estimated at £100,000, after changing straight line depreciation for six years. All profits except depreciation are cash-based.

The company's cost of capital is 10%.

Required

Using the following table, and any further calculations necessary, calculate:

*   The net present value of the project using a discount factor of 10%.

*   The payback period in years

*   The discounted payback period, to the nearest year (using 10% discount)

*   The estimated internal rate of return to the nearest whole %

*   The accounting rate of return to the nearest whole % (using average investment)

Year	Cash Flow	Disc Factor 10%	Disc Cash Flow 10%	Disc Factor 15%	Disc Cash Flow 15%
0		1.000		1.000	
1		0.909		0.870	
2		0.826		0.756	
3		0.751		0.658	
4		0.683		0.572	
5		0.621		0.497	
6		0.564		0.432	
Net Present Values					

7 Performance indicators

this chapter covers...

We start this chapter by examining what performance indicators can tell us and learn some of the 'ground rules' that will help us to develop, use and interpret them. We will see how making comparisons is invaluable, and how benchmarking can play its part in making sense of the data.

Next we will start our examination of ratios by looking at those connected with profitability and how the resources of the business are used to generate profit. The last groups of ratios are those concerned with examining the statement of financial position to understand issues like liquidity.

We will then learn how to interpret ratios, and their limitations.

Next, we examine the issues surrounding quality, including the categories of the cost of quality.

We will then examine non-financial indicators which are numerical, for example, number of customer complaints or number of employee-days absence. We will then go on to discuss qualitative measures that are not expressed numerically, but may refer to attitudes and opinions.

The balanced scorecard is a technique for grouping performance measurements under four categories (or 'perspectives'), and this idea is discussed and illustrated in the next section.

Finally, we examine the issues concerned with divisional performance, including using the measures of return on investment and residual income, and the alternatives for transfer pricing.

MEASURING THE PERFORMANCE OF ORGANISATIONS

performance indicators

It is important to be able to measure the performance of an organisation in a way which allows managers to see where improvements can be made. In Chapters 3 and 4 we have studied the analysis of cost variances. These are examples of performance measurements which can be used:

- to monitor the use of resources
- to help with control of the business
- to help with planning for the future

A list of variances for one cost centre for one period is not particularly informative. The usefulness of variances depends on being able to compare them with target levels, with the variances for other time periods or with those for other similar cost centres.

In this chapter we will consider different ways of measuring the performance of an organisation (or of a part of an organisation). For example, we can calculate profit as a percentage of sales, sales revenue per employee, the percentage of orders which are delivered late, and many other measures. An individual measurement is called a **performance indicator**. What we have seen above for variance analysis applies to any performance indicator.

A performance indicator may be used for:

- identifying problems
- controlling costs
- measuring the utilisation of resources
- measuring an individual's performance
- planning

Examples of performance indicators include:

- the direct materials usage variance, which may identify a problem relating to wastage of materials
- the administration cost as a percentage of sales, which may help with control of costs
- the number of hours of machine down time, which is relevant to how well resources are being used
- profit as a percentage of sales revenue, which may indicate how well a company has been managed
- the number of product units rejected on inspection, which may help with planning production levels

The usefulness of a performance indicator depends on:

- comparing with standards, budgets or targets
- comparing with other periods of time
- comparing with other similar organisations

A range of factors can have an impact on performance indicators, and should be taken into account when evaluating performance. These include (but are not limited to) the following:

- The learning effect – this relates to the fact that individuals (and organisations) may become more efficient as time goes on, as everyone gets more used to the way things are done. However, performance will not continue to improve forever, so the impact of the learning effect should not be over-estimated.

- Economies of scale – where activity levels increase there may be opportunities to reduce cost due to (for example) bulk discounts or spreading fixed costs over a greater number of outputs.

- Mechanisation – where manual operations are replaced by mechanical or computer-controlled operations the performance should improve. However, the type of costs will often change, for example, reduced labour costs may be replaced by increased costs related to non-current assets.

One key area that most organisations will want to focus on is its performance in terms of productivity and efficiency. Although both these terms concentrate on the relationship between inputs and outputs, there are some important distinctions in what they are measuring.

Productivity measures the quantity of output (for example units produced) and compares this to some form of input (for example number of employees or value of non-current assets).

Efficiency takes the inputs of a process and assesses how economically they are used to produce the output. In this way, efficiency takes account of the value of the outputs in relation to the value of the inputs. Measures of efficiency therefore examine how well resources have been used to generate profits.

making comparisons – consistency

Comparisons can give very useful information. However, we must be sure that figures being compared really are 'comparable'. In other words, they must have been prepared in a **consistent** way, so that we are comparing 'like with like'.

For example, the Net Profit figures for a business over a number of years can be compared provided that the same accounting policies have been applied throughout. A change in the policy for depreciation, for example, would affect the profit figures and they would not be comparable.

data for performance measurement

The diagram below shows that there are different kinds of data that may be used for performance measurement.

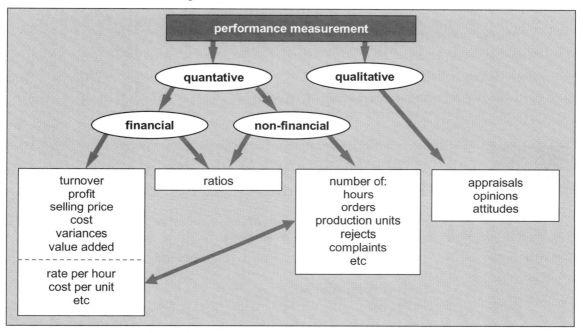

Quantitative data is data which can be stated in numbers, and this can be split into:

- Financial or Monetary data which is in terms of money and

- Non-financial or non-monetary data, which is in terms of units other than money, such as numbers of hours.

Qualitative data is data which cannot be put in numerical terms. It can consist of people's opinions or judgements, for example the views of students about a teacher. Such data is used for performance measurement, particularly in appraisal schemes for types of work where there is no clear-cut numerical measure of performance. A combination of quantitative and qualitative data is often used.

The examples shown in the above diagram include variances as an example of financial data. You have seen in your earlier studies that variances are given in money terms. The other point to note about variances is that each variance comes from two pieces of information and is the difference between them. An alternative way of comparing two pieces of information is to calculate a ratio or percentage, and this is one of the most common ways of arriving at a useful measure of performance. Percentages are particularly useful when comparisons are being made.

---

tutorial note – dealing with percentages

In order to express a ratio as a percentage, it is necessary to multiply by 100. This can be done using the % function on a calculator.

In all the formulas which follow, we have shown 'x 100' as well as indicating that the answer is a percentage by using the % sign.

When using these formulas:

either multiply by 100

or   use the % button on your calculator.

Case Study

LITTLE LIMITED AND LARGE LIMITED: PERFORMANCE INDICATORS AS PERCENTAGES

Little Ltd and Large Ltd are companies which operate in the same industry. For a given period, we have the following data:

	Little Ltd	Large Ltd
	£000s	£000s
Turnover (sales revenue)	465	2,550
Gross profit	185	895

At a glance, it is not easy to compare these figures because of the difference in size. If we calculate the gross profit as a percentage of sales revenue, we obtain more useful information for comparison:

Little Ltd Gross profit percentage = $\dfrac{185}{465}$ x 100%   =   39.8%

Large Ltd Gross profit percentage = $\dfrac{895}{2,550}$ x 100%   =   35.1%

We can then see that Little Ltd is translating a greater proportion of its sales revenue into gross profit than Large Ltd. This is an example of a performance indicator.

financial indicators: calculating averages

Although total amounts of money such as sales, profits and costs may be used for performance measurement, it is often more informative to calculate an average 'per employee', 'per hour', 'per unit of output' and so on. This is a simple calculation which relates the financial data to the size of the organisation in some way.

practical examples

1 If sales orders amount to £32million for the year and there are 16 sales representatives, then Average sales orders per representative = £32m ÷ 16 = £2m

2 If materials cost £87,000 in total for output of 29,000 units of a product, then Average cost of materials per unit = £87,000 ÷ 29,000 = £3

3 If training costs for the year total £171,000 and there are 450 employees, then Average expenditure on training per employee = £171,000 ÷ 450 = £380

RATIO ANALYSIS

Ratio analysis generally refers to the calculation of a set of ratios or percentages using data from the financial and management accounts of a business. The income statement (profit and loss account) and the statement of financial position (balance sheet) are used in the analysis, which can then be used to evaluate the performance of the business, particularly by:

- comparing with budgets or targets

- comparing with other periods of time

- comparing with other similar organisations

In the case of limited companies, people outside the company can look at the final accounts and calculate ratios, for example when deciding whether to buy shares in the company. This analysis will add to the available information, but should not be used on its own.

In order to make meaningful comparisons between organisations or time periods, the accounts must have been prepared on the same basis – applying the principle of consistency by comparing like with like. It is very difficult to achieve this, especially when using published accounts. In this case, it is essential to study the notes to the accounts, which may give important information about accounting policies and the breakdown of certain figures. Even so, details of the methods used may not be given and therefore the ratios calculated must be used with care.

The aim should always be to provide useful information for the purpose for which it is required. It is not sufficient to put figures into formulas (or into a computer program) without thinking of the factors that may affect them.

sources of data for ratios

In this chapter we consider the ratios which can be calculated from the statement of profit or loss (income statement) and the statement of financial position of a business. We will do this in a number of stages:

1   We will consider first the ratios calculated from the statement of profit or loss separately, before linking sales and profits with the statement of financial position.

2   The key measure of profit in relation to the assets shown on the statement of financial position is return on capital employed.

3   Our third section on ratio analysis will include ratios relating to the current assets and current liabilities of the organisation.

PROFITABILITY RATIOS

In the Case Study comparing Little Limited and Large Limited, the calculation of gross profit as a percentage of sales revenue gives useful information. It shows what proportion of the sales revenue remains as gross profit, after the cost of sales is taken out. Little Ltd's gross profit percentage of 39.8%, for example, means that, out of every £100 of sales revenue, there is £39.80 gross profit. Large Ltd keeps only £35.10 gross profit out of every £100 of sales revenue.

Similar percentages can be calculated comparing each of the figures on an income statement with the sales revenue. These show what proportion or 'slice' of sales revenue is being used for each type of cost and how big a slice is kept in profits.

Profit percentages are calculated on the basis of Sales Revenue. This can be done for Gross Profit and Net Profit. In the accounts of a company, several versions of profit are given, before and after interest and tax. To measure the performance of the company, the 'Operating Profit' is used for many ratios, because this is the profit from the main trading activities of the company.

- *gross profit margin (percentage)* $= \dfrac{gross\ profit}{sales} \times 100\%$

- *operating profit margin* $= \dfrac{operating\ profit}{sales} \times 100\%$

Profit percentages are indicators of the profitability of the business.

It must be remembered that the choice of methods for depreciation of assets and for inventory valuation can make a difference to profit figures.

Any other figure from the statement of profit or loss can also be calculated as a percentage of sales, particularly if it appears to need investigation. For example, if selling expenses have increased from one period to the next, it may be useful to calculate for each period:

- *selling expenses as a percentage of sales* $= \dfrac{\text{selling expenses}}{\text{sales}} \times 100\%$

- ***or*** *any type of expense as a percentage of sales* $= \dfrac{\text{expense}}{\text{sales}} \times 100\%$

Similarly, if details of the costs of materials and wages are available, we can calculate, for any type of cost:

- *cost as a percentage of sales* $= \dfrac{\text{cost}}{\text{sales}} \times 100\%$

Whether costs behave as fixed or variable costs in relation to activity levels makes a difference to how we would expect the ratios to behave. A higher revenue figure often results from a higher volume of sales, which would mean that total variable costs would also be higher. Total fixed costs, however, would not be expected to change with the volume. In percentage terms, this means that we would expect:

- a variable cost to remain relatively stable as a percentage of revenue

- a fixed cost as a percentage of revenue to decrease as revenue increases

  For example, the direct materials cost of a product may be expected to be 12% of the sales revenue and this percentage would stay approximately the same for different numbers of units. On the other hand, if a fixed cost is £90,000 per year:

  - compared with annual sales of £900,000, the fixed cost would be 10%
  - but compared with annual sales of £1,200,000, it would be only 7.5%.

Case Study

PERFORM LIMITED: USING BENCHMARK RATIOS

Perform Limited is a manufacturing company that uses benchmark ratios based on a budget to compare with actual performance. The following operating statement has been compiled from actual data for the most recent period.

	£
Sales Revenue	9,400,000
Cost of Sales	6,080,000
Gross Profit	3,320,000
Selling and Distribution Expenses	1,415,000
Administration Expenses	1,170,000
Operating Profit	735,000

The following table shows the benchmark ratios for the company.

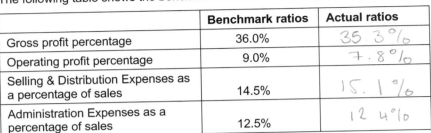

	Benchmark ratios	Actual ratios
Gross profit percentage	36.0%	35.3%
Operating profit percentage	9.0%	7.8%
Selling & Distribution Expenses as a percentage of sales	14.5%	15.1%
Administration Expenses as a percentage of sales	12.5%	12.4%

The sales revenue and the selling prices are in line with the budget.

required

- Calculate the ratios shown in the table relating to actual performance, rounded to one decimal place.

- Suggest possible areas of cost that could have contributed to the performance falling below expectations.

solution

	Benchmark ratios	Actual ratios
Gross profit percentage	36.0%	35.3%
Operating profit percentage	9.0%	7.8%
Selling & Distribution Expenses as a percentage of sales	14.5%	15.1%
Administration Expenses as a percentage of sales	12.5%	12.4%

The gross profit percentage and the operating profit percentage are both below benchmark.

Since the sales revenue and selling prices are in line with the budget, the volume of sales must also be as expected. This means that the reduced gross profit percentage must be due to increased costs of production. The difference in actual gross profit and the benchmark ratio of 0.7% of sales represents additional cost of approximately £66,000. We do not have sufficient information to narrow the cause down within that category.

The reduced gross profit contributes to the reduced operating profit, which is 1.2% of sales (approximately £113,000) below benchmark. The other factor is the cost of selling and distribution expenses that are greater than expected. since sales volume is in line with the budget, volume cannot have an impact on any variable costs within this category. The cause must therefore be cost increases which will need to be identified. The administration costs are slightly below benchmark and appear to be under control.

return on capital employed (ROCE)

By 'capital employed' we mean the money being used to finance the running of a business. This is normally represented by the owners' capital, together with any long-term liabilities such as loans that make more money available. The statement of financial position shows another way of looking at this, as the value of the non-current and current assets less the current liabilities.

Capital employed is the essential funding used by managers for the fixed assets, for keeping the business going and therefore for making sales and profits. It is important for investors to see that this funding is being put to good use. 'Return on Capital Employed' is a performance indicator that compares the profit with the amount of long-term finance being used by management.

Return on Capital Employed is a key ratio which therefore shows how well the management of an organisation has used the assets (or the resources shown on the statement of financial position) to generate profits.

To calculate ROCE, the profit is expressed as a percentage of the capital employed in the business.

Because there are alternative ways to express 'capital employed' we can use either of the following formulas to achieve the same result.

$$ROCE = \frac{operating\ profit}{non\text{-}current\ assets + net\ current\ assets} \times 100$$

$$ROCE = \frac{operating\ profit}{capital + non\text{-}current\ liabilities} \times 100$$

Note that 'non-current assets + net current assets' is also known as 'net assets'. 'Capital employed' is therefore equal to 'net assets'.

Notice that in these ratios, the operating profit is used. This is the profit before interest and tax that arises from operations, and is usually shown in the operating statement. If you are asked to calculate one of these ratios you may be provided with a figure for 'capital employed' or 'net assets'.

THICKE LTD AND THINN LTD:
COMPARING PERFORMANCE

Thicke Ltd and Thinn Ltd are two companies that both operate in the DIY goods retail market. Thicke is a long established company that trades from several retail sites, but Thinn is a more recently opened company that operates online from a central distribution site. The companies have the following data for the last financial period.

	Thicke Ltd £	Thinn Ltd £
Sales Revenue	15,150,000	6,950,000
Cost of sales	12,500,000	5,940,000
Gross profit	2,650,000	1,010,000
Distribution costs	450,000	295,000
Administration costs	600,000	95,000
Marketing costs	150,000	380,000
Operating profit	1,450,000	240,000
Capital Employed	18,125,000	2,400,000

required

- Complete the following table to show performance ratios for both companies, rounded to two decimal places.

	Thicke Ltd	Thinn Ltd
Gross profit %	17.49%	14.53%
Distribution costs as % of sales	2.97%	4.24%
Administration costs as % of sales	3.96%	1.37%
Marketing costs as % of sales	0.99%	5.47%
Operating profit %	9.57%	3.45%
Return on Capital Employed % (ROCE)	8%	10%

- comment on what the ratios reveal about the companies' performance.

solution

	Thicke Ltd	**Thinn Ltd**
Gross profit %	17.49	14.53
Distribution costs as % of sales	2.97	4.24
Administration costs as % of sales	3.96	1.37
Marketing costs as % of sales	0.99	5.47
Operating profit %	9.57	3.45
Return on Capital Employed % (ROCE)	8.00	10.00

Thicke Ltd is maintaining a higher gross profit margin than Thinn Ltd, and this is also reflected in a higher operating profit margin. While Thinn Ltd has lower administration costs as a percentage of sales, all their other costs reveal higher percentages of sales than Thicke Ltd's. The result is that Thinn Ltd's operating profit as a percentage of sales is just over a third of that recorded by Thicke Ltd.

While this may seem to show poor cost control by Thinn Ltd, it could simply be in line with their business model. By selling online they are able to undercut traditional retailers (hence the lower gross profit percentage), but have higher distribution costs and invest more in marketing to increase customer awareness.

However, despite having higher operating costs than Thicke Ltd, Thinn Ltd has a higher return on capital employed. This key measure shows that their method of operation needs fewer assets to produce profits. This makes sense as an online sales operation does not require expensive shops.

asset turnover

Asset Turnover is another important ratio which links the statement of financial position with the income statement. It measures how well the assets have been used during a period to generate sales revenue.

Asset Turnover is the number of times the value of the assets has been obtained in Turnover (Sales).

For example, an asset turnover ratio of 3 times would mean that, for every £1 of value in the assets, there had been £3 of sales revenue. Any improvement in asset turnover means that more sales revenue is being obtained per £1 value of the assets used. This can lead to improvements in the amount of profit and in ROCE, provided that the profit margin is not cut too much. We see below how asset turnover, operating profit margin and ROCE are linked.

Again there may be different definitions of the value of the assets, but we will use the non-current assets plus net current assets as above.

$$asset\ turnover\ =\ \frac{turnover\ (sales\ revenue)}{non\text{-}current\ assets\ +\ net\ current\ assets}$$

The denominator could alternatively be shown as 'total assets – current liabilities'.

As already noted, 'Net Assets' is normally identical to 'Capital Employed'. In the following Case Study note that 'non-current assets plus net current assets' is equal to 'net assets'.

THICKE LTD AND THINN LTD: ASSET TURNOVER

The following abbreviated details refer to the previous Case Study.

	Thicke Ltd	Thinn Ltd
	£	£
Sales Revenue	15,150,000	6,950,000
Operating Profit	1,450,000	240,000
Net Assets	18,125,000	2,400,000

required

Calculate the asset turnover figures (rounded to two decimal places) for both companies and comment on what they reveal.

solution

	Thicke Ltd	Thinn Ltd
Asset Turnover	0.84	2.90

Workings:

| Thicke Ltd: | £15,150,000 / £18,125,000 | = 0.84 |
| Thinn Ltd: | £6,950,000 / £2,400,000 | = 2.90 |

Notice that these figures are not percentages. They are sometimes referred to as 'times' (for example '2.90 times').

The indicators show that Thinn Ltd is more successful at generating sales from its net assets than Thicke Ltd. As we already noted, Thicke Ltd has a number of expensive shops, whereas Thinn Ltd just has one distribution centre.

ROCE and operating profit margin

There is an important link between ROCE, Asset Turnover and the Operating Profit margin (ie Operating Profit as a percentage of Sales):

ROCE = operating profit margin x asset turnover

because:

$$\frac{Operating\ Profit}{Non\text{-}current\ \&\ net\ current\ assets} = \frac{Operating\ Profit}{\cancel{Sales}} \times \frac{\cancel{Sales}}{Non\text{-}current\ \&\ net\ current\ assets}$$

The sales (turnover) figure can be cancelled in the calculation of the right hand side of this equation (see lines).

The following diagram illustrates these connections:

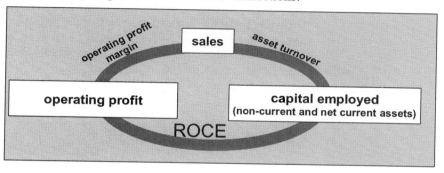

We can use the figures from the previous Case Study to illustrate this.

	Thicke Ltd	Thinn Ltd
Operating Profit %	9.57	3.45
Return on Capital Employed %	8.00	10.00
Asset Turnover	0.84	2.90

ROCE = Operating profit margin x asset turnover

For Thicke Ltd:

     8.00% = 9.57% x 0.84

For Thinn Ltd:

     10.00% = 3.45% x 2.90

Both these are valid, subject to minor rounding errors.

This arithmetical connection emphasises that both operating profit % and asset turnover contribute to return on capital employed.

Compared to Thinn Ltd, although Thicke Ltd has a higher operating profit %, it has a lower asset turnover (i.e. fewer sales generated from its net assets). The result is a return on capital employed that is lower than that of Thinn Ltd.

CURRENT ASSETS AND LIABILITIES

An important aspect of the management of a business is the control of the current assets of inventory, receivables and cash.

Usually a certain level of inventory is necessary in order to avoid running out of inventory and losing production and sales. Keeping too much inventory, however, incurs additional costs of storage and means that the money tied up in inventory cannot be used for other purposes. Offering customers credit may boost sales, but it is important to collect the money from receivables within a reasonable time. Similarly, cash is needed on a day-to-day basis, but surplus cash should be invested in order to earn extra income. In each case a suitable balance must be achieved.

Control of the current liability of payables means taking advantage of the credit terms offered by suppliers, but making sure they can be paid on time.

RECEIVABLES, PAYABLES AND INVENTORY INDICATORS

An organisation needs to keep levels of receivables, payables and inventory that are appropriate for the type of business. Ratios used to measure these levels are usually calculated in terms of numbers of days or months, to estimate:

- the average time taken to collect money from trade receivables
- the average time taken to pay trade payables
- the average time that goods or materials remain in inventory

The limitations of these estimates are discussed below. The usefulness of the ratios is in making comparisons and identifying trends. For example, if the average time taken to collect money from receivables decreases over several time periods, this suggests that control of receivables is improving.

receivable collection

Cash should be received within the time allowed by the normal credit terms for customers. It is possible to *estimate* the time being taken for customers to pay, by using the formula:

$$receivables'\,collection\,period = \frac{trade\,receivables}{revenue} \times 365\,days$$

Notice that the formula gives an average time, based on the closing receivables.

If customers are normally allowed two months' credit, for example, the receivables' collection period should not be much above 60 days (remembering that the closing receivables figure may not be typical). As usual, comparison over time is more useful and may show whether control of receivables is improving or not.

When making comparisons between organisations, remember that some businesses allow customers longer credit periods in order to increase sales.

In effect, customers are borrowing from the business, because sending goods without receiving payment is like lending money. Conversely, suppliers are lending to the business. It makes sense, therefore, to try to collect the money back from customers more quickly than paying amounts due to suppliers. However, suppliers who are not paid on time may refuse to supply goods or services in future.

payables' payment period

The **Payables' Payment Period** can be estimated in a similar way to the Receivables' Collection Period, but here it is credit purchases (or cost of sales) which are relevant.

$$payables' \ payment \ period = \frac{trade \ payables}{cost \ of \ sales} \ \text{x} \ \ 365 \ days$$

Again, the formula gives an average, based on the closing trade payables figure, which may not be typical.

inventory holding period

This is the length of time taken for inventory to be sold, or the average age of inventory. The inventory figure used in the formula may be the average of the opening and closing inventory, which is calculated in the usual way for an average (mean) of two items, by adding them together and dividing the total by 2:

$average \ inventory = 0.5 \ \text{x} \ (opening \ inventory + closing \ inventory)$

If the opening inventory is not known, the closing inventory figure is used.

$$average \ age \ of \ inventory \ \ = \ \frac{average \ inventory}{cost \ of \ sales} \ \ \text{x} \ 365 \ days$$

or,

$$average \ age \ of \ inventory \ \ = \ \frac{closing \ inventory}{cost \ of \ sales} \ \ \text{x} \ 365 \ days$$

It can be argued that the closing inventory gives an equally good estimate. The average based on the opening and closing inventory may not be a fairer reflection, especially if the trade is seasonal.

The speed with which inventory should be sold depends on the type of business. For example, fresh fruit must be sold within a few days, whereas non-perishable goods may be kept for longer periods. In some businesses, such as manufacturing ice cream, toys or fireworks, the level of inventories will vary considerably with the seasons. The statement of financial position date may happen to coincide with particularly high (or low) inventories and the inventory turn will appear to be very slow (or fast) moving. We need more information about the business to be able to comment further.

Note the correspondence between the pairs of figures used in the last three ratios:

■ trade receivables are related to revenue

■ trade payables are related to cost of sales

■ inventory is related to cost of sales

working capital cycle

The combined impact of receivables, payables and inventory days can be shown by calculating the working capital cycle in days. This ratio shows us how much time on average passes between the payment for inventory purchased and the receipt of money for the goods once they have been sold.

Working capital cycle = Inventory days + receivable days – payables days

Note that the inventory and receivable days are added together (as they represent current assets), but payables days are deducted because they relate to current liabilities. A greater number of working capital cycle days indicates a greater investment in working capital (or working capital requirement).

ratios: the whole picture

We now look at a Case Study which incorporates a number of the ratios described so far in this Chapter. It shows how ratios can be used in business decision making.

TUBS AND POTS LIMITED: RATIO ANALYSIS

Tubs and Pots Ltd supplies plant holders to local garden centres. The company has now been offered a contract to supply a national chain of home and garden superstores. The following information shows extracts from the statement of financial position and the income statement as forecast for the next year:

- on the basis of continuing with the current local trade ('Current Trade')
- on the basis of acceptance of the contract ('With Contract')

	Current Trade £	With Contract £
Current Assets:		
Inventory	6,000	20,000
Trade Receivables	14,000	52,000
Cash at Bank	4,000	
	24,000	72,000
Current Liabilities		
Trade Payables	12,000	70,000
Bank Overdraft		7,000
	12,000	77,000
Revenue	70,000	204,000
Cost of Sales	38,000	124,000

required

Task 1

Using the above information, calculate the following indicators for the current trade and for the acceptance of the contract:

1. Receivables' Collection Period
2. Payables' Payment Period
3. Average age of inventory (using the closing inventory)
4. Gross Profit in £
5. Gross Profit percentage (on Sales)

Task 2

Identify the changes which will take place in the business of Tubs and Pots Ltd if the contract is accepted and comment on the findings.

solution

Task 1: calculation of ratios

Check that you can carry out these calculations before looking at the workings at the end of the solution.

		current trade	with contract
1	Receivables' Collection Period	73 days	93 days
2	Payables' Payment Period	115 days	206 days
3	Average age of inventory	58 days	59 days
4	Gross Profit in £	£32,000	£80,000
5	Gross Profit percentage (on Sales)	45.7%	39.2%

Task 2: analysis of ratios

The forecasts show that, with the contract, **revenue** would increase to nearly three times the current level and the management of the company would need to consider whether such expansion within one year is feasible. There would also be higher **inventory levels** and the company would go into an **overdraft** situation. Building up inventories means that **cost of sales** is increased to more than three times the current level, which could have contributed to the need for an overdraft. Another reason for the overdraft could be purchases of non-current assets.

The **Receivables' Collection Period** increases to about 3 months with the contract, and the Payables' Payment Period to over 6 months. The **average age of inventory** stays about the same. With the contract, there is a decrease in the **Gross Profit Margin** (Gross Profit as a percentage of Sales). Although the gross profit has more than doubled, the impact on the operating profit should also be reviewed.

The managers of Tubs and Pots Ltd need to investigate the risks attached to acceptance of this contract. If non-current assets are purchased, longer-term finance would be more suitable than an overdraft. They also need more working capital to avoid the problems with liquidity. The increased collection period indicates that the national chain would take longer to pay for the goods than the current customers. It appears risky to plan for over 6 month payables' payment period <u>unless</u> such terms have been agreed with the suppliers.

It would be important to consider the length and security of the contract. The forecasts given are for one year only and show that Gross Profit Margin would decrease. This could be caused by the national chain insisting on paying lower prices for the goods. over a number of years it may be possible to improve on this, by reducing costs. The management of Tubs and Pots Ltd should also consider the effect on their current trade with their local customers.

Workings		current trade	with contract
1	$\dfrac{\text{Receivables} \times 365}{\text{Revenue}}$	$\dfrac{£14,000 \times 365}{£70,000}$	$\dfrac{£52,000 \times 365}{£204,000}$
2	$\dfrac{\text{Payables} \times 365}{\text{Cost of sales}}$	$\dfrac{£12,000 \times 365}{£38,000}$	$\dfrac{£70,000 \times 365}{£124,000}$

3	Closing inventory x 365 Cost of sales	£6,000 x 365 £38,000	£20,000 x 365 £124,000
4	Revenue – Cost of sales	£70,000 – £38,000	£204,000 – £124,000
5	Gross profit x 100% Revenue	£32,000 x 100% £70,000	£80,000 x 100% £204,000

Case Study

VOLUMIZER LIMITED: ADJUSTING VOLUMES AND PRICES

situation

Volumizer Limited is developing a new product and a colleague has prepared forecast information based upon two scenarios. The forecast operating statement and data from the statement of financial position for both scenarios is shown below.

- Scenario 1 is to set the price at £18 per unit with sales of 60,000 units each year.
- Scenario 2 is to set the price at £12 per unit with sales of 120,000 units each year.

Forecast Operating Statement	Scenario 1 £	Scenario 2 £
Revenue	1,080,000	1,440,000
Cost of production		
Direct (Raw) Materials	300,000	600,000
Direct Labour	120,000	192,000
Fixed Production overheads	360,000	360,000
Total cost of sales	780,000	1,152,000
Gross profit	300,000	288,000
Selling and distribution costs	74,000	122,000
Administration costs	50,000	50,000
Operating profit	176,000	116,000
Other data:		
Total Net Assets	1,500,000	1,500,000
Inventory	130,000	192,000
Receivables	175,000	250,000
Payables	63,000	126,000

required

Complete the table on the next page to show the performance indicators. Round percentages and values to two decimal places, and days to the nearest whole day.

	Scenario 1	Scenario 2
Gross profit margin		
Operating profit margin		
Return on capital employed		
Direct materials cost per unit £		
Direct labour cost per unit £		
Fixed production cost per unit £		
Inventory days		
Receivables days		
Payables days		
Working capital cycle days		

Draft a report for the Finance Director covering the following:

(a) An explanation of why the gross profit margins are different, referring to the following:

- Sales price and Sales volume
- Materials cost
- Labour cost
- Fixed costs

(b) An explanation of why the net profit margins are different.

(c) The implications for liquidity of the two scenarios.

(d) A recommendation, with reasons, as to which course of action to take.

s o l u t i o n

	Scenario 1	Scenario 2
Gross profit margin	27.78%	20.00%
Operating profit margin	16.30%	8.06%
Return on capital employed	11.73%	7.73%
Direct materials cost per unit £	5.00	5.00
Direct labour cost per unit £	2.00	1.60
Fixed production cost per unit £	6.00	3.00
Inventory days	61	61
Receivables days	59	63
Payables days	29	40
Working capital cycle days	91	84

To: Finance director	Subject: Scenarios 1 & 2
From: Accounting technician	Date:

(a) Why are the gross profit margins different?

- Sales Price / Sales Volume
  The sales price is 50% higher under scenario 1, which will result in an increase in the gross profit margin. The sales volume under scenario 2 is double that of scenario 1. This only affects the gross profit margin percentage because not all the production costs are variable.

  - Materials
    The materials cost per unit is constant at £5.00 per unit, and therefore does not affect the gross profit margin. There is no economy of scale.

  - Labour
    Labour cost per unit is £2.00 for scenario 1 decreasing to £1.60 for scenario 2. The more units that are produced, the lower the labour cost per unit. This will improve the margin for scenario 2. The lower labour cost per unit may be because of economies of scale in production.

  - Fixed costs
    Fixed costs are constant in total, and so as the volume of production increases, the fixed cost per unit decreases. This will increase the margin for Scenario 2.

(b) Why are the net profit margins different?

The net profit margins are different partly due to the reduction in gross profit for Scenario 2, and partly due to the increased sales and distribution costs in Scenario 2.

(c) Implications for liquidity

The working capital requirement for scenario 2 is £74,000 greater than for Scenario 1. This is made up of increased value of inventory and receivables, less increased payables. This is in spite of only a modest decrease in working capital cycle days. since there is no change in total net assets under each scenario, this extra working capital will probably come from cash reserves or overdraft. This will put a strain on the resources.

(d) Recommendation, with reasons, as to which course of action to take

Based purely on the forecast information, scenario 1 is the best option creating the largest return, and without the negative impact on working capital. However, the sales volume is lower than scenario 2, and so the market share is lower. It may be worth considering what the demand level would be if the selling price were set somewhere between £12 and £18 per unit, and modelling that scenario before making a final decision.

LIMITATIONS OF RATIO ANALYSIS

In the introduction to this section, it was emphasised that one set of ratios alone does not give very useful information. Ratios for other time periods or other organisations are useful for comparison, as are target ratios.

The principle of **comparing like with like** should be applied in ratio analysis, but this is not always straightforward. Some of the ratios can be defined in different ways, so the particular definition used should be made clear. Even so, detailed information may not be given, for example to split sales into cash sales and credit sales.

When using the **published accounts of companies**, it is not possible to guarantee that we are comparing like with like, as different policies (including those regarding depreciation, inventory valuation and goodwill, for example) will affect the results.

For any organisation, there is also the possibility that the statement of financial position does not show a typical position, intentionally or otherwise. A single transaction the next day may make it look quite different. The statement of financial position reflects the conditions for a particular season of the year and in trades with seasonal variations, this can make a big difference to the ratios.

Discussion of a particular case may include looking for ways in which the ratios could have been distorted. For example, high levels of spending on research, training or marketing may reduce profits in one period, but bring much greater benefits in a later period. The reverse is also true: cutting these costs may improve the profit ratios in the short term, but in the long term sales and profits would suffer.

When making comparisons over different time periods, the ratios are based on historical costs as shown in the accounts. If there has been inflation during the time periods, a better comparison can be made by making adjustments for this before calculating the ratios.

Before drawing firm conclusions from ratio analysis, these limitations should be considered. However, the analysis can give useful information, particularly in showing how items in the financial statements relate to each other and in identifying trends.

QUALITY AND TOTAL QUALITY MANAGEMENT

Throughout the second half of the 20th Century there were further developments in cost management techniques. One of these, 'Total Quality Management', became popular in the 1980s. It starts from an understanding that the quality of a product or service can be defined as 'its fitness for the customer's purpose'. This is important as it emphasises the purpose that the customer will have for the item.

For a product or service to be of high quality, it does not necessarily mean that it uses very expensive materials or highly skilled staff to provide it. What is important is that it **satisfies the customer**. This means that the product or service must:

- be fit for the purpose for which it is purchased

- represent value for money to the customer.

In modern consumer-led societies, customers have access to a wide choice of products and services and make greater demands on suppliers. It is therefore increasingly important for businesses to pay more attention to the requirements of consumers. For example, there is fierce competition for market share between the main supermarket chains in the UK. If they all sell similar products at similar prices, the quality of the service they provide becomes a factor. Attention turns to reducing queues at the tills, providing in-store restaurants and other ways of increasing customer satisfaction.

total quality management

Total Quality Management (TQM) means that quality management becomes the aim of every part of an organisation.

The basic principle is one of continuous improvement, in order to eliminate faulty work and prevent mistakes. Mistakes carry a cost:

- wastage of materials

- idle time

- the cost of reworking

- the loss of customer goodwill, resulting in lost sales

- the cost of replacements

- the cost of dealing with customers' complaints

The concept of continuous improvement and getting more 'right first time' will reduce these costs. Other costs will be incurred in quality management, but the intention is that in the long term the organisation will benefit.

implementing TQM

If TQM is to be introduced, it must become the philosophy of everyone in the organisation, and apply to every activity, including administration, purchasing, sales, marketing and distribution, as well as production. Training and motivation of staff is essential, so that an attitude of seeking improvement is encouraged. Everyone should be allowed to put forward ideas. Groups of employees may form 'quality circles' and have regular meetings to discuss their ideas for quality improvements.

Each person within an organisation has customers. These may be internal users of his/her work – i.e. colleagues – as not everyone deals directly with the external customers. If the quality of the work for the next immediate user is monitored, mistakes will be reduced throughout the organisation.

The involvement of all staff of an organisation means that many different types of knowledge and skills are being used. These may be in engineering, design, information technology, materials handling, office management and many other areas. Specialist consultants may also be needed from outside the organisation.

the costs of quality

The costs relating to quality management can be grouped under four headings:

Prevention costs The costs associated with preventing faulty output, for example training employees in quality control

Appraisal costs The costs of checking quality, like inspection costs

Internal failure costs The costs of rectifying problems within the organisation, for example having to scrap sub-standard products

External failure costs The costs incurred when sub-standard products reach the customer, including repairs and loss of goodwill

the benefits of Total Quality Management

Organisations which develop a culture of TQM and continuous improvement expect that the costs will be outweighed by the benefits. The benefits include:

- reduction of Internal Failure Costs
- reduction of External Failure Costs
- improved reputation and goodwill of customers
- increased sales
- better motivated staff due to improved job satisfaction

- reduction of staffing costs in some areas (typically in middle management, as senior management develops closer links to the operational workforce)

- improved ethical standards or behaviour

TOGS: THE ACTUAL COST OF QUALITY

situation

Togs manufactures clothes for a number of UK retail stores. The company has unfortunately allowed its quality systems to slip in recent years.

The fabric supplies are not inspected before cutting and making up the garments.

The finished garments are inspected, and on average 120 items per month are found to have fabric faults. Of these, 20 must be scrapped. The remainder are sold as seconds at a discount of £15 on the normal price.

A further 40 garments per month are returned by retailers because of fabric faults, which have been missed by the inspectors in the factory. The retailers do not pay for these, and they are not replaced. Some retailers do not reorder from the company.

The returned garments are all sold as seconds at the reduced price.

The variable cost of manufacture is £48 per garment.

A management consultant suggests that Togs should:

1   Identify the costs of quality, in money terms where possible and state in which of the four types of cost of quality each cost should be categorised.

2   Think about and suggest ways in which improvements could be made.

solution

1   The costs of quality and types of cost

- The cost of scrapping 20 garments is the cost of making them, which is:

  20 x £48 = £960 per month.

  This is an internal failure cost.

  Note: We use the variable cost of making the garments, because the fixed costs (by definition) are not increased by making additional items.

- The cost of selling the faulty goods as seconds is £15 per garment, as this is the reduction in contribution from the discounted selling price. The cost of seconds found on inspection is:

  100 x £15 = £1,500 per month.

  This is an internal failure cost.

- The cost of selling the other faulty goods, which are returned by retailers, as seconds is:

  40 x £15 = £600 per month.

  This is an external failure cost, because the faulty goods went out of the factory. Additional external failure costs will result from the lost orders from retailers and loss of reputation amongst customers, but we do not have sufficient information to measure these.

2   how can improvements be made?

The situation could be improved by inspection of the fabric as it is received. This would give rise to appraisal costs. An alternative would be to negotiate contract terms with the supplier to include guarantees regarding the quality of the fabric. Immediate action could be taken to improve the inspection of finished goods and avoid sending faulty goods to retailers. Although this alone would not reduce the total number of substandard goods, it would avoid the external failure cost of lost goodwill and future sales.

NON-FINANCIAL INDICATORS

A **non-financial indicator** is a measurement which is expressed in numbers, but not in money terms, the possible units being very varied: for example hours, transactions, units of product, customers and so on.

Non-financial indicators can take many forms, because they can be designed to measure aspects of any kind of work. They are useful in both manufacturing and service industries and can be applied in both profit-making and non-profit making organisations. They are particularly useful for measuring quality.

Some examples of possible non-financial indicators are given below. Several indicators may be used together for the same activity. You may have other examples from the workplace.

In assessments, you may be asked to suggest how a particular aspect of the work of an organisation could be assessed.

Activity or aspect to be measured	Non-financial indicator
Automated production	Hours of machine down time
Absenteeism	Employee-days absence
Telephone helpline	Average time in seconds taken to answer calls
Quality of service	Number of customer complaints
Input of data to computer	Number of errors per 1000 inputs
Customer satisfaction	Number of repeat orders
Quality of output	Number of units rejected per 1000

QUALITATIVE (NON-NUMERICAL) MEASURES

Some aspects of work are very difficult to measure in terms of numbers, for example: motivation of others, team working, helpfulness to customers.

When numerical indicators are not suitable, **opinions** and **attitudes** have to be recorded, perhaps by customer surveys. Surveys often ask customers to give ratings, say on a scale of 1 to 5, but these are only an aid to obtaining an overall view, not an accurate measurement.

Appraisal schemes within an organisation may involve collecting feedback from colleagues. For example, those present at a meeting may be asked their opinion as to the how well the person chairing the meeting carried out that task. Work relationships can affect the judgements given (and vice versa), so the usefulness of this feedback may be limited.

PERFORMANCE MEASUREMENT IN SERVICE ORGANISATIONS

It is more difficult to measure the performance of a service organisation or department than one which produces tangible goods. Services cannot be checked before being provided in the same way as products can be inspected for faults.

The usual financial measures and ratios can be used for profit-making service organisations. (Non-profit-making organisations are considered in the next section of this chapter.)

Non-financial and qualitative measures, discussed earlier in this chapter, are often applicable to services. For example:

■ Average waiting times for customers can be calculated and compared to a target.

■ The number of customer complaints indicates the level of customer satisfaction.

The appropriate performance indicators to use depend on the type of service being provided and what its aims must be. From the organisation's point of view, financial indicators are likely to be important. If you then consider what features of the service would be important to customers, you can see which items of data are available to measure those features.

The **financial** and **customer** aspects or perspectives discussed in this section form part of the 'Balanced Scorecard', which can be applied to any kind of profit-making organisation, which is discussed later in this chapter.

PERFORMANCE MEASUREMENT IN NON-PROFIT MAKING ORGANISATIONS

Non-profit making organisations include charities and clubs as well as some public sector organisations. Without the objective of profit, there may be no single aim by which 'success' can be measured.

Performance indicators need to be designed to measure how well the organisation has achieved its aims. Much of the section on service organisations above applies to non-profit making organisations, many of which do provide services. Instead of profit, value for money is the main financial criterion. This is usually defined as:

- **economy:** controlling expenditure on costs

- **efficiency:** relating 'outputs' to inputs, meaning that obtaining more from the money spent shows greater efficiency

- **effectiveness:** relating 'outputs' to the aims of the organisation, so that achieving more of what it sets out to do shows greater effectiveness

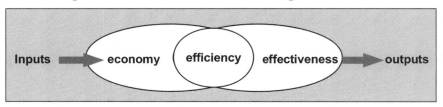

Economy can be measured in the same way as costs in businesses, by comparing with budgets and calculating variances for example.

A possible indicator for **efficiency** is the cost per unit, where units of output can be defined. For example, in a nursing home, the cost of a resident day could be calculated.

Effectiveness may be measured by comparison with targets or with other similar organisations.

Some aspects of non-profit-making activities can only be assessed by qualitative measures: opinions and judgements of experts, users or those who provide the funding. Representatives of government agencies or funding bodies may carry out observations or inspections, as in schools for example.

The general principles of performance measurement apply to these organisations as well as to businesses:

- comparability – comparing like with like

- comparison with standards, budgets or targets

- comparison with similar organisations

- comparison over time, to look for trends

ETHICAL AND COMMERCIAL CONSIDERATIONS

The choice of performance indicator to use in a particular situation can affect the way people approach their work. It is important to make sure that the measurement of performance motivates employees to work efficiently and in the best interests of the organisation as a whole.

If the particular measure being used can be manipulated by workers, so that their performance looks good, it may encourage behaviour that is not in fact beneficial to the organisation as a whole. We learned in our study of standard costing that responsibility for variances may be allocated to individual managers, and that this may cause unhelpful behaviour.

If people take action to improve particular measures of performance in the short term, their behaviour may have adverse effects for the organisation later on. For example, profits may be improved by cutting down on training costs. Eventually, the lack of training may result in inefficiencies or mistakes, which will then reduce the profits. Looking at ways in which a performance indicator can be manipulated may be part of its evaluation, because the results are not useful or meaningful if they can easily be changed by such behaviour.

If targets are set in terms of a particular measure of performance, they should be:

- achievable, but encouraging improvement
- within the area of responsibility of the person being measured
- comparing like with like
- seen to be fair and meaningful

A system for assessing people's work is more likely to motivate them as part of the organisation 'team' if they can see that it is fair and that they can attain the required level by being efficient. The result should be to encourage behaviour that benefits the organisation as a whole.

Sometimes using target indicators can encourage unethical behaviour. This would include manipulation of performance indicators to support an individual manager's apparent performance as already discussed. Unethical behaviour can also impact on those outside the organisation.

For example, suppose a manager who is responsible for paying suppliers was assessed according to how high the 'payables days' indicator was. There would be a great temptation to delay payments, particularly to those suppliers who had little commercial leverage over the organisation. As well as being unethical, this practice could lead to difficulties negotiating new supplies contracts, and could even result in rumours circulating in the industry that the organisation was unable to make payments.

Unethical practices could arise from judging a credit control manager purely on the basis of reducing 'receivables days'. This could result in unacceptably aggressive tactics to chase money owed, which could also result in losing customers.

Great care must therefore be taken when using performance indicators as targets for individual managers that it does not encourage unethical behaviour.

THE BALANCED SCORECARD

The Balanced Scorecard is a way of viewing the performance of a profit-making organisation from four **perspectives**, relating to profits, customers, quality and development, as follows:

- **the financial perspective** is concerned with satisfying the shareholders or owners of a business and relates to profits. Suitable indicators include ROCE and profit margin

- **the customer perspective** is concerned with customer satisfaction and loyalty. It relates to customers' views of the business and suitable indicators include delivery times and numbers or amounts of orders from previous customers

- **the internal perspective** is concerned with technical excellence and consumer needs, which relate to quality. Suitable indicators are those which assess quality and value

- **the innovation and learning perspective** is concerned with the need for continual improvement of existing products and the ability to develop new products to meet customers' changing needs, so it is related to development. Suitable indicators may include the percentage of turnover attributable to new products or a measure of research and development expenditure

In a given case, you may be asked to identify ways of measuring these four perspectives. You will need to look for data available in the Case Study which you can connect with each aspect of the business and be prepared to develop new performance indicators. The next Case Study illustrates this type of task. Note particularly how the 'average delay in fulfilling orders' is calculated. The method is very similar to that used for the average age of inventory or receivables. You need to be able to apply general principles like this in different situations.

Sometimes, a task is set the other way round: you are asked to say which perspective is being measured by a given indicator. It is important to read the tasks carefully and make sure you answer the right question!

HSB LTD: THE BALANCED SCORECARD

You are employed by HSB Ltd, a company with several subsidiaries, and you have been asked to apply the balanced scorecard to monitor the performance of the subsidiaries. The following information relates to Subsidiary H for the period ended 31 December 20-3. You also have available the financial accounts of Subsidiary H for the same year. Extracts are given here.

	£000s
Gross sales	3,500
Less: returns	70
Sales	3,430
Operating profit	825
Analysis of sales by products:	
Sales of new products	1,350
Sales of existing products	2,080
Sales as above	3,430
Analysis of sales by customers:	
Sales to new customers	650
Sales to existing customers	2,780
Sales as above	3,430
Value of orders placed for delivery during the year	4,250

required

Identify and calculate, from the available information, one performance indicator which you could use in monitoring each of the four perspectives in the balanced scorecard.

solution

Monitoring the balanced scorecard for subsidiary H for the year ended 31 December 20-3:

- The *financial* perspective could be measured by operating profit margin, which is (825 ÷ 3,430) x 100% = 24%.

- The *customer* perspective could be measured by repeat custom as a percentage of sales, which is (2,780 ÷ 3,430) x 100% = 81 %.

- An alternative would be the average delay in fulfilling orders. The unfulfilled orders amount to £4,250,000 – £3,430,000 = £820,000 and this could be used as a fraction of turnover to calculate (820 ÷ 3,430) x 365 days, giving 87 days as the average delay.

- The *internal* perspective could be measured by the percentage of sales returns, which is (70 ÷ 3,500) x 100% = 2%.

- The *innovation and learning* perspective could be measured by the percentage of sales derived from new products, which is (1,350 ÷ 3,430) x 100% = 39%.

RESPONSIBILITY CENTRES

As already mentioned, an important area of management accounting is the monitoring and control of costs. This is usually carried out by making certain managers responsible for each of the various aspects of the organisation and the costs that are incurred there. This concept is known as responsibility accounting. Standard costing usually makes good use of the idea of responsibility accounting.

Responsibility accounting often divides the organisation into 'responsibility centres' of three main types.

cost centres

These are responsibility centres where costs are charged and can be monitored and controlled. They are parts of the organisation that incur costs but do not have any direct income, and therefore the manager responsible for a cost centre could only be held accountable for the costs incurred there. We have already seen the role that cost centres can play in absorption costing where costs are allocated or apportioned to cost centres before being absorbed into product costs.

profit centres

Profit centres are parts of the organisation where costs are incurred, but income is generated as well. This means that profit can be calculated, and the manager responsible would be accountable for the amount of profit based on both the income and the expenditure in that responsibility centre. The profit would be measured in monetary amount, and also as a percentage of sales income.

investment centres

Investment centres are responsibility centres where the manager is responsible for income and expenditure (as in a profit centre), but also for the level of investment. The investment could be in the form of non-current (fixed) assets, and also could include elements of working capital such as inventory (stock), receivables (debtors), and payables (creditors) and maybe also cash. An investment centre is in effect a mini business within the main organisation. Monitoring would be carried out by comparing the profit with the investment, often by measures such as return on investment or return on capital employed.

DIVISIONAL PERFORMANCE

In this section we are going to examine how organisations that include autonomous or semi-autonomous divisions can report and manage performance. Divisions of an organisation are often set up as investment centres, as the managers of divisions will have control over profitability and investment.

We will discuss how indicators like 'return on investment' or measuring 'residual income' may be used. We will also see the impact that setting any transfer price can have.

return on investment

Return on investment is calculated as operating profit of the division as a percentage of the investment in the division. The return on investment is equivalent to the accounting rate of return that we examined in the last chapter. There we were looking at future returns, but when measuring divisional performance, we will be considering historical returns. Using the idea of responsibility accounting, both the operating profit and investment in the division should be controllable by the divisional manager.

If the accounts for the organisation include a separate statement of financial position for each division, then the investment may be taken from this document. In that case the return on investment could be based on the 'net assets' or 'capital employed' of the division, and it would be the equivalent of return on capital employed (depending on the exact definition used).

Where an organisation has several divisions, using return on investment as a measure of performance provides a way of fairly comparing different divisions, irrespective of their size. Since it is also comparable with 'whole company' ratios like ROCE, it is widely understood amongst managers.

worked example

Alpha Ltd has two divisions. Each division generated £20 million operating profit. Division A uses an investment of £80 million, and Division B has an investment of £200 million.

The return on investment for each division is:

Division A (£20 million / £80 million) x 100%   =25%

Division B (£20 million / £200 million) x 100% =10%

While 'return on investment' is widely used as a measure of divisional performance, it is not without problems. Its use could encourage divisional managers to make decisions that would increase their division's return, even if it reduced the return for the whole business.

worked example – continued

To use the figures from the previous example, a manager of Division A would be likely to reject a future project with a return on investment of 20%, since it would dilute the division's performance. The manager of Division B may accept a future project with a return of 12%, since it would increase Division B's overall return.

If the whole company's cost of capital was 15%, then both these decisions would reduce the overall return of the company. The Division A project at 20% return would have increased the company return if it were accepted, while the Division B project should be rejected as it would generate a lower return than the company cost of capital.

Another situation where divisional return on investment could lead to actions that may not benefit the whole company may occur if the markets for the divisions' products overlapped. Then one division may increase its market share (and therefore return on investment), while adversely affecting another division.

We will also see shortly how the setting of transfer prices between divisions can have an impact on behaviour and returns.

residual income

Divisional performance can also be measured by using the idea of 'residual income'. This is defined as the operating profit of the division minus a cost of capital charge based on the investment in the division. This measure can be useful where both the profit and the investment in the division are controllable by the divisional manager.

The cost of capital charge would be set by the managers in the head office (not the division), and it would reflect the cost of capital to the organisation. This percentage would then be applied to the investment in the division.

We will now return to the earlier example to see how this would work.

worked example

Using residual income, Division A and Division B would have results calculated as follows:

	Division A	Division B
Operating profit	£20 million	£20 million
Less Cost of Capital Charge at 15%	£12 million	£30 million
Residual Income	£ 8 million	(£10 million)

With this reporting measure being used it is more likely that the future project decisions would be made correctly, as if they generated more than the cost of capital, then they would also increase residual income.

One drawback of using residual income in isolation would be that it makes comparison of divisions of different sizes difficult. This could be mitigated by setting target or budget residual income figures for each division.

transfer pricing

Transfer pricing refers to the prices charged when goods (or services) are supplied from one division of an organisation to another. For example, a car manufacturer may have several divisions that make different components, that are then supplied to the division that deals with final assembly.

The basis on which transfer prices are calculated will have a major effect on the profitability of both the supplying division and the receiving division, including return on investment and residual income. If set too high, then excess profit will be made by the supplying division at the expense of the receiving division, and if too low, then the effect will be the opposite.

Organisations can choose how to set transfer prices. The broad alternative methods are as follows:

- Market price

- Price negotiated between divisions

- Cost plus a profit mark-up

- Full (absorption) cost

- Marginal cost

It is vital when deciding how transfer prices are set, that the method is perceived as fair by all parties. In this way all managers will be motivated, and they will see the performance indicators as reliable.

We will now briefly examine each of the main methods to see what the main issues are.

Market price is perhaps the best option, since neither party benefits from transferring at more or less than a fair value. This will only apply if there is a competitive market for the items being transferred – for example if the supplying division also sells the same items outside the organisation.

A price negotiated between the two divisions can produce a fair outcome. However, this can be a time-consuming exercise, and where one of the parties has no other option of where to buy or sell, then the other division will have an unfair advantage.

Cost plus a profit mark-up should ensure that the supplying division makes some profit. Provided the mark-up is not too high, the receiving division should generally be content. However, this system may not always motivate divisional managers, particularly if they have the alternative to buy or sell on the open market at a different price.

Full absorption cost would normally leave the supplying division without any profit from the transactions. The only exception would be if the quantity supplied to the other division was more than planned, in which case the overheads would be spread over more units, reducing the cost. However, if the quantity was lower than planned, then the supplying division would incur a loss. The receiving division would benefit from this pricing mechanism in all situations.

Marginal cost would provide a worse situation for the supplying division than full absorption cost. The division would be unable to generate a profit from the transactions, and the receiving division would have a substantial advantage. However, for the company as a whole, using marginal cost can optimise performance, at the expense of poor measures of divisional performance. This is because the receiving division will have accurate information about the marginal cost to the organisation of producing the product.

Chapter Summary

- Data which is collected for performance measurement may be quantitative (numerical) data in terms of money or other units, or it may be qualitative data consisting of opinions or attitudes. A combination of quantitative and qualitative data can be used.

- Comparisons are more useful than single sets of data, provided the data being compared has been prepared on a consistent basis, to compare like with like. Comparison may be made with standards, budgets or targets; with other periods of time; with other similar organisations, and to assess the viability of plans.

- The methods and techniques used for performance measurement include Ratio Analysis – ie the calculation of percentages and ratios from the financial accounts or project forecasts.

- The quality of a product or service can be considered as its fitness for the customer's purpose. The intention of quality management is that the additional costs of getting more 'right first time' will be outweighed by the benefits.

- There are costs attached both to poor quality and to making improvements. These costs are grouped under the headings: Prevention costs; Appraisal costs; Internal failure costs; External failure costs.

- Non-financial and qualitative measures of performance are useful for service organisations, and should be designed to measure the aspects of the service which are important to customers.

- Financial performance measurement for non-profit making organisations is based on value for money, which is achieved through economy, efficiency and effectiveness.

- The 'balanced scorecard' looks at an organisation from the financial, customer, internal and innovation and learning perspectives and identifies ways of measuring each of these aspects of its performance.

- Divisional performance can be measured through the application of responsibility accounting, using measures like return on investment and residual income. Care in the setting of transfer prices between divisions is important to motivate managers and ensure that the performance measurement is valid.

<table>
<tr><td rowspan="13">Key
Terms</td></tr>
</table>

performance indicator		an individual measurement used to evaluate the performance of an organisation or part of an organisation
productivity		the aspect of the performance of an organisation which could be measured by the level of output
efficiency		the aspect of the performance of an organisation which could be measured by relating the value of the output to the inputs
benchmarking		the setting of standards or targets for the activities of an organisation
financial indicator		a performance indicator measured in money terms
ratio analysis		the analysis of the financial accounts of an organisation by calculating ratios and percentages

gross profit margin (percentage)

$$\frac{\text{Gross Profit} \times 100\%}{\text{Revenue}}$$

operating profit margin

$$\frac{\text{Operating Profit} \times 100\%}{\text{Revenue}}$$

**ROCE
(return on capital
employed)**

$$\frac{\text{Operating profit} \times 100\%}{\text{Capital employed}}$$

**asset turnover
(number of times)**

$$\frac{\text{Revenue}}{\text{Total assets} - \text{current liabilities}}$$

receivables period

$$\frac{\text{Trade receivables} \times 365 \text{ days}}{\text{Revenue}}$$

payables period

$$\frac{\text{Trade payables} \times 365 \text{ days}}{\text{Cost of sales}}$$

inventory holding period

$$\frac{\text{Inventory} \times 365 \text{ days}}{\text{Cost of sales}}$$

working capital cycle period

inventory days + receivables days − payable days

balanced scorecard

the concept of performance measurement from the point of view of four perspectives: financial, customer, internal and innovation and learning

return on investment

$$\frac{\text{operating profit}}{\text{investment}} \times 100\%$$

residual income

operating profit − cost of capital charge

Activities

7.1 The following income statements relate to a small retail shop selling stationery and gifts:

Toni Jones Statement of Profit or Loss for the year ended:

	31 May 20-3		31 May 20-2	
	£000s	£000s	£000s	£000s
Sales		525		450
Less: cost of sales				
Opening inventory	50		30	
Purchases	408		335	
Less: Closing inventory	(80)	378	(50)	315
Gross profit		147		135
Less: Expenses:				
Administration	25		24	
Selling	38	63	30	54
Operating profit		84		81

Required:

For Toni Jones for the given years, calculate:

(a) Gross profit percentage.

(b) Operating profit percentage.

(c) Each expense as a percentage of Sales.

Comment briefly on the original figures and on the percentages calculated.

7.2 Using the following information, complete the performance indicators shown in the table below. Calculate percentages and values to two decimal places and days to the nearest day.

Sales volume (units)	84,000
	£
Revenue	462,000
Cost of production	
Direct (raw) materials	193,200
Direct labour	121,800
Fixed production overheads	92,400
Total cost of sales	407,400
Gross profit	54,600
Selling and distribution costs	14,000
Administration costs	23,000
Operating profit	17,600
Other data:	
Total net assets	150,000
Inventory	21,200
Receivables	75,000
Payables	33,000

Selling price per unit £	
Gross profit margin	
Operating profit margin	
Return on capital employed	
Direct materials cost per unit £	
Direct labour cost per unit £	
Fixed production cost per unit £	
Full production cost per unit £	
Inventory days	
Receivables days	
Payables days	
Working capital cycle days	

7.3 Scinso Soft Ltd has developed a product that softens skin and is claimed to produce the appearance of a youthful complexion. The product competes with many other products in the marketplace. The market leader is Laurelle plc, which sells to over 60% of the market. You have been given the following information about Scinso Soft Ltd and Laurelle plc for the year ended 31 May 20-0.

Statements of Profit or Loss		Scinso Soft Ltd	Laurelle plc
		£000	£000
Sales revenue		4,500	22,000
Cost of production:			
Direct materials		1,200	3,300
Direct labour		750	2,200
Fixed production overheads		600	3,000
Total cost of sales		2,550	8,500
Gross profit		**1,950**	**13,500**
Selling and distribution costs		500	1,000
Administration costs		375	750
Advertising costs		250	10,000
Operating profit		**825**	**1,750**
Other Information		**Scinso Soft Ltd**	**Laurelle plc**
Number of units sold	**Units**	600	2,200
	000		
Net assets	£000	5,000	8,500

Calculate the performance indicators for Scinso Soft Ltd and Laurelle plc and complete the following table (give answers to two decimal places):

	Scinso Soft Ltd	Laurelle plc
Selling price per unit		
Material cost per unit		
Labour cost per unit		
Fixed production overheads per unit		
Gross profit margin		
Operating profit margin		
Advertising cost as % of turnover		
Return on capital employed		

7.4 Pacer is a company that manufactures deodorant that it sells through discount retailers. The market leader is Greenapple whose deodorant is sold through major supermarkets. Greenapple is able to take advantage of its market share to maintain its selling price, and invests heavily in advertising and promotion. The companies have the following data for the last financial period.

	Pacer	Greenapple
Sales volume (units)	23,500,000	280,000,000
	£000	£000
Sales Revenue	18,800	616,000
Cost of sales:		
Direct materials	4,935	67,200
Direct labour	7,050	78,400
Fixed overhead	1,880	16,800
Gross profit	4,935	453,600
Distribution costs	1,410	19,600
Administration costs	1,460	94,600
Marketing costs	705	274,300
Operating profit	1,360	65,100
Net assets	16,850	812,000

Required:

- Complete the following table to show performance ratios for both companies, rounded to two decimal places

	Pacer	Greenapple
Sales price per unit £		
Direct materials per unit £		
Direct labour per unit £		
Fixed overhead per unit £		
Gross Profit %		
Distribution Costs as % of Sales		
Administration Costs as % of Sales		
Marketing Costs as % of Sales		
Operating Profit %		
Return on Capital Employed %		

- Draft a report that explains the differences in the companies' strategies and the impact this has on their performance.

7.5 The costs of quality are divided into four categories:

1 Prevention costs

2 Appraisal costs

3 Internal failure costs

4 External failure costs

Required:

State the category to which each of the following types of cost belongs:

(a) Investigation of faults.

(b) Training production staff to use new equipment.

(c) The loss of customer loyalty due to poor quality goods.

(d) Costs resulting from loss of production due to machine breakdown.

(e) Inspection of raw materials when received.

(f) The cost of scrapping output.

(g) Claims from customers relating to defective products.

7.6 Wessit Housing Association is considering offering a contract for double-glazing its properties to one of two suppliers, Staylite Ltd and Temeglass Ltd. The following information has been extracted from the most recent annual report and accounts of the two companies.

	Staylite Ltd	Temeglass Ltd
	£000s	£000s
Sales	7,660	9,500
Gross profit	3,467	4,522
Operating profit	403	627
Interest charges	45	2
Non-current Assets (net book value)	600	800
Current assets	198	307
Current liabilities	182	156
Debentures	450	0
Share capital and reserves	166	951
Average number of employees	16	18

Required:

(a) Calculate the following ratios for each of the two companies:
- gross profit margin
- operating profit margin
- return on capital employed
- asset turnover
- sales per employee
- operating profit per employee

(b) Using the given information and the ratios you have calculated, comment on the profitability of the two suppliers.

(c) State which of the performance indicators you have calculated may be used to indicate how efficient the companies are.

(d) State which of the performance indicators you have calculated may be used to indicate the productivity of the companies.

(e) Explain the limitations of the above analysis, in particular from the point of view of Wessit Housing Association's decision about the contract.

(f) Suggest one further indicator which Wessit Housing Association should seek to obtain (not necessarily from the report and accounts) before making this decision.

7.7 Use ticks to complete the following table to show which perspective of the balanced scorecard is being measured by each performance indicator.

	Financial perspective	Customer perspective	Internal perspective	Innovation and learning perspective
Average delivery time				
Gross profit margin				
% sales to existing customers				
Return on capital employed				
% of rejects				
Number of new products				
Research and development expenditure as % sales				

7.8 A company has three divisions, X, Y, and Z. Details of the divisional operating profits and investments are shown in the following table.

The company cost of capital is 12%.

Complete the table to show the return on investment (to two decimal places), and the residual income of each division.

	Division X	Division Y	Division Z
Operating profit £	850,000	189,000	2,150,000
Investment £million	4.5	3.6	12.1
Return on investment %			
Residual income £			

8 Statistical techniques

this chapter covers...

In this chapter we will explain how to calculate key statistical indicators which will help us to analyse past data and to forecast what may happen in the future.

We will start by examining time series – strings of data that occur over time. We will see how a formula can be used to represent a straight line on a graph (regression analysis), and how this can be used to predict data at various points.

Next we will see how some data moves in regular cycles over time, and how this, together with the underlying trend, can be used to develop forecasts. We will show how averaging techniques can be used to detect the trend in given data.

The third section concerns the use of index numbers. These can be used to compare numerical data over time – for example prices of commodities or general price inflation. We will see how to carry out various calculations using index numbers that can be useful.

Finally we will examine the concept of probability and expected values, and see how sensitivity analysis can be used.

TIME SERIES ANALYSIS

Time series analysis involves analysing numerical trends over a time period. It is often used to examine past and present trends so that future trends can be forecast. The term 'trend analysis' is used to describe the technique that we will now examine. At its simplest the concept is based on the assumption that data will continue to move in the same direction in the future as it has in the past.

Using the sales of a shoe shop as an example we will now look at a range of techniques for dealing with trends.

an identical annual change

A shoe shop 'Comfy Feet' has sold the following numbers of pairs of shoes annually over the last few years:

20-1	10,000
20-2	11,000
20-3	12,000
20-4	13,000
20-5	14,000
20-6	15,000
20-7	16,000

It does not require a great deal of arithmetic to calculate that if the trend continues at the previous rate – an increase of 1,000 pairs a year – then shoe sales could be forecast at 17,000 pairs in 20-8 and 18,000 pairs in 20-9. Of course this is a very simple example, and life is rarely this straightforward. For example, for how long can this rate of increase be sustained?

average annual change

A slightly more complex technique could have been used to arrive at the same answer for the shoe shop. If we compare the number of sales in 20-7 with the number in 20-1, we can see that it has risen by 6,000 pairs. By dividing that figure by the number of times the year changed in our data we can arrive at an average change per year. The number of times that the year changes is 6, which is the same as the number of 'spaces' between the years (or alternatively the total number of years minus 1).

Shown as an equation this becomes:

Average Annual Sales Change =

$$\frac{(Sales\ in\ Last\ Year - Sales\ in\ First\ Year)}{(Number\ of\ Years - 1)} = \frac{(16,000 - 10,000)}{(7 - 1)}$$

$$= \ +1,000, \text{ which is what we would expect.}$$

The + 1,000 would then be added to the sales data in 20-7 of 16,000 (the last actual data) to arrive at a forecast of 17,000.

This technique is useful when all the increases are not quite identical, yet we want to use the average increase to forecast the trend. A negative answer would show that the average change is a reduction, not an increase. We will use this technique when estimating the trend movement in more complicated situations.

This is not the only way that we can estimate the direction that data is moving over time, and it does depend on the data (including especially the first and last points) falling roughly into a straight line. We will note alternative methods that can be used later in this section.

constructing a graph

The same result can be produced graphically. Using the same shoe shop example we can extend the graph based on the actual data to form a forecast line.

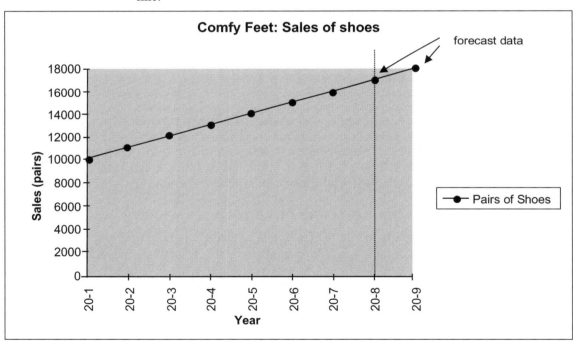

If in another situation the actual data does not produce exactly equal increases, the graph will produce the same answer as the average annual change provided the straight line runs through the first and last year's data points.

using a formula

The data in the example could have been expressed in the following formula:

$$y = mx + c$$

where

y is the forecast amount

m is 1,000 (the amount by which the data increases each year)

x is the number of years since the start year (20-1)

c is 10,000 (which is the sales figure in the start year of 20-1)

If we wanted a forecast for the year 20-9, we could calculate it as:

Forecast	=	(1,000 x number of years since 20-1) + 10,000
y (the forecast)	=	(1,000 x 8) + 10,000
	=	18,000, which is what we would expect.

This formula works because the formula is based on the equation of a straight line.

using a formula for more calculations

The formula of a straight line ($y = mx + c$) that we have just used to calculate a forecast for 'y' can also be used to work out other information. The formula always has the following components:

- a fixed value ('c' in the formula $y = mx + c$); this is the point where the straight line starts from

- a gradient value ('m' in the formula); this determines how steep the line is, and whether it is going up (when 'm' is positive) or going down (when 'm' is negative)

The formula can be used (for example) to predict prices, costs or demand. Sometimes the formula is shown in a slightly different style (for example $y = a + bx$), but the components are still the same.

We will now use the formula to demonstrate how different elements can be calculated.

practical example

For example, suppose we are told that the price of a component over time is believed to increase based on the formula $Y = a + bX$, where

- Y is the price in £, and

- X is the year number

We are told that in year number 4 the price was £68, and in year number 8 the price was £76.

We would like to calculate 'a' and 'b' in the formula, and then use this information to predict the price in year 11.

We can use a calculation to determine how much the price is moving by each year:

	Price		Year
	£76		8
	£68		4
Differences	£8	divided by	4	= £2 per year

This is the 'gradient' amount 'b', and we can use it to calculate the amount 'a' by using price information from either of the years that we know. For example, using year 4 data and putting it into the formula gives:

£68 = a + (£2 x 4 [the year number])

£68 = a + £8 So a must be £60

Now we have the full formula that we can use for any year:

Y = £60 + £2 x X

In year 11, this would give a price of:

Y = £60 + (£2 x 11) = £82

If you are provided with more than two pairs of data, then using the highest and the lowest will probably give the most reliable answer.

We will now use an example to illustrate the use of the formula to predict demand.

Sales of a national daily newspaper have been declining steadily for several years. The demand level is believed to follow the formula $Y = a + bX$, where Y is the demand in numbers of newspapers, and X is the year number. Calculations have already been carried out to establish the values of 'a' and 'b', which are:

- a is 200,000
- b is -2,500

Note that 'b' is a negative figure, so each year the demand decreases.

You are asked to calculate the expected sales in year 14.

If we insert the known data into the formula, we can calculate the demand for year 14 as follows:

Y = 200,000 – (2,500 x 14) Y = 165,000

linear regression

In the last section on time series analysis we saw that when some historical data moves in a consistent and regular way over time we can use it to help estimate the future trend of that data. We also saw that in these circumstances the data can be represented by

■ a straight line on a graph, and / or

■ an equation of the line in the form $y = mx + c$

to help us develop the trend.

Linear regression is the term used for the techniques that can be used to determine the line that best replicates that given data. You should be aware of the techniques in general terms, and be able to appreciate their usefulness. You may be given historical data or the equation of a line and asked to use it to generate a forecast.

Where data exactly matches a straight line (as with the 'Comfy Feet' data) there is no need to use any special techniques. In other situations the following could be used:

■ **Average annual change**. This method was described earlier, and is useful if we are confident that the first and last points (taken chronologically since we are looking at data over time) are both representative. It will smooth out any minor fluctuations of the data in-between. We will see this method used in the 'Seasonal Company' Case Study later in this chapter.

■ **Line of best fit**. Where the data falls only roughly into a straight line, but the first and last points do not appear to be very representative, the average annual change method would give a distorted solution. Here a line of best fit can be drawn onto the data points on a graph that will form a better estimate of the movement of the data. The graph on the next page illustrates a situation where the line of best fit would provide a better solution than the average annual change method.

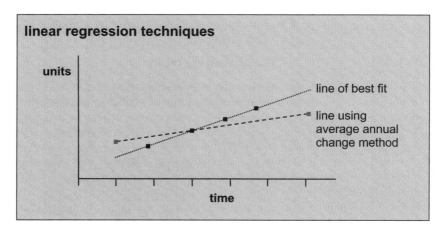

■ **Least squares method**. This is a mathematical technique for developing the equation of the most appropriate line. It is more accurate than drawing a line of best fit onto a graph by eye, but the calculations involved are outside the scope of this book.

In the following example the regression line has already been calculated, and is used to forecast the cost of materials.

---

practical example

A colleague has calculated the least squares regression line (the line of best fit) as

$y = 15.75 + 1.65x$

where y is the cost per kilogram in £ and x is the period. April X5 is period 32.

You are asked to forecast the cost per kilogram for July X5.

The figures are inserted into the formula as follows (July X5 is period 35)

$y = 15.75 + (1.65 \times 35)$

Forecast cost per kilogram (y) = £73.50

All linear regression techniques assume that a straight line is an appropriate representation of the data. When looking at time series this means that we are assuming that the changes in the data that we are considering (known as the dependent variable) are in proportion to the movement of time (the independent variable). This would mean that we are expecting (for example) the sales level to continually rise over time. When we use time series analysis we must remember that sometimes data does not travel forever in a straight line, even though they may do so for a short time. For example share prices on the stock market do not continue to go up (or down) steadily, but often move in a more erratic way.

TIME SERIES ANALYSIS AND SEASONAL VARIATIONS

There are four main factors that can influence data which is generated over a period of time:

■ **The underlying trend**

This is the way that the data is generally moving in the long term. For example the volume of traffic on our roads is generally increasing as time goes on.

■ **Long-term cycles**

These are slow moving variations that may be caused by economic cycles or social trends. For example, when economic prosperity generally increases this may increase the volume of traffic as more people own cars and fewer use buses. In times of economic depression there may be a decrease in car use as people cannot afford to travel as much or may not have employment which requires them to travel.

■ **Seasonal variations**

This term refers to regular, predictable cycles in the data. The cycles may or may not be seasonal in the normal use of the term (eg Spring, Summer etc). For example, traffic volumes are always higher in the daytime, especially on weekdays, and lower at weekends and at night.

■ **Random variations**

All data will be affected by influences that are unpredictable. For example, flooding of some roads may reduce traffic volume along that route, but increase it on alternative routes. Similarly the traffic volume may be influenced by heavy snowfall.

The type of numerical problems that you are most likely to face will tend to ignore the effects of long-term cycles (which will effectively be considered as a part of the trend) and random variations (which are impossible to forecast). We are therefore left with analysing data into underlying trends and seasonal variations, in order to create forecasts.

The technique that we will use follows the process in the diagram below.

The process is as follows:

1 The historical actual data is analysed into the historical trend and the seasonal variations.

2 The historical trend is used to forecast the future trend, using the techniques examined in the last section.

3 The seasonal variations are incorporated with the forecast future trend to provide a forecast of where the actual data will be in the future.

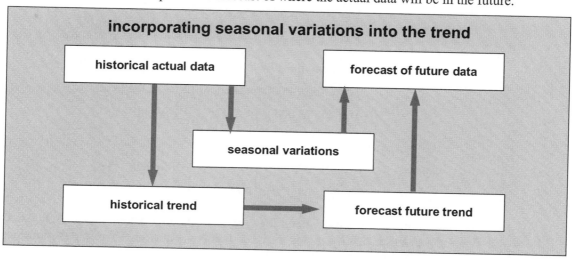

incorporating seasonal variations into the trend

historical actual data

forecast of future data

seasonal variations

historical trend

forecast future trend

forecasting using deseasonalised data

If we know (or can estimate fairly accurately) the seasonal variations, then we can use this information together with actual data to work out what the trend is. The term 'deseasonalised data' means data from which the seasonal variations have been stripped away – in other words the trend. We can then extrapolate this trend. This means forecasting how the trend will move in the future.

The seasonal variations for unit sales of a product have been calculated to be the following percentages of the underlying trend:

Quarter 1	−15%
Quarter 2	+25%
Quarter 3	+10%
Quarter 4	−20%

In year 5 the actual unit sales results are as follows:

Quarter 1	42,500
Quarter 2	75,000
Quarter 3	77,000
Quarter 4	64,000

From these figures we can calculate the 'deseasonalised' data – the trend figures. We need to be careful because the seasonal variations are calculated as percentages of the trend.

Quarter 1   The trend must be greater than 42,500 by 15% of the trend.

Therefore 42,500 must equal 85% of the trend

Trend = 42,500 x 100 / 85   = 50,000

Quarter 2   The trend must be lower than 75,000 by 25% of the trend.

Therefore 75,000 must equal 125% of the trend

Trend = 75,000 x 100 / 125   = 60,000

Using the same logic:

Quarter 3   Trend = 77,000 x 100 / 110   = 70,000

Quarter 4   Trend = 64,000 x 100 / 80   = 80,000

Having identified the trend for year 5 as 50,000, 60,000, 70,000 and 80,000 we can see that it is rising by 10,000 units per quarter. Therefore the forecast for year 6 can be worked out as follows:

Year 6	Quarter 1	Quarter 2	Quarter 3	Quarter 4
Extrapolated Trend	90,000	100,000	110,000	120,000
Seasonal Variations	−15%	+25%	+10%	−20%
Forecast	76,500	125,000	121,000	96,000

In a task the analysis of actual data may have been carried out already, or you may be asked to carry out the analysis by using 'moving averages'. If you are using moving averages it is important that:

- your workings are laid out accurately

- the number of pieces of data that are averaged corresponds with the number of 'seasons' in a cycle

- where there is an even number of 'seasons' in a cycle a further averaging of each pair of averages takes place

moving averages

A moving average is the term used for a series of averages calculated from a stream of data so that:

- every average is based on the same number of pieces of data, (eg four pieces of data in a 'four point moving average'), and

- each subsequent average moves along that data stream by one piece of data so that compared to the previous average it

  - uses one new piece of data and

  - abandons one old piece of data.

This is easier to calculate than it sounds! For example, suppose we had a list of six pieces of data relating to the factory output over two days where a three-shift pattern was worked as follows:

Day 1	Morning Shift	14 units
	Afternoon Shift	20 units
	Night Shift	14 units
Day 2	Morning Shift	26 units
	Afternoon Shift	32 units
	Night Shift	26 units

If we thought that the shift being worked might influence the output, we could calculate a three-point moving average. The workings would be as follows:

First moving average:	$(14 + 20 + 14) \div 3$	$=$ 16
Second moving average:	$(20 + 14 + 26) \div 3$	$=$ 20
Third moving average:	$(14 + 26 + 32) \div 3$	$=$ 24
Fourth moving average	$(26 + 32 + 26) \div 3$	$=$ 28

Notice how we move along the list of data. In this simple example with six pieces of data we can't work out any more three-point averages since we have arrived at the end of the numbers after only four calculations.

Here we chose the number of pieces of data to average each time so that it corresponded with the number of points in a full cycle. By choosing a three-point moving average that corresponded with the number of shifts we always had **one** example of the output of **every** type of shift in our average. This means that any influence on the average by including a night shift (for example) is cancelled out by also including data from a morning shift and an afternoon shift.

We must be careful to always work out moving averages so that exactly one complete cycle is included in every average. The number of 'points' is chosen to suit the data.

When determining a trend line, each average relates to the data from its mid point, as the following layout of the figures just calculated demonstrates.

		Output	**Trend (Moving Average)**
Day 1	Morning Shift	14 units	
	Afternoon Shift	20 units	16 units
	Night Shift	14 units	20 units
Day 2	Morning Shift	26 units	24 units
	Afternoon Shift	32 units	28 units
	Night Shift	26 units	

This means that the first average that we calculated (16 units) can be used as the trend point of the afternoon shift on day 1, with the second point (20 units) forming the trend point of the night shift on day 1. The result is that we:

■ know exactly where the trend line is for each period of time, and

■ have a basis from which we can calculate 'seasonal variations'

Even using our limited data in this example we can see how seasonal variations can be calculated. **A seasonal variation is simply the difference between the actual data at a point and the trend at the same point.** This gives us the seasonal variations shown in the following table, using the figures already calculated.

		Output	Trend	Seasonal Variation
Day 1	Morning Shift	14 units		
	Afternoon Shift	20 units	16 units	+ 4 units
	Night Shift	14 units	20 units	− 6 units
Day 2	Morning Shift	26 units	24 units	+ 2 units
	Afternoon Shift	32 units	28 units	+ 4 units
	Night Shift	26 units		

The seasonal variation for the afternoon shift, calculated on day 1, is based on the actual output being 4 units greater than the trend at the same point (20 minus 16 units).

Case Study

THE AVERAGE COMPANY:
MOVING AVERAGES AND FORECASTS

The Average Company has sales data that follows a 3 period cycle. The sales units shown in the table below have been compiled from actual data in periods 11 to 19.

Period	Actual Data	3 Point Moving Averages (Trend)	Seasonal Variations
11	7,650		
12	7,505		
13	7,285		
14	7,590		
15	7,445		
16	7,225		
17	7,530		
18	7,385		
19	7,165		

r e q u i r e d

(a) Using a 3 point moving average, calculate the trend figures and the seasonal variations.

(b) Extrapolate the trend to periods 20 to 25, and using the seasonal variations forecast the sales units for those periods.

solution

(a) The 3 point moving averages can be calculated for each period except the first and the last. The seasonal variations are calculated as (actual data – trend).

Period	Actual Data	3 Point Moving Averages (Trend)	Seasonal Variations
11	7,650		
12	7,505	7,480	+25
13	7,285	7,460	–175
14	7,590	7,440	+150
15	7,445	7,420	+25
16	7,225	7,400	–175
17	7,530	7,380	+150
18	7,385	7,360	+25
19	7,165		

(b) The trend calculated from 3 point moving averages can be seen to be reducing by 20 each period, and so can be easily extrapolated.

The seasonal variations operate on a 3 period repeating cycle, so can be inserted. The forecast data is then calculated as (extrapolated trend + seasonal variations).

Period	Forecast Data	Extrapolated Trend	Seasonal Variations
20	7,470	7,320	+150
21	7,325	7,300	+25
22	7,105	7,280	-175
23	7,410	7,260	+150
24	7,265	7,240	+25
25	7,045	7,220	-175

INDEX NUMBERS

Index numbers are used to assist in the comparison of numerical data over time. A commonly used index is the Retail Price Index that gives an indication of inflation by comparing the cost of a group of expenses typically incurred by households in the UK from year-to-year. There are many other types of index numbers that have been created for specific purposes, for example:

■ the average wage rate for a particular job, or for all employment

■ the average house price either by region or throughout the UK

■ the market price of shares (eg the FTSE 100 index)

- the quantities of specific items that are sold or used (eg litres of unleaded petrol)

- the quantities of a group of items that are sold or used (eg litres of all motor fuel)

- the manufactured cost of specific items or a range of items (sometimes called 'factory gate' prices)

Many government indices and other indicators are available at www.gov.uk/government/statistics. If you have the opportunity, have a look at the enormous range of data that can either be downloaded free, or can be purchased in government publications.

When using published statistics it is important to make sure that they are specific enough to be useful for your purpose. For example, data on the growth in the population of the West of England will be of limited use if you are trying to forecast the sales in a bookshop in Taunton. Of far more use would be details of proposed housing developments within the immediate area, including the numbers of new homes and the type of households that form the developers' target market.

leading and lagging indicators

Some indicators can be classified as 'leading' indicators, whilst others are known as 'lagging' indicators. This means that some indicators naturally give advance warning of changes that may take place later in other indicators. For example, an index that monitors the prices of manufactured goods ('factory gate' prices) will react to changes before they have filtered through to retail price indices. The index of 'factory gate' prices can therefore be considered to be a 'leading' indicator of retail prices, and give early warning of implications to industrial situations.

In a similar way, an index recording the volume of manufactured output from factories will lag behind an index measuring the volume of purchases of raw materials made by industrial buying departments.

weightings of indices

Those indices that are based on information from more than one item will use some form of weighting to make the results meaningful.

For example, while an index measuring the retail price of premium grade unleaded petrol is based on a single product and therefore needs no weighting, this would not be true for a price index for all vehicle fuel. In this case it will require a decision about how much weight (or importance) is to be placed on each component of the index. Here the relative quantities sold of types of fuel (for example unleaded petrol and diesel) would be a logical way to weight the index. This would ensure that if petrol sales were double those for diesel, any price changes in petrol would have twice the impact on the index than a price change in diesel.

As the purchasing habits of consumers change, then the weighting and composition of complicated indices like the Retail Price Index and the Consumer Price Index are often changed to reflect this. This will include changes to the weighting of certain items, for example due to the increase in the proportion of household expenditure on holidays. It can also involve the addition or deletion of certain items entirely (for example the inclusion of certain fast foods). You may have seen news items from time to time about the revision of items contained within the RPI or CPI as consumers' tastes change.

calculations using index numbers

Whatever type of index we need to use, the principle is the same. The index numbers represent a convenient way of comparing figures.

For example, the RPI was 82.61 in January 1983, and 245.8 in January 2013. This means that average household costs had nearly tripled in the 30 years between. We could also calculate that if something that cost £5.00 in January 1983 had risen exactly in line with inflation, it would have cost £14.88 in January 2013. This calculation is carried out by:

$$\textit{historical price} \quad x \quad \frac{\textit{index of time converting to}}{\textit{index of time converting from}}$$

ie   £5.00   x $(245.8 \div 82.61)$ =   £14.88

This is an increase of $\dfrac{(£14.88 - £5.00)}{£5.00}$ x 100 =   197.6%

You may be told that the 'base year' for a particular index is a certain point in time. This is when the particular index was 100. For example the current RPI index was 100 in January 1987.

Index numbers referring to costs or prices are the most commonly used ones referred to in the unit studied in this book. If we want to use cost index numbers to monitor past costs or forecast future ones, then it is best to use as specific an index as possible. This will then provide greater accuracy than a more general index.

For example, if we were operating in the food industry, and wanted to compare our coffee cost movements with the average that the industry had experienced, we should use an index that analyses coffee costs in the food industry. This would be much more accurate than the RPI, and also better than a general cost index for the food industry.

practical example

The following table shows the actual material costs for January for years 20-2 to 20-5, together with the relevant price index.

Period	Actual costs (£)	Cost index	Costs at January 20-2 prices
January 20-2	129,300	471	
January 20-3	131,230	482	
January 20-4	135,100	490	
January 20-5	136,250	495	

Required: Restate all the actual costs at January 20-2 prices, to the nearest £.

Solution

Period	Actual costs (£)	Cost index	Costs at January 20-2 prices
January 20-2	129,300	471	129,300
January 20-3	131,230	482	128,235
January 20-4	135,100	490	129,861
January 20-5	136,250	495	129,644

Case Study

TURNER LIMITED: ADJUSTING TO REAL TERMS

Sales revenue and Net Profit figures are given for Turner Ltd for the five years ended 31 December 20-5. A suitable index for Turner Ltd's industry is also given.

	20-1	20-2	20-3	20-4	20-5
Sales revenue (£000s)	435	450	464	468	475
Net Profit (£000s)	65	70	72	75	78
Industry Index	133	135	138	140	143

required

Calculate the sales revenue and profit in terms of year 20-5 values and comment on the results.

solution

To put each figure into 20-5 terms, it is divided by the index for its own year and multiplied by the index for 20-5, ie 143. For example:

Sales revenue Year 20-1 $\frac{435}{133}$ x 143 = 467.7

Sales revenue Year 20-2 $\frac{450}{135}$ x 143 = 476.7 and so on.

In year 20-5 terms:

	20-1	20-2	20-3	20-4	20-5
Sales revenue (£000s)	467.7	476.7	480.8	478.0	475.0
Net Profit (£000s)	69.9	74.1	74.6	76.6	78.0

The adjusted figures compare like with like in terms of the value of the pound, and the Net Profit still shows an increasing trend throughout, but the sales revenue decreases in the last two years.

creation of an index

You may be required to create an index from given historical data, and we will now see how this is carried out.

Suppose that you are provided with the following prices for one unit of a certain material over a period of time:

Month	Jan	Feb	March	April	May	June
Price	£29.70	£30.00	£28.30	£30.09	£31.00	£31.25

The first thing to do is to decide which point in time is to be the base point – the price at this point will be 100 in our new index. In this example we will first use January as our base point, but later we will see how another date could have been chosen.

Next, the price of another date (we'll use February) is divided by the price at the base point. The result is then multiplied by 100 to give the index at that point (ie February):

(£30.00 / £29.70) x 100 = 101.01

Note that the index number is not an amount in £s, it is just a number used for comparison purposes. In this example we've rounded to two decimal places – and we will need to be consistent for the other figures.

If we carry out the same calculation for the March price we get the following:

(£28.30 / £29.70) x 100 = 95.29

Notice that here the answer is less than 100, which makes sense because the price in March is lower than the price in January. Checking that each index number is the expected side of 100 (ie higher or lower) is a good idea and will help you to detect some arithmetical errors.

The full list of index numbers is as follows – make sure that you can arrive at the same figures.

Month	Jan	Feb	March	April	May	June
Price	£29.70	£30.00	£28.30	£30.09	£31.00	£31.25
Index	100.00	101.01	95.29	101.31	104.38	105.22

We could have chosen a different date to act as our base point – if we chose March, then the calculation for January would have been:

$$(£29.70 / £28.30) \times 100 = 104.95$$

Then the full list of index numbers would have been as follows:

Month	Jan	Feb	March	April	May	June
Price	£29.70	£30.00	£28.30	£30.09	£31.00	£31.25
Index	104.95	106.01	100.00	106.33	109.54	110.42

Again, make sure that you could arrive at the same figures.

Don't forget that although we have used the creation of a price index in the above example, you could also be asked to create an index from any suitable historical data. Whatever the type of data, the arithmetic required is the same.

PROBABILITY AND EXPECTED VALUE

Sometimes when we are trying to predict what will happen in the future there is a range of possibilities. If we do not have reliable historical data to base our prediction on, we cannot use techniques like time series analysis. Instead, it can be useful to produce a forecast in the form of a range of possibilities. Judgement can then be used to assign a **probability** to each possible outcome.

Probability is expressed as a decimal with a value between 0 and 1. A probability of 0 means that there is no chance of this occurring, and a probability of 1 shows that the outcome definitely will happen. Between these extremes, probabilities indicate the likelihood of an event occurring. A probability of more than 0.5 indicates that an outcome is more likely than not to occur.

For example, we may be planning to attend an outside event on a certain date in the future, If we are concerned about the likelihood of rain on that day we could attempt to use judgement (or the judgement of an expert) to assign probabilities to each possibility. These could then be expressed as follows:

Outcome	Probability
No rain	0.6
Rain	0.4
Total	1.0

This is known as a **probability distribution**. Note that the probability of all the possible outcomes must add up to 1. In this case it indicates that there is more chance of it being a dry day than of it raining.

If we were planning to attend the event to sell ice cream, then we may be able to estimate the sales we could make depending on the outcome. For example, we may estimate that if there is no rain our sales would be £2,000. If there was rain the sales are estimated at £500.

By linking each profit to the relevant probability, we could calculate the **expected value** of the sales on that day, as follows:

Outcome	Probability	Sales	Weighted Sales	
No rain	0.6	£2,000	£2,000 x 0.6 =	£1,200
Rain	0.4	£500	£500 x 0.4 =	£200
Total	1.0		Expected value	£1,400

The expected value is a weighted average of the financial outcomes.

The expected value in this example is the average sales that could be expected if the circumstances of this particular day could be repeated many times. This example is very simple so that the process can be explained. We will now see how probabilities and expected values can be more useful by using a more complicated Case Study.

Case Study

PREDICTIONS LTD:
PROBABILITY AND EXPECTED VALUES

situation

A company is considering launching one of two new products, and it has carried out market research on them both. This research has been combined with accounting data to provide the following profit outcomes for each product. The following table shows this data, together with the expected values.

Product A			Product B		
Probability	Profit £'000	Weighted Profit £'000	Probability	Profit £'000	Weighted Profit £'000
0.1	50	5	0.2	70	14
0.2	80	16	0.4	110	44
0.4	100	40	0.2	120	24
0.2	150	30	0.1	140	14
0.1	200	20	0.1	150	15
Expected value		111	Expected value		111

required

Analyse the data to distinguish between the likely profitability of the two products. Make a recommendation as to which product you consider to be the best alternative.

solution

At first glance, since both products have the same expected value of £111,000 profit, they both seem to be of equal benefit.

However, by looking at the probability distributions in more detail we can make several further points.

- Product A has a profit range of £50,000 to £200,000, but Product B has a smaller profit range of between £70,000 and £150,000. Product B would avoid the risk of the low £50,000 profit but also of the high £200,000 profit that Product A demonstrates.
- The most likely single outcome for Product A is a profit of £100,000, but this is only a four in ten chance. The most likely outcome for Product B is £110,000, again with a 0.4 probability.
- If we consider grouping some probabilities together, we can deduce that Product A has a 0.7 probability of profits of £100,000 or more. This is calculated by adding together the probabilities of £100,000, £150,000, and £200,000. Calculating the equivalent figures for Product B, we see that it has a higher (0.8) probability of a profit of £110,000 or more.

Overall Product B would be considered the best option, based on it having a narrower range of profits, a higher single most likely profit, and a more likely profit of £110,000 or more.

SENSITIVITY ANALYSIS

Sensitivity analysis is concerned with examining forecast data to see how sensitive it is to changes in assumptions or levels of accuracy. It can be used with many types of forecast data, including those that we have studied in this chapter.

Time series forecasts can be examined to see what effect a change of 5% or 10% would make to the forecasts, and how that would impact on other data – for example budgets or decision making.

Costs or other data forecast using index numbers could be examined to see the effect of changes in both the forecast and data that flows from it.

In the last section we saw how probability distributions can be used to help our understanding of data and make decisions. This is a form of sensitivity analysis, since we are considering each outcome in the range and seeing how likely it is to occur and what impact it would have. The last Case Study that we looked at is good example of how sensitivity analysis can help us make decisions.

Chapter Summary	■ A time series is formed by data that occurs over time. If the data increases or decreases regularly (in a 'straight line') then it can be represented by a formula. The formula can then be used to predict the data at various points.
	■ Some data moves in regular cycles over time, and the distances that the data is from the underlying trend are known as seasonal variations. Information about the underlying trend and the seasonal variations can be used to forecast data.
	■ Moving averages can be used to split data into the trend and the seasonal variations.
	■ Index numbers can be used to compare numerical data over time. Examples of the use of index numbers are for prices of commodities or general price inflation.
	■ Probability and expected values can be used to help us understand situations where there is a range of possible outcomes.

Key Terms	**time series analysis**	the examination of historical data that occurs over time, often with the intention of using the data to forecast future data
	trend	the underlying movement in the data, once seasonal and random movements have been stripped away
	seasonal variations	regular variations in data that occur in a repeating pattern
	extrapolation of data	using information about a known range of data to predict data outside the range (for example in the future)
	deseasonalised data	data that has had seasonal variations stripped away
	linear regression	using a mathematical formula to demonstrate the movement of data over time. This technique is sometimes used to help forecast the movement of the trend
	index numbers	a sequence of numbers used to compare data, usually over a time period
	probability	the likelihood of an event occurring, expressed as a decimal between 0 and 1
	probability distribution	the range of outcomes linked to their probabilities that will total 1.0
	expected value	the weighted average outcome, based on the sum of all the outcomes multiplied by their probabilities
	sensitivity analysis	the analysis of uncertain data to establish the impact of different outcomes

Activities

8.1 Sales (in units) of a product are changing at a steady rate and don't seem to be affected by any seasonal variations. Use the data given for the first three periods to forecast the sales for periods 4 and 5.

Period	1	2	3	4	5
Sales (units)	212,800	210,600	208,400		

8.2 Sales (in units) of a product are changing at a broadly steady rate and don't seem to be affected by any seasonal variations. Use the average change in the data given for the first five periods to forecast the sales for periods 6 and 7.

Period	1	2	3	4	5	6	7
Sales (units)	123,400	123,970	124,525	125,085	125,640		

8.3 The table below shows the last three months' cost per kilo for material Beta, together with estimated seasonal variations:

Month	Jan	Feb	March	April	May
Actual Price £	6.80	6.40	7.00		
Seasonal Variation £	+0.40	−0.10	+0.40	−0.30	−0.40
Trend £					

- Calculate the trend figures for January to March, and extrapolate them to April and May.
- Forecast the actual prices in April and May

8.4   Computer modelling has been used to identify the regression formula for the monthly total of a specific indirect cost as

$Y = £13.20 x + £480.00$

Where y is total monthly cost

And   x is monthly production in units

Calculate the total monthly cost when output is:

- 500 units, and
- 800 units

State whether the total cost behaves as a:

- Fixed cost, or
- Variable cost, or
- Semi-variable cost, or
- Stepped cost.

8.5   The regression formula for monthly sales of a certain product (in units) has been identified as:

$Y = 1200, + 13X$

Where Y is total monthly sales, and X is the month number.

January 20-9 was month 30

Forecast the monthly sales in August 20-9

8.6 A company has sales data that follows a 3 period cycle. The sales units shown in the table below have been compiled from actual data in periods 30 to 36.

Period	Actual data	3 point moving averages (Trend)	Seasonal variations
30	3,500		
31	3,430		
32	3,450		
33	3,530		
34	3,460		
35	3,480		
36	3,560		
37			
38			
39			
40			

Complete the table to show your responses to the following:

(a) Using a 3 point moving average, calculate the trend figures and the seasonal variations for periods 31 to 35.

(b) Extrapolate the trend to periods 37 to 40, and using the seasonal variations forecast the sales units for those periods.

8.7 The table below shows details of 5 unrelated materials. Complete the blank parts of the table. Show all figures to two decimal places.

Material	Old price £	New price £	New price as index number with old price as base	% increase in price
A	2.13	2.16		
B	10.25	11.00		
C	3.60	3.75		
D	240.00		105.00	
E	68.00		124.00	

8.8 The table below shows details regarding purchases of a specific material. Complete the table to show the actual cost per kilo (to the nearest penny) and create an index based on the cost per kilo with January as the base, to the nearest whole number.

	January	February	March
Total cost £	20,000	24,000	25,000
Total quantity	2,000 kilos	2,200 kilos	2,140 kilos
Cost per kilo £			
Cost index			

8.9 **Situation**

A company is considering launching one of two new products, and it has carried out market research on them both. This research has been combined with accounting data to provide the following profit outcomes for each product. The following table shows this data.

Product X			Product Y		
Probability	Profit £'000	Weighted Profit £'000	Probability	Profit £'000	Weighted Profit £'000
0.1	100		0.2	70	
0.1	120		0.3	100	
0.6	150		0.2	150	
0.1	180		0.2	200	
0.1	200		0.1	220	
Expected value			Expected value		

Required

- Complete the table to calculate the expected value of the profit for each product.

- Analyse and comment on the likely profitability of the two products. Make a recommendation as to which product you consider to be the best alternative.

Answers to chapter activities

CHAPTER 1: PREPARING BUDGETS

1.1 **(a)** The speed at which the craftsmen work, and their working hours will determine their output. Since they can sell all that they produce their output will be the principal budget factor.

(b) The transport requirements of the turkey supplier will form the principal budget factor. The transport company and the turkey supplier will have a common activity level over the coming year.

(c) The maintenance requirements of the Manchester trams will form the principal budget factor. This will in turn depend upon maintenance schedules for the current fleet, plus that for any additional trams to be acquired.

(d) The demand from the staff at the business park for baked potatoes seems likely to easily outstrip supply, based on the figures given. The capacity of the outlet would therefore form the principal budget factor.

1.2 **Situation**   **Contact**

(a) You want to identify the production capacity of the firm.   Production planning manager

(b) You want to forecast the price of raw materials.   Buyer or purchasing manager

(c) The draft budget is ready for review.   Budget committee

1.3 **Cost**   **Budget**

(a) Production wages   Cost of Production

(b) Printing recruitment application forms   Personnel

(c) Advertising   Marketing

(d) Customer demand survey   Marketing

(e) Raw materials   Cost of Production

(f) Spare parts for production machines   Maintenance

(g) Warehouse extension   Capital Expenditure

(h) Sales commission paid to staff   Marketing

1.4

Situation	Suggested Accounting Treatment
Holiday pay for production workers	Charge to production in a labour hour overhead rate
Material wastage in production	Direct cost
Cost of the purchasing department	Activity based charge to production cost centres
Administrative wages	Allocate to administrative overheads
Computing services	Allocate to administrative overheads
Production equipment maintenance	Charge to production in a machine hour overhead rate
Depreciation of production equipment	Charge to production in a machine hour overhead rate
Redecoration of the sales showroom	Allocate to marketing overheads

1.5

Period	October	November	December
Sales (units)	20,400	21,600	24,000
Opening inventory	4,080	4,320	
Closing inventory	4,320	4,800	
Production (units)	20,640	22,080	

1.6 The production budget (in units) for month 5 equals:

Budgeted Sales Units	1,800	units
– Opening Inventory of Finished Goods	(500)	units
+ Closing Inventory of Finished Goods	400	units
Production budget	1,700	Units

The raw materials usage budget is based on the raw material required to satisfy the production budget:

Raw Materials Usage = (1,700 units × 4 kilos per unit)	= 6,800 kilos
The raw material purchases budget for month 5 will equal:	
Raw materials usage budget	6,800 kilos
– opening Inventory of raw materials	(1,200) kilos
+ closing Inventory of raw materials	1,500 kilos
Raw materials purchases budget	7,100 kilos

1.7   Direct labour hours needed:

25,430 units × 9 minutes / 60 = 3,815 hours (rounded up)

Basic rate hours available:

22 employees × 160 hours   = 3,520 hours

Overtime hours required:

3,815 hours − 3,520 hours   = 295 hours

1.8   Answer is (b) 600 hours

Working: 72,000 units at 12 per hour = 6,000 hours needed

Basic time 30 staff × 180 hours = 5,400 hours

Overtime hours 6,000 − 5,400 = 600 hours

1.9   Total number of units to be produced: = 27,365 units

Maximum number of units to be made in-house:

(22 employees × (160 + 20) hours) / (9 minutes / 60)   = 26,400 units

Number of units to be sub-contracted:

27,365 − 26,400   = 965 units

1.10 **(a)**

Product	Units	Hours per unit	Hours required
A	240	1.5	360
B	210	2.0	420
C	170	3.0	510
Total hours for department Y			1,290

(b)   1,290 / 300 = 4.3 machines required (round up to 5 machines)

Therefore number of machines to hire is 2.

1.11

Units of Zapp	Jan	Feb	Mar	Apr	May	Jun	Total
Sales	5,000	4,000	6,500	5,000	6,500	5,000	32,000
Less opening inventory of Finished Goods	(3,000)	(2,000)	(3,250)	(2,500)	(3,250)	(2,500)	
Add closing inventory of Finished Goods	2,000	3,250	2,500	3,250	2,500	2,500	
Production Budget	4,000	5,250	5,750	5,750	5,750	5,000	31,500
Litres of Woo	**Jan**	**Feb**	**Mar**	**Apr**	**May**	**Jun**	**Total**
Materials Usage – Woo (Production × 2 litres)	8,000	10,500	11,500	11,500	11,500	10,000	63,000
Less opening inv'ry of Woo	(8,000)	(10,500)	(11,500)	(11,500)	(11,500)	(10,000)	
Add closing inv'ry of Woo	10,500	11,500	11,500	11,500	10,000	10,000	
Materials Purchase – Woo	10,500	11,500	11,500	11,500	10,000	10,000	65,000
Litres of Koo	**Jan**	**Feb**	**Mar**	**Apr**	**May**	**Jun**	**Total**
Materials Usage – Koo (Production × 3 litres)	12,000	15,750	17,250	17,250	17,250	15,000	94,500
Less opening inv'ry of Koo	(16,000)	(15,750)	(17,250)	(17,250)	(17,250)	(15,000)	
Add closing inv'ry of Koo	15,750	17,250	17,250	17,250	15,000	15,000	
Materials Purchase – Koo	11,750	17,250	17,250	17,250	15,000	15,000	93,500
	Jan	*Feb*	*Mar*	*Apr*	*May*	*Jun*	*Total*
Direct Labour (Hours) (Production × 0.5 hour)	2,000	2,625	2,875	2,875	2,875	2,500	15,750

1.12

<table>
<tr><td colspan="3"><u>**Workings schedules**</u></td><td colspan="3"><u>**Operating budget**</u></td></tr>
<tr><td></td><td></td><td></td><td></td><td>**Units**</td><td>**£**</td></tr>
<tr><td>**Materials**</td><td>**kg**</td><td>**£**</td><td>Sales revenue @ £2.60 each</td><td>29,000</td><td>**75,400**</td></tr>
<tr><td>Opening inventory</td><td>2,100</td><td>2,000</td><td></td><td></td><td></td></tr>
<tr><td>Purchases</td><td>15,500</td><td>27,125</td><td>Opening inventory of finished goods</td><td>4,000</td><td>7,000</td></tr>
<tr><td>Sub-total</td><td>17,600</td><td>29,125</td><td></td><td></td><td></td></tr>
<tr><td>Used</td><td>**16,600**</td><td>**27,375**</td><td>**Cost of production**</td><td>30,000</td><td></td></tr>
<tr><td>Closing inventory</td><td>1,000</td><td>**1,750**</td><td>Materials</td><td></td><td>**27,375**</td></tr>
</table>

Closing inventory of materials is to be valued at budgeted purchase price (£27,125 / 15,500) = £1.75 per kilo

Labour	**24,000**
Production Overhead	**8,625**
Total	**60,000**

Labour

	Hours	**£**
Basic time @ £12 per hour	**2,000**	**24,000**

Closing inventory of finished goods*	5,000	**10,000**

*Valued at budgeted production cost per unit

Cost of goods sold
(£7,000 + £60,000 - £10,000)

57,000

It takes 4 minutes to make each item 30,000 production units takes 30,000 x 4min divided by 60 = 2,000 hours

Gross profit	**18,400**

Production overhead	**Hours**	**£**	**Non-Production Overheads**	
Variable @ £2.00 per labour hour	**2,000**	**4,000**	Administration	3,000
Fixed		4,625	Marketing	4,000
Total Production Overheads		**8,625**	Total	7,000

Operating profit	**11,400**

1.13

Materials Budget:	Kilos	£
Opening inventory	2,055	2,135
Purchases	10,320	10,836
Sub-total	12,375	12,971
Used in production	10,275	10,766
Closing inventory	2,100	2,205

Labour Budget:	Hours	£
Basic rate	1,650	19,800
Overtime	63	1,008
Total	1,713	20,808

Overhead Budget:	£
Variable overhead: 1,713 hours × £3.00	5,139
Fixed overhead	8,497
Total overhead	13,636

Operating Budget:

	£	£
Sales revenue (7,000 × £15)		105,000
Cost of goods sold:		
Opening inventory of finished goods (2,000 × £6.50)		13,000
Cost of production (6,850 units):		
Materials	10,766	
Labour	20,808	
Overhead	13,636	
		45,210
Closing inventory of finished goods (1,850 × £6.60)		12,210
Cost of goods sold (7,000 units)		46,000
Gross profit		59,000
Administration	16,500	
Marketing	23,450	
		39,950
Operating profit		19,050

1.14 **Cash Budget**   **May**

                                                              £
Opening cash balance   (480)
Receipts:
Customer receipts   6,500
Payments:
For purchases   (2,000)
For wages   (1,040)
For overheads   (1,320)
For capital exp.   0
Total payments   (4,360)
Closing cash balance   1,660

1.15

                                                    £   £
Receipts: (£56,500 + £2,000)   58,500
Payments:
Materials (£15,500 + £1,200)   16,700
Wages   19,500
Expenses (£14,650 + £650)   15,300
                                                 ———————
                                                 51,500
Net cash flow   7,000

CHAPTER 2: USING BUDGETS

2.1

	Advantages	Disadvantages
Overtime:	Known staff abilities	Overtime premium rate
	Good utilisation of own equipment	Staff may not wish to work overtime
	Consistent supervision by regular supervisors	Tiredness causing quality problems
Sub-contracting:	Quality may be contractors' responsibility	Cost (a profit is made by sub-contractor)
	Credit may be available	Process out of organisation's control
	No overheads	

2.2 There is labour available to make **175,000**[1] units in normal time. Therefore, **12,500**[2] hours of overtime will be needed.

The raw material contract will provide enough material to make **150,000**[3] units. Therefore, **100,000**[4] kg will have to be purchased on the open market.

Quality control can test **192,000**[5] units in the year. It will be necessary to make alternative arrangements for **8,000**[6] units.

Workings:

(1)   50 × 1,750 hours = 87,500 hours available

  87,500 hours will make 87,500 / 0.5 hours = 175,000 units

(2)   Units made in overtime is 200,000 − 175,000 = 25,000 units

  These will take 25,000 × 0.5 hours = 12,500 hours

(3)   300,000 kg / 2 kg per unit = 150,000 units

(4)   Remaining 50,000 units require 50,000 × 2 kg = 100,000 kg

(5)   16,000 units × 12 months = 192,000 units

(6)   200,000 − 192,000 = 8,000 units

2.3 170,000 / 20,000 = 8.5, so we must go up to the next step. Therefore, to manage the current output of 170,000 units there must be 9 supervisors, with a maximum output of (9 × 20,000) = 180,000 units.

Budgeted supervision cost must be £360,000 / 9 = £40,000 per supervisor.

(a) 160,000 units requires 8 supervisors, costing £320,000

(b) 175,000 units requires 9 supervisors, costing £360,000

(c) 185,000 units requires 10 supervisors, costing £400,000

2.4

Operating Budget	First Scenario	Alternative Scenario
Selling price per unit	£17.00	£17.34
Sales volume	150,000	144,000
	£	£
Sales revenue	2,550,000	2,496,960
Costs:		
Materials	600,000	576,000
Labour	637,500	612,000
Depreciation	312,000	288,000
Energy	123,600	118,800
Occupancy costs	235,000	244,400
Total costs	1,908,100	1,839,200
Operating profit	641,900	657,760
Increase / (decrease) in profit		15,860

2.5 **Monthly Operating Statement**

Volume	34,000		
	Flexed Budget	Actual	Variance F/A
	£	£	£
Revenue	2,720,000	2,856,000	136,000 F
Costs			
Material	476,000	510,000	34,000 A
Labour	612,000	616,250	4,250 A
Distribution	6,800	7,000	200 A
Energy	161,000	164,000	3,000 A
Equipment hire	36,000	35,000	1,000 F
Depreciation	182,000	180,000	2,000 F
Marketing	231,000	235,000	4,000 A
Administration	186,000	189,000	3,000 A
Total	1,890,800	1,936,250	45,450 A
Operating Profit	829,200	919,750	90,550 F

2.6

Original Budget		Flexed Budget	Actual	Variance Fav (Adv)
60,000	Sales volume (units)		57,300	
£		£	£	£
960,000	Sales revenue	916,800	945,250	28,450
	Costs:			
138,000	Materials	131,790	134,950	(3,160)
234,000	Labour	223,470	222,390	1,080
72,000	Distribution	68,760	70,400	(1,640)
85,000	Energy	83,650	82,350	1,300
88,000	Equipment hire	88,000	86,950	1,050
91,400	Depreciation	91,400	92,300	(900)
59,600	Marketing	59,600	65,300	(5,700)
66,500	Administration	66,500	65,250	1,250
834,500	Total costs	813,170	819,890	(6,720)
125,500	Operating profit (loss)	103,630	125,360	21,730

CHAPTER 3: STANDARD COSTING – DIRECT COSTS

3.1 The following statements are true: (b), (c), (d) and (f). All the other statements are false.

3.2 (a)

One Unit of X	Quantity	Cost per unit of input £	Total cost £
Direct Materials	0.75 (kg)	10.00	7.50
Direct Labour	0.20 (hr)	13.00	2.60
Fixed Overheads	1	7.00	7.00
Total			17.10

(b) 20,000 units x £17.10 = £342,000

3.3 Using the budget data to calculate the standard data for one unit:

Direct Materials   40,000 kg ÷ 20,000   = 2 kg
                                @ £300,000 ÷ 40,000   = £7.50 per kg
                                                      = £15.00 per unit

Direct Labour   10,000 hrs ÷ 20,000   = 0.5 hrs
                                @ £120,000 ÷ 10,000   = £12.00 per hr
                                                        = £6.00 per unit

Direct Material Price Variance: (37,000 kg x £7.50) – £278,000 = £500 A

Direct Material Usage Variance: £7.50 x ([2 kg x 19,000 units] – 37,000 kg) = £7,500 F

Direct Labour Rate Variance: (9,800 hrs x £12.00) – £117,200 = £400 F

Direct Labour Efficiency Variance: £12.00 x ([0.5 hr x 19,000 units] – 9,800 hrs) = £3,600 A

3.4 **(a)** Direct material price variance
(610 sq metres x £25) – £15,400 = £150 Adverse

(b) Direct material usage variance
((300 windows x 2 sq metres) x £25) – (610 sq metres x £25) = £250 Adverse

(c) Direct labour rate variance
(145 hours x £16) – £2,440 = £120 Adverse

(d) Direct labour efficiency variance
((300 windows x 0.5 hours) x £16) – (145 hours x £16) = £80 Favourable

3.5 Using the budget data to calculate the standard data for one unit:

Variable Materials   3,000 kg ÷ 30,000   = 0.1 kg
   @ £75,000 ÷ 3,000   = £25 per kg
   = £2.50 per unit

Variable Labour   15,000 hrs ÷ 30,000   = 0.5 hrs
   @ £150,000 ÷ 15,000   = £10.00 per hr
   = £5.00 per unit

Variable Material Price Variance: (3,100 kg x £25.00) – £81,000 = £3,500 A

Variable Material Usage Variance: £25 x ([0.1 kg x 32,000 units] – 3,100 kg) = £2,500 F

Variable Labour Rate Variance: (15,900 hrs x £10.00) – £155,000 = £4,000 F

Variable Labour Efficiency Variance: £10.00 x ([0.5 hr x 32,000 units] – 15,900 hrs) = £1,000 F

3.6 Direct Material Price Variance: (71,500 kg x £9.45) – £678,700 = £3,025 A

Direct Material Usage Variance: £9.45 x ((96 kg x 700 units) – 71,500 kg) = £40,635 A

[**Note:** 5 hours 6 minutes = 5.1 hours.]

Direct Labour Rate Variance: (3,850 hrs x £12.60) – £48,440 = £70 F

Direct Labour Efficiency Variance: £12.60 x ([5.1 hr x 700 units] – 3,850 hrs) = £3,528 A

3.7 (c) £3,000 A

3.8 **(a)** (d) 1,000

(b) This is an adverse variance.

3.9

Email
To: Production Manager From: Accounting Technician Subject: Reasons for Direct Cost Variances

The following are likely reasons for the variances shown in the recent report.

Direct Material Price Variance £2,960 Favourable

This variance appears to be the result of the new contract that was agreed with the material supplier. This is effectively a bulk discount which was able to be negotiated due to the additional requirements for material due to the increased production level.

Direct Material Usage Variance £5,350 Adverse

The most likely cause of this variance is the excess material wastage created when the machine was not working correctly.

Direct Labour Rate Variance £9,260 Adverse

This variance has occurred despite the anticipated pay increase not having been paid (which would normally have led to a favourable variance). The most likely reason is the additional overtime worked which would have resulted in enhanced pay for the hours concerned. Some overtime was due to catching up with production following the machine problems, but overtime may also have been used to increase production above the budgeted level. This should be investigated to determine whether this was the case.

Direct Labour Efficiency Variance £5,150

This variance relates to the labour time taken to produce the output. The problem with the machine working slowly would have contributed to this, as would the extra idle time that occurred when the machine broke down and had to be repaired.

3.10   Labour efficiency variance (excluding idle time):
(5,000 units x 0.75 hr x £10) – (3,850 hrs x £10)   = £1,000 A

Labour idle time variance:
(150 hrs x £10)   = £1,500 A

3.11

	£	Adverse / Favourable
Labour rate variance	36.00	Favourable
Labour efficiency variance (excluding idle time)	75.00	Adverse
Idle time variance	300.00	Adverse

CHAPTER 4: STANDARD COSTING – OVERHEADS AND SALES

4.1 **(a)** Variable overhead expenditure variance:
(2,420 direct labour hours x £1.50) – £3,910 = £280 Adverse

(b) Variable overhead efficiency variance:
(5 hours x 500 units x £1.50) – (2,420 hours x £1.50) = £3,750 – £3,630 = £120 Favourable

4.2 **(a)** Variable overhead expenditure variance:
(1,900 machine hours x £20*) – £38,600 = £600 Adverse
* Standard hourly rate = £30 / 1.5

(b) Variable overhead efficiency variance:
(1.5 hours x 1,250 units x £20) – (1,900 hours x £20) = £37,500 – £38,000 = £500 Adverse

4.3 **(a)** Absorption rate = Budgeted overheads / budgeted output
= £500,000 / 25,000 units   = £20 per unit

Fixed overhead volume variance:
Actual output x absorption rate – Budgeted output x absorption rate
= (30,000 x £20) – (25,000 x £20) = £100,000 F
The volume variance is favourable because actual volume is greater than budgeted.

(b) Fixed overhead expenditure variance:
Budgeted cost of fixed overheads – Actual cost of fixed overheads
= £500,000 – £480,000   = £20,000 F
The expenditure variance is favourable because actual costs are less than budgeted.

4.4 **(a)** Fixed overhead expenditure variance:
£60,000 – £58,000 = £2,000 F

(b) Fixed overhead volume variance
£12 per unit* x (3,500 units – 5,000 units) = £18,000 A
*Absorption rate = £60,000 / 5,000 units = £12 per unit

4.5 **(a)** Fixed Overhead Expenditure Variance
£440,000 – £428,000 = £12,000 F

Fixed Overhead Volume Variance
(2,150 x £200) – (2,200 x £200)   = £10,000 A

(b) One disadvantage of absorbing overheads on a per-sofa basis is that each sofa will absorb an identical amount of overheads. This may not be appropriate if different types of sofa use different amounts of resource – for example, some sofas may take longer to manufacture.

(c)

	Favourable	Adverse	
Budgeted / Standard fixed cost for actual production (2,150 x £200)			£430,000
Variances	**Favourable**	**Adverse**	
Fixed overhead expenditure	£12,000		
Fixed overhead volume		£10,000	
Total variance	£2,000		–£2,000
Actual fixed cost for actual production			£428,000

4.6 **(a)** £94,600 ÷ 2,200   = £43 per hour

    (b) Exp = £94,600 – £99,000   = £4,400 A
       Vol = £43 x (2,500 – 2,200)   = £12,900 F
       Total = (2,500 x £43) – £99,000 = £8,500 F

    (c) Valid: 3, 4

4.7 **(a)** £448,000 ÷ 14,000   = £32 per hour

    (b) 14,000 ÷ 2,000   = 7 hours each

    (c) 7 x 1,800   = 12,600 hours

    (d) Exp = £448,000 – £455,000   = £7,000 A
       Vol = £32 x (12,600 – 14,000) = £44,800 A

    (e) Reconciliation:

Overhead Absorbed	£403,200
Expenditure Variance	£7,000 A
Volume Variance	£44,800 A
Actual Overhead	£455,000

4.8 **(a)** (5,100 desks x 5 std hrs) + (7,000 chairs x 2 std hrs) = 39,500 std hrs for actual production

    (b) £600,000 / 40,000 standard direct labour hours = £15 per standard direct labour hour

    (c) Variances:
    Fixed Overhead Expenditure Variance
      £600,000 – £603,500 = £3,500 A
    Fixed Overhead Volume Variance
      (39,500 std hrs x £15) – (40,000 bud std hrs x £15) = £7,500 A
    Total Fixed Overhead Variance
      (39,500 std hrs x £15) – £603,500 = £11,000 A

4.9

Situation	Fixed Overhead Expenditure Variance			Fixed Overhead Volume Variance		
	Adverse	Favourable	No impact	Adverse	Favourable	No impact
Production manager awarded a pay increase	✓					✓
Unplanned additional day's holiday shut down			✓*	✓		
Additional direct labour staff used to increase production			✓		✓	
Unplanned pay rise given to direct labour staff			✓			✓**
New maintenance contract implemented with reduced costs		✓				✓
Additional shift working (including supervisors) used to increase production	✓				✓	

*Unless there are heating and lighting savings that would result in a favourable variance.
**Unless pay rise increases motivation and speed of working

4.10 Sales price variance   £1,350,000 – (£130 x 10,000 units)   = £50,000 F

Sales volume variance   (10,000 units x £80) – (10,600 units x £80)   = £48,000 A

Total sales variance   £50,000 F – £48,000 A   = £2,000 F

CHAPTER 5: COST MANAGEMENT TECHNIQUES

5.1 Cost Driver Rates

Receiving Deliveries Inwards	£20,000 / 500 deliveries	= £40.00 per delivery
Issuing Goods to Production	£100,000 / 500,000 issues	= £0.20 per issue

Usage of Activity per year

Simplex	Receiving Deliveries	£40.00 x 10 deliveries	= £400
	Issuing Goods	£0.20 x 100 issues	= £20
Complex	Receiving Deliveries	£40.00 x 200 deliveries	= £8,000
	Issuing Goods	£0.20 x 1,000 issues	= £200

Revised Unit Costs

		Simplex		Complex
		£		£
Original Cost		70.00		145.50
Less original Stores overhead		(5.00)		(10.00)
ABC Stores overhead				
Receiving	(£400 / 2,000)	0.20	(£8,000 / 200)	40.00
Issuing Goods	(£20 / 2,000)	0.01	(£200 / 200)	1.00
Revised Cost using ABC		65.21		176.50

5.2

	Added value	Non-added value
(a) Moving engines made in one location to another factory for installing in cars		✓
(b) Holding meeting to decide on the colour of paint to use on new range of products		✓
(c) Applying several coats of paint to prestige products	✓	
(d) Fitting strings to electric guitars by a musical instrument manufacturer	✓	
(e) Waiting by production workers for materials to be delivered		✓
(f) Clearing waste materials away from production area		✓

5.3 **(a)** Expected total sales revenue from Digisnap = £480 x 25,000 = £12,000,000

(b) Target operating profit from Digisnap = 22% x £12,000,000 = £2,640,000

(c) Total target cost for Digisnap = £12,000,000 – £2,640,000 = £9,360,000

(d) Target operating profit per unit of Digisnap = £2,640,000/25,000 = £105.60

(e) Target cost per unit of Digisnap = £480 – £105.60 = £374.40

5.4 **(a)**

	£
Sales price per unit	50.00
Profit margin (40% of £50)	20.00
Total costs (£50 – £20)	30.00
Fixed cost per unit	16.00
Labour cost per unit	6.00
Maximum material cost per unit	8.00
Target cost per kilogram (£8 x 1,000/200)	40.00

(b) The trade price per kilogram quoted on the supplier's price list is £50 per kilogram. The purchasing manager has negotiated a discount of 15%. The discount should be **rejected** because the £50 reduces to **£42.50** which is **above** the Target cost. The cost gap is **£2.50** per kilogram.

(c) The minimum percentage discount needed to achieve the Target cost is **20%**.

5.5

Year	Cash Inflow £000	Cash Outflow £000	Net Cash Flow £000	Discount Factor	Present Value £000
0	0	1,900	–1,900	1.000	–1,900
1	0	1,900	–1,900	0.909	–1,727
2	0	4,650	–4,650	0.826	–3,841
3	5,600	3,350	2,250	0.751	1,690
4	7,700	3,500	4,200	0.683	2,869
5	3,500	0	3,500	0.621	2,174
	Totals		1,500		–735

5.6 Based on the information given, activity based costing would appear to be most appropriate for the Radical Company. It is the only system that would cope with accurately costing the range of products outlined. For example, the developments and design costs for items that are constantly updated are likely to be greater than those with unchanged specifications. Similarly, the size of batches and lengths of production runs would have a cost impact that only ABC would recognise.

CHAPTER 6: DECISION MAKING TECHNIQUES

6.1

(1)

	Units	Per Unit £	Total £
Lost contribution on 400 gram can sales	1,000,000	0.64	−640,000
200 gram can sales:			
Additional revenue	2,200,000	0.55	1,210,000
Material cost	2,200,000	0.07	−154,000
Labour cost	2,200,000	0.03	−66,000
Increase fixed costs			−110,000
Net increase / (reduction) in profit			240,000

(2)

	Units	Per Unit £	Total £
Lost contribution on 400 gram can sales	1,000,000	0.64	−640,000
200 gram can sales:			
Additional revenue	2,200,000	0.55	1,210,000
Buy-in cost	2,200,000	0.20	−440,000
Increase fixed cost			−15,000
Net increase / (reduction) in profit			115,000

(3) The company should make their own 200 gram cans of beans, as this provides the most additional profit.

6.2

	Aye £000	Bee £000	Total £000
Sales	320	160	480
Total variable costs	165	100	265
Fixed costs related to products	25	15	40
Product contribution	130	45	175
Whole business fixed costs			140
Operating Profit			35

Since the Bee product is making a contribution of £45,000 to the overall profitability, this would be lost if the product were discontinued. Therefore the product should not be discontinued.

6.3 **(a)**

	Shiver	Shake	Total
Production (units)	10,000	15,000	25,000
Total contribution £	180,000	285,000	465,000

(b)

	Shiver	Shake	Total
Contribution per kg of material £	9.00	7.60	
Production (units)	12,000	4,800	16,800
Material usage (kg)	24,000	12,000	36,000
Total contribution £	216,000	91,200	307,200

6.4

	Exe	Wye
Contribution per kg material	£20	£12.50
Contribution per labour hour	£40	£50

Using X to denote number of Exes, and Y to denote number of Wyes:

Material constraint	$2X + 2Y = 10,000$
Labour constraint	$X + 0.5Y = 3,500$
Multiply labour equation by 2 gives	$2X + Y = 7,000$
Deducting this from material equation	$Y = 3,000$
Substituting for Y in either equation	$X = 2,000$
For graph:	
Material constraint	When $Y = 0$, $X = 5,000$
Labour constraint	When $X = 0$, $Y = 5,000$

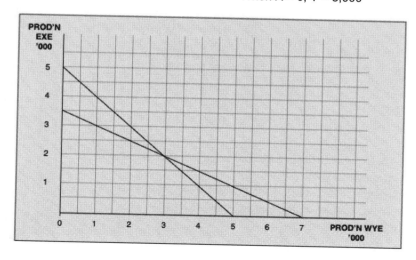

The graph could alternatively be drawn by using the alternative axis for each product.

	Exe	Wye	Total
Production (units)	2,000	3,000	5,000
Materials required (kg)	4,000	6,000	10,000
Labour required (hours)	2,000	1,500	3,500
Contribution	£80,000	£75,000	£155,000

6.5

	Year 0	Year 1	Year 2	Year 3
Net cash flows £	−60,000	25,000	25,000	25,000
Discount factor	1.000	0.909	0.826	0.751
Present values £	−60,000	22,725	20,650	18,775
Net present value £				2,150

6.6

	Year 0	Year 1	Year 2	Year 3
Cash inflows £	0	38,500	38,500	39,500
Cash outflows £	74,500	1,500	9,500	1,500
Net cash flows £	−74,500	37,000	29,000	38,000
Discount factor	1.000	0.909	0.826	0.751
Present values £	−74,500	33,633	23,954	28,538
Net present value £				11,625

6.7

Year	Cash Flow	Disc Factor 10%	Disc Cash Flow 10%	Disc Factor 15%	Disc Cash Flow 15%
0	−1,200,000	1.000	−1,200,000	1.000	−1,200,000
1	300,000	0.909	272,700	0.870	261,000
2	300,000	0.826	247,800	0.756	226,800
3	300,000	0.751	225,300	0.658	197,400
4	300,000	0.683	204,900	0.572	171,600
5	300,000	0.621	186,300	0.497	149,100
6	300,000	0.564	169,200	0.432	129,600
Net Present Values			+106,200		−64,500

The net present value of the project using a discount factor of 10% is + £106,200

The payback period in years is 4 years

The discounted payback period is 5 years to the nearest year

The estimated internal rate of return to the nearest whole %

10% + (106,200 / 170,700) x 5%   = 13%

The accounting rate of return to the nearest whole %

(100,000 / 600,000) x 100% =17%

CHAPTER 7: PERFORMANCE INDICATORS

7.1 (a) – (c)

	31 May 20-3	**31 May 20-2**
Gross Profit % of Sales	28%	30%
Operating Profit % of Sales	16%	18%
Administration expense as % of Sales	4.8%	5.3%
Selling expense as % of Sales	7.2%	6.7%

Comments: Looking at the original figures, it can be seen that Sales Revenue, Purchases and Expenses have all increased in the second year. Administration, which would probably be expected to be a fixed cost, has remained relatively stable. Inventory levels have built up in both years. Profits have also increased.

Looking at the ratios, the percentage Gross Profit has decreased slightly, which could be due to increased purchase costs or having to reduce selling prices, or both. The expenses together still represent 12% of Sales, and as would be expected for a fixed cost, the administration percentage has gone down slightly. The selling expense, however, has increased as a proportion of sales, possibly due to increased advertising to generate more sales. The reduction in Operating Profit percentage results from the decreased Gross Profit margin.

Toni Jones should consider whether there is a problem with the build-up of inventory – are there goods which do not sell? Also the reasons for the decrease in Gross Profit margin and increase in selling expenses should be investigated.

7.2

Selling price per unit £	5.50
Gross profit margin	11.82%
Operating profit margin	3.81%
Return on capital employed	11.73%
Direct materials cost per unit £	2.30
Direct labour cost per unit £	1.45
Fixed production cost per unit £	1.10
Full production cost per unit £	4.85
Inventory days	19
Receivables days	59
Payables days	30
Working capital cycle days	48

7.3

	Scinso Soft Ltd	Laurelle plc
Selling price per unit	£7.50	£10
Material cost per unit	£2.00	£1.50
Labour cost per unit	£1.25	£1.00
Fixed production overheads per unit	£1.00	£1.36
Gross profit margin	43.33%	61.36%
Operating profit margin	18.33%	7.95%
Advertising costs as % of turnover	5.56%	45.45%
Return on capital employed	16.50%	20.59%

7.4

	Pacer	Greenapple
Sales price per unit £	0.80	2.20
Direct materials per unit £	0.21	0.24
Direct labour per unit £	0.30	0.28
Fixed overhead per unit £	0.08	0.06
Gross Profit %	26.25	73.64
Distribution Costs as % of Sales	7.50	3.18
Administration Costs as % of Sales	7.77	15.36
Marketing Costs as % of Sales	3.75	44.53
Operating Profit %	7.23	10.57
Return on Capital Employed %	8.07	8.02

Report

Strategies and Performance of Pacer and Greenapple

Both companies sell a similar product with similar costs per unit. Greenapple uses a slightly more expensive material, but this is offset by economies of scale that bring down the direct labour and fixed overhead costs per unit. Despite the similar unit costs, Pacer sells its deodorant at just over a third the price of Greenapple's product. This is the reason for the large difference in gross profit percentages.

While Pacer has other costs totalling just over 19% of sales value, Greenapple's other costs are over 63% of sales value. This is mainly due to the marketing costs which appears to be necessary to maintain the high quantity of sales despite the high selling price.

The result is operating profit percentages that are 7.23% for Pacer and 10.57% for Greenapple. However the return on capital employed for both companies are very similar at just over 8%.

7.5   Prevention costs: (b)

Appraisal costs: (e)

Internal failure costs: (a) (d) (f)

External failure costs: (c) (g)

7.6   Wessit Housing Association

(a)   The ratios for each of the two companies are:

	Staylite Ltd	Temeglass Ltd
Gross profit margin	45.3%	47.6%
Operating profit margin	5.3%	6.6%
Return on capital employed	65.4%	65.9%
Asset turnover	12.44 times	9.99 times
Sales per employee	£478,750	£527,778
Operating profit per employee	£25,188	£34,833

(b)   Indicators of the profitability of the two companies include the profit margins and ROCE. Temeglass Ltd appears to be more profitable using any of these indicators.

(c)   The main performance indicators which may be used to indicate efficiency are ROCE and operating profit margin. (Profit per employee may also be significant.)

(d)   The performance indicator which may be used to indicate the productivity of the companies is sales per employee, although this is not ideal because comparative selling prices and volumes of output are not known. Output per employee would be a better indicator. Profit per employee could also be used here.

(e)   The limitations of the above analysis are:

When using the published accounts of companies, it is not possible to guarantee that we are comparing like with like, as different policies (including those regarding depreciation, inventory valuation and goodwill, for example) will affect the results. Also there is the possibility that the statement of financial position does not show a typical position. In this case, only one year's results are available for each company, so it is not possible to see whether there are any significant trends.

(f)   A further indicator which Wessit Housing Association should seek to obtain would be some measure of quality or value for money. Suggestions include selling prices, product specifications, or some indication of customer satisfaction. The companies may be able to show their previous work and it would be particularly useful to the housing association to obtain opinions or references from previous customers. Numbers of customer complaints would be another possible measure, if available.

7.7

	Financial perspective	Customer perspective	Internal perspective	Innovation and learning perspective
Average delivery time		✓		
Gross profit margin	✓			
% sales to existing customers		✓		
Return on capital employed	✓			
% of rejects			✓	
Number of new products				✓
Research and development expenditure as % sales				✓

7.8

	Division X	Division Y	Division Z
Operating profit £	850,000	189,000	2,150,000
Investment £million	4.5	3.6	12.1
Return on investment %	18.89	5.25	17.77
Residual income £	310,000	(243,000)	689,000

CHAPTER 8: STATISTICAL TECHNIQUES

8.1

Period	1	2	3	4	5
Sales (units)	212,800	210,600	208,400	206,200	204,000

8.2

Period	1	2	3	4	5	6	7
Sales (units)	123,400	123,970	124,525	125,085	125,640	126,200	126,760

Average change (125,640 – 123,400) / 4 = 560

8.3

Month	Jan	Feb	March	April	May
Actual Price £	6.80	6.40	7.00	6.40	6.40
Seasonal Variation £	+0.40	–0.10	+0.40	–0.30	–0.40
Trend £	6.40	6.50	6.60	6.70	6.80

8.4   500 units   Total cost   (£13.20 x 500) + £480.00 = £7,080

800 units   Total cost   (£13.20 x 800) + £480.00 = £11,040

The total cost behaves as a semi-variable cost.

8.5   August 20-9 will be month 37

Forecast sales   1,200 + (13 x 37)   = 1,681 units

8.6 (a) and **(b)**

Period	Actual data	3 point moving averages (Trend)	Seasonal variations
30	3,500		
31	3,430	3,460	−30
32	3,450	3,470	−20
33	3,530	3,480	+50
34	3,460	3,490	−30
35	3,480	3,500	−20
36	3,560		
37	3,490	3,520	−30
38	3,510	3,530	−20
39	3,590	3,540	+50
40	3,520	3,550	−30

8.7

Material	Old price £	New price £	New price as index number with old price as base	% increase in price
A	2.13	2.16	101.41	1.41%
B	10.25	11.00	107.32	7.32%
C	3.60	3.75	104.17	4.17%
D	240.00	252.00	105.00	5.00%
E	68.00	84.32	124.00	24.00%

8.8

	January	February	March
Total cost £	20,000	24,000	25,000
Total quantity	2,000 kilos	2,200 kilos	2,140 kilos
Cost per kilo £	10.00	10.91	11.68
Cost index	100	109	117

8.9

Product X			Product Y		
Probability	Profit £'000	Weighted Profit £'000	Probability	Profit £'000	Weighted Profit £'000
0.1	100	10	0.2	70	14
0.1	120	12	0.3	100	30
0.6	150	90	0.2	150	30
0.1	180	18	0.2	200	40
0.1	200	20	0.1	220	22
Expected value		150	Expected value		136

The expected value of Product X is higher than Product Y.

The most likely outcome for Product X is a profit of £150,000, and this has a probability of 0.6, showing that this outcome is more likely than not.

The most likely outcome for Product Y is only £100,000, and this itself has only a 3 in 10 chance of occurring.

The likelihood of Product X realising a profit of at least £150,000 is 80%, while the likelihood for Product Y realising at least £150,000 is only 50%, with an even chance that the profit will be less than this.

All the indicators therefore point to Product X proving a better option.

Index

for your notes

for your notes

for your notes

for your notes